Barth's Theological Ontology of Holy Scripture

Princeton Theological Monograph Series

K. C. Hanson, Charles M. Collier, D. Christopher Spinks, and Robin Parry, Series Editors

Recent volumes in the series:

Brian C. Howell
In the Eyes of God:
A Contextual Approach to Biblical Anthropomorphic Metaphors

Sarah Morice-Brubaker
The Place of the Spirit: Toward a Trinitarian Theology of Location

Joas Adiprasetya
An Imaginative Glimpse:
The Trinity and Multiple Religious Participations

Anthony G. Siegrist
Participating Witness: An Anabaptist Theology of
Baptism and the Sacramental Character of the Church

Kin Yip Louie
The Beauty of the Triune God:
The Theological Aesthetics of Jonathan Edwards

Mark R. Lindsay
Reading Auschwitz with Barth
The Holocaust as Problem and Promise for Barthian Theology

Dick O. Eugenio
Communion with the Triune God
The Trinitarian Soteriology of T. F. Torrance

Brendan Thomas Sammon
The God Who Is Beauty
Beauty as a Divine Name in Thomas Aquinas and Dionysius
the Areopagite

Barth's Theological Ontology of
Holy Scripture

Alfred H. Yuen

Foreword by
John Webster

PICKWICK *Publications* · Eugene, Oregon

BARTH'S THEOLOGICAL ONTOLOGY OF HOLY SCRIPTURE

Princeton Theological Monograph Series 211

Pickwick Publications
An Imprint of Wipf and Stock Publishers
199 W. 8th Ave., Suite 3
Eugene, OR 97401

www.wipfandstock.com

ISBN 13: 978-1-62032-911-5

Cataloging-in-Publication data:

Yuen, Alfred H.

    Barth's theological ontology of Holy Scripture / Alfred H. Yuen ; foreword by John Webster.

    xii + 186 pp. ; cm. —Includes bibliographical references and index.

    Princeton Theological Monograph Series 211

    ISBN 13: 978-1-62032-911-5

    1. Barth, Karl, 1886–1968. 2. Bible—Criticism, interpretation, etc. I. Webster, J. B. (John Bainbridge), 1955–. II. Title. III. Series.

BS511.3 .Y83 2014

Manufactured in the U.S.A.

Contents

Foreword by John Webster | vii

Abbreviations | ix

Introduction | 1

1 Scripture: Early Convictions | 16

2 Being Taught: The Bible and the Reformed Scripture Principle | 53

3 *Dominus Illuminatio Mea*: The School of the Biblical Witness | 122

4 *Dominus et Vivificantem*: Biblical Witnesses as Children of God | 141

Conclusion | 165

Bibliography | 175

Index | 185

Foreword

IT IS ONE OF the curiosities of the reception of Barth's theology that, though he is commonly acclaimed as a theologian of the Word, relatively little attention has been devoted to his doctrine of Holy Scripture. There have been studies of aspects of his exegesis and his hermeneutics, of his attitudes to the methods of historical criticism, and of the way in which is dogmatic thought is shaped by biblical narrative. But what Barth had to say about the nature of Scripture remains under-explored, especially in English-language scholarship, where the only full-dress treatment of the theme—Klass Runia's *Karl Barth's Doctrine of Holy Scripture*—is ill-informed and deeply unsympathetic. A number of explanations for the neglect might be adduced: lack of interest in bibliology on the part of contemporary mainstream Protestant theologians; palpable hostility towards Barth's teaching about the nature of Scripture on the part of a vocal adherents of a dominant strand of confessional Reformed theology, who judge him a treacherous occasionalist who refuses to identify Scripture and Word of God; the gravitation of Barth's more sympathetic readers to other elements of his theology of revelation, above all its Christological principles. Barth himself, of course, shares some of the responsibility for steering readers away from the topic. Like some of his nineteenth century forebears, he worried that a doctrine of Scripture, and especially of biblical inspiration, risked collapsing the free presence and activity of divine speech into an inert textual deposit, and he deployed the idea of Scripture as witness to revelation as a way of avoiding the peril.

Yet Barth's unease with one strand of the Reformed tradition's varied teaching on the nature of the Bible—a strand which he did not, perhaps, understand as fully as he should—ought not to make readers inattentive to the many things which he had to say in the topic, especially in his earlier writings. As Barth built up his interpretation of the particular genius of Reformed Christianity in the 1920s, he lighted upon a number of its *differentia*: its insistence that the telos of salvation is moral renewal; its confessional mobility; and its dedication to the Scripture principle, to which this study gives its attention. Its core proposal—that, by virtue of the Holy Spirit's action, both the scriptural writings and their readers have their ontological centre in divine self-communication—is laid out by an attentive study of representative writings, pastoral and theological, from Barth's student days to the first volume of the *Church Dogmatics*. It possesses the qualities Barth himself looked for in study of theologians from the past: attentiveness, sympathy, willingness to follow another's questions and answers, a sense of the weightiness of the matter by which another's mind and spirit are engaged. It is an invitation to consider a grand theme in a grand thinker.

John Webster
University of St. Andrews

Abbreviations

Anselm	*Anselm: Fides Quaerens Intellectum. Anselm's Proof of the Existence of God in the Context of his Theological Scheme.* Karl Barth. Translated by I. W. Robertson. London: SCM Press, 1960; Pittsburgh: The Pickwick Press, 1975.
B-Th	*Karl Barth-Eduard Thurneysen: Briefwechsel.* Karl Barth and Eduard Thurneysen. Edited by E. Thurneysen. Zürich: TVZ, 1973.
B-Bultmann	*Letters 1922-1966.* Karl Barth and Rudolph Bultmann. Edited by B. Jaspert. Zürich: TVZ, 1994.
B-Rade	*Karl Barth-Martin Rade: Ein Briefwechsel.* Karl Barth and Martin Rade. Gütersloh: Gütersloher Velagshaus, 1981.
CD	*Church Dogmatics.* Karl Barth. Translated by G. T. Thomson et al. Edinburgh: T. & T. Clark, 1956–1975.
ChD	*Die christliche Dogmatik im Emtwurf: 1 Band: Die Lehre vom Worte Gottes: Prolegomena zur christlichen Dogmatik 1927.* Karl Barth. Edited by H. Stoevesandt. Zürich: TVZ, 1982.
"Das Scriftprinzip"	"Das Schriftprinzip der reformierten Kirche." Karl Barth. *Vorträge und kleinere Arbeiten 1922-1925.* Zürich: TVZ, 1990, 500–44.

Abbreviations

EJE	*Erklärung des Johannes-evangeliums (kapitel 1-8) Vorlesung Münster, Wintersemester 1925/1926, wiederholt in Bonn, Sommersemester 1933.* Karl Barth. Edited by W. Fürst. Zürich: TVZ, 1976.
ET	English translation.
GD	*The Göttingen Dogmatics: Instruction in the Christian Religion.* Vol. 1. Karl Barth. Translated by G.W. Bromiley and edited by H. Reiffen. Grand Rapids: Eerdmans, 1991.
PT	*Die protestantische Theologie im 19. Jahrhundert.* Karl Barth. Zürich: TVZ, 1985.
RevT	*Revolutionary Theology in the Making: Barth-Thurneysen Correspondence, 1914–1925.* Karl Barth and Eduard Thurneysen. Translated by J. D. Smart. Richmond, VA: John Knox Press, 1964.
Römerbrief 1919	*Der Römerbrief* (Erste Fassung) *1919.* Karl Barth. Edited by H. Schmidt. Zürich: TVZ, 1985.
Römerbrief 1922	*Der Römerbrief 1922.* Karl Barth. Zürich: TVZ, 1984.
UCR I	*Unterricht in der christlichen Religion, I. Prolegomena, 1924.* Karl Barth. Edited by H. Reiffen. Zürich, TVZ, 1985.
UCR II	*Unterricht in der christlichen Religion 2: Die Lehre von Gott/Die Lehre vom Menschen 1924/1925.* Karl Barth. Edited by H. Stoevesandt. Zürich: TVZ, 1990.
UCR III	*Unterricht in der christlichen Religion 3: Die Lehre von der Versöhnung/Die Lehre von der Erlösung 1925/1926.* Karl Barth. Edited by H. Reiffen. Zürich, TVZ, 1985.

TRC   *The Theology of the Reformed Confessions.* Karl
Barth. Translated by D. L. Guder and J. J. Guder.
Louisville: John Knox Press, 2002.

TVZ   Theologischer Verlag Zürich.

WGWM   *The Word of God and the Word of Man.* Karl
Barth. Translated by D. Horton. London: Hodder
and Stoughton, 1928.

ZZ   *Zwischen den Zeiten.*

Introduction

[I]t is characteristic of what is said and intended and denoted in the Bible, again in the sense of those who said it, that if it is to reveal and establish itself at all as substance and object, it must do so of itself. How can it be otherwise, when what is said is God's revelation, the lordship of the triune God in His Word by the Holy Ghost? To what is said—and even as they say it, and the biblical witnesses themselves attest it—there belongs a sovereign freedom in fact of both speaker and hearer alike. The fact that it can be said and heard does not mean that it is put at the power and disposal of those who say and hear it. What it does mean is that as it is said and heard by them it can make itself said and heard. It is only by revelation that revelation can be spoken in the Bible and that it can be heard as the real substance of the Bible. If it is to be witness at all, and to be apprehended as such, the biblical witness must itself be attested by what it attests. . . . In fact of it, the unfortunate possibility that the matter of which the word speaks may be alien to us does not excuse us. Nor does it permit us, instead of proceeding from the substance of the word, to go first to the word, i.e., to the humanity of the speakers as such. But if that is the case, we obviously not excused or permitted by the mystery which is the obvious source of this fatal possibility: the mystery of the sovereign freedom of the substance. . . . We have to know the mystery of the substance if we are really to meet it, if we are really to be open and ready, really to give ourselves to it, when we are told it, that it may really meet us as the substance. And when it is a matter of understanding, the knowledge of this mystery will create in us a peculiar fear and reserve which is not at all usual to us. We will then know that in the face of this subject-matter there can be no question of our achieving, as we do in others, the confident approach which masters and subdues the matter. It is

> rather a question of our being gripped by the subject-matter—not gripped physically, not making an experience of it and the like, although (ironically) that can happen—but really gripped, so that it is only as those who are mastered by the subject-matter, who are subdued by it, that we can investigate the humanity of the word by which it is told us.[1]

THUS KARL BARTH IN the second part-volume of the *Church Dogmatics*, one that, which first saw the light of day as university lectures at Basel, was completed shortly after his Gifford Lectures at the University of Aberdeen in 1937.

Arguably, it is a substantial statement about the nature of Scripture: what Scripture is in virtue of its employment[2] by "the triune God in His Word by the Holy Ghost." If Barth's pneumatological, bibliological reference informs his characterization of Scripture, I suggest that the significance of the reference has been somewhat overlooked in a number of recent readings on his view of Scripture. In his view of Scripture, Barth understood the Spirit as unbound,[3] external,[4] and necessary[5] to the regeneration of the

---

1. *CD* I/2, 469–71.

2. Cf. the concept of God's use of Scripture in Kelsey, "The Bible and Christian Theology," 400–401.

3. For recent critiques of Barth's primacy of God's absolute freedom from Scripture, see, for example, M. D. Thompson's critique in his "Barth's Doctrine of Scripture," 168–97: "His commitment to God's absolute and unconditional freedom and his embrace of a particular way of understanding being and becoming fit awkwardly with the biblical presentation of God as one who freely binds himself to his promise and of God's Word as an inspired text that cannot be broken" (197); for a similar, but more developed reading, see, Vanhoozer, "A Person of the Book? Barth on Biblical Authority and Interpretation," 26–59 (esp. 57–58), and Ward, *Word and Supplement*, 106–36.

4. For recent readings in which the profile of Barth's soteriological concept of externality is marginal at best, see, for example, D. Gibson's thoughtful reading of Barth's scriptural orientation as "positing . . . the relationship between revelation and the Bible," *Reading the Decree*, 185–88; similarly, Bentley, *The Notion of Mission in Karl Barth's Ecclesiology*, 25–30; in his notable essay, Bender strangely downplays the significance of Barth's concept of externality, "Scripture and Canon in Karl Barth's Early Theology," 183–84; likewise, P. McGlasson asserts that "the text of the Bible, the language of its witness, is not distant from its divine Object," (*Jesus and Judas*, 41–43); Thompson's reading tends to stress an intrinsic relation of the text to revelation, "Witness to the Word," 168–97; K. Runia's analysis of the *CD* material describes the Spirit's illumination and inspiration as permanent in the biblical writers, *Karl Barth's Doctrine of Holy Scripture*, 33–35; for a more qualified account of Runia's point, see, Wood, *Barth's Theology of Interpretation*, 8 n. 127.

5. Our *theological* employment of the term, "ontology" or "ontotheology," which

biblical witnesses as *peccatores iusti* in the consequence of the asymmetry,[6] externality, and unidirectionality of their hidden, new person to the old.[7] Consequently, with respect to God's unbound, pure deity in his relation to the biblical witnesses, if Scripture is wholly gratuitous—unnecessary—to his entire being, then Scripture and the reading church are therefore—contingent—upon his unbound action to which they are entirely bound. I suggest that Barth's bibliological notion of contingence considers God's transcendence in God's immanence: the ontological weight in Barth's well-known talk of God's lordship is on Scripture and theology, and on creation—but *not* on God. As Barth wrote, "God is Lord of the wording of His Word. He is not bound to it but it to Him. He has free control over the wording of Holy Scripture. He can use it or not use it. He can use it in this way or in that way."[8] My account of Barth's reference to the Spirit's scriptural self-presence keeps in view the emphasis on the Spirit's deity as well as the Spirit's oneness in being with the Father and Son. It goes without saying, though it should be said for clarity, that in my reading I do neither

---

Barth did not use *verbatim* but are arguably appropriate in part because of his soteriological primacy of divine action, stresses a concept of God that is substantially different from Kant's, Heidegger's and their expressions in the church. Cf. Heidegger, "The Onto-Theo-logical Constitution of Metaphysics," 70–71 (esp. 125). Heidegger, "Kant's Thesis about Being," 339–43; 362. For an excellent treatment of Heidegger's construal of the relation of theology to Western concept of being, see Thomson, *Heidegger on Ontotheology*, 15ff. D. Stephen Long argues that in Heidegger's construal of "ontotheology" "'God' is at most a supporting framework that props up transcendentalism by way of providing a secure ground for a transcendental standpoint" ("Radical Orthodoxy," 127–28).

6. Cf. H. Kirchstein's careful reading of Barth tends towards a problematic, direct identity between the divine and human spheres. *Der souveräne Gott und die Heilige Schrift*, 30–31. Similarly, see also, *contra* Abraham, *Canon and Criterion in Christian Theology*, 363–90 (esp. 367, 384). Unlike our use of the term "ontology," Abraham's primacy of ontology or "canonical heritage" posits revelation in the so-called "canonical materials, persons, and practices" "working in harmony": there is apparently no qualitative distinction between text and interpretation. (29; 467) By positing God's presence and work in the church's coinherence with Scripture, Scripture can then be thought as domestic in *certain* readers. Cf. Vickers, "Canonical Theism and the Primacy of Ontology," 159–60; 173. "When canonical theists speak of the primacy of ontology over epistemology, we intend to call attention to the transforming presence and work of the triune God in the life of the church." See also, Thesis XXI: "Canonical theism gives intellectual primacy to ontology over epistemology" (5).

7. *CD* I/1, 466. "Grace is the Holy Spirit received, but we ourselves are sinners. This is true. If we say anything else we do not know the deity of the Holy Spirit in God's revelation."

8. *CD* I/1, 139.

hold nor argue that Barth is infallible. Instead, my intention is quite simply a plausible and self-delimited account of his view of Scripture. In sum, whether or not Barth's view of the Spirit is valid—an important question that far exceeds the modest scope of my reading—my reading of Barth's pneumatological reference suggests Barth's arguably crucial, bibliological commitment to a key principle: "*opera trinitatis ad extra sunt indivisa.*"[9]

If this reading of Barth's bibliological emphasis on the pure deity of God is plausible, I suggest, for instance, that Barth's characterization of God's relation to Scripture and the church has less to do with what R.W. Jenson describes as Barth's "Spirit-avoidance"[10] or what R.D. Williams calls the "linear view of revelation."[11] Jenson complains that Barth (apparently) relegates the Spirit from a full agent to an impersonal power, while Williams speaks of Barth's (alleged) subordination of the Spirit to the Father and the Son. Their readings tend to reduce Barth's account of God's saving economy to mere epistemological issues. And this sort of tendency in reading Barth risks giving the impressions, for instance, that God is vulnerable to churchly or creaturely transference; that human ideas about God can be

9. Cited in a creedal reflection in which Barth talks about the gratuity of the knowledge of the Spirit in the creaturely "spirit" on one hand and a logical necessity to confess the deity and operation of the Spirit—"in the light of the principle"—in theology's talk of creation and revelation on the other. Whether it is always explicit throughout the entire career of his writings on Scripture, Barth's commitment is crucial for grasping his approach to the Spirit's relation to Scripture: for instance, a significant, theologically necessary reference to the work of the Spirit—in indivisible unity with the Father and Son—in Barth's description of the anthropological and creaturely orientation of the biblical witnesses. For the immediate context of the citation, see *CD* I/1, 472.

10. Jenson, "You Wonder Where the Spirit Went," 296–304 (esp. 302, 304).

11. Williams, "Barth on the Triune God," in *Karl Barth*, 147–93 (esp. 161–81); for a recent, thoughtful essay on the topic, see Ables, "The Grammar of Pneumatology in Barth and Rahner," 208–24 (esp. notes 7–8). Ables, however, seems to downplay Barth's rejection of any sort of divinization of creature or insistence on the irreducible, Creator-creature ontological distinction (222). I think that by speaking of that distinction in Barth's thought one needs not suggest that the decision of God as Saviour and Redeemer can be posited ontologically in the human and henceforth hermeneutically applied. For a discussion on Barth's account of the ontological distinction with respect to deification, see, for example, McCormack, "Participation in God, Yes, Deification, No: Two Modern Answers to an Ancient Question," 347–74. As we shall see in the following chapters, Barth speaks of the knowledge of that distinction prominently in terms of divine action that is ever *new* as it is always *free*—free, that is, crucially, it is in his nature that God can rest: "This God is not only a God of action," Barth argues, "as the founding of the Sabbath tells us with special beauty. He can not only work; He can also rest from all his works" (*CD* I/1, 322). The notion of divine rest is arguably important for considering Barth's language of divine action and decision, but is often overlooked.

read back into the being and action of God; and that the Spirit lacks genuine freedom in the Godhead, and particularly in relation to the Word. But I suggest in my reading of Barth that these impressions are distortions of his convictions about God; about God's relation to Scripture and to the church; and about the deity and agency of the Spirit of the triune God. As Barth wrote on the relation between the Spirit and Scripture in the reception of the latter by virtue of the former as the ends *and* means of the knowledge of God in Jesus Christ:

> Man remains man, the man who can deceive himself and others; the sign remain a sign, which may fade again and disappear. But the Holy Spirit remains the Holy Spirit wholly and utterly the Spirit of promise. Even and especially the child of God in the New Testament sense will never for a moment or in any regard cease to confess: "I believe that I cannot of my own reason or power believe in Jesus Christ my Lord or come to him." God remains the Lord even and precisely when He "fills" us. No other intercedes with Him on our behalf except Himself. "In thy light we see light" (Ps. 36.9). The deity of the Holy Spirit is thus demanded. The essentiality, the directness of the work of the Holy Spirit is demanded.[12]

Suppose that what concerns Jenson and Williams is Barth's account of the Spirit's freedom in the Godhead, especially in relation to the Word. Barth's writings on Scripture, however, do not attest the concern.[13] On the contrary, I suggest that Barth's aforesaid view on Scripture is arguably informed by his

---

12. *CD* I/1, 464–65. Barth goes on to dismiss any idea of domestication of the Spirit in faith or the believer: "We are not grasping at more but at less and ultimately at nothing at all, if in addition to the guarantee which is identical with God Himself we think we must grasp at an unequivocal experience, at a guarantee of the guarantee so to speak, in order that we may then decide for certainty of faith, as though a certainty for which we must first decide could be the certainty of faith."

13. Cf. Barth's related affirmations of the Spirit's freedom from the Son, and the Spirit's deity as one being and Sache in the Godhead in "Das Schriftprinzip," 527–28. "We object that in the Catholic teaching on revelation the *being* of revelation (Offenbart*sein*) means revealed*ness* (Offenbart*heit*)—Christ and Spirit one nature, one essence, one subject, a thing that *is* not a person *here* who *acts*; ["revelation"] that the catholic church so triumphantly finds, without having to search, *has*, without having to receive; we object that it knows or speaks nothing of the crisis of its one real, confrontational Word of God (*gegenüberstehenden Gotteswortes*), real, that is, not just principally and eternally, but also concretely and contemporarily." See also: "according to the testimony of Scripture the Holy Spirit is no less and no other than God Himself, distinct from Him whom Jesus calls His Father, distinct also from Jesus Himself, yet no less than the Father, and no less than Jesus, God Himself, altogether God" (*CD* I/1, 459).

conviction about the Spirit's freedom in relation to the Word, the Spirit's freedom as characteristic of the freedom and action of the triune God.

Although I argue that Barth's view of Scripture is pneumatologically informed in the terms of his commitment to the logical priority of the belief in God's indivisible, immanence and transcendence, I do not pretend that my self-consciously limited, focused reading of Barth's concept of Scripture can address every legitimate question concerning his pneumatology and doctrine of God (and their implication in theological anthropology of the reader, theology of interpretation, and so on)—neither is that the purpose or objective of the book. More closely, my reading does not pretend to do anymore than scratching the surface of the relation between Scripture and Spirit in Barth's bibliological writings. Succinctly put, it is *not* primarily a reading of Barth's pneumatology or concept of interpretation: it is rather a reading of Barth's theological concept of *Scripture*—what Scripture *is* in terms of its content, nature, and ends by virtue of the activity of the triune God. *Occasionally*, this focus on Barth's concept of *Scripture* would help lead us to, I wish to show, Barth's teachings about the Spirit and about God. Once again, however, the thesis is about Barth's view of *Scripture*, not about his pneumatology in any depth or as a whole: I intend simply to indicate Barth's reference to the Spirit as a significant and visible feature of the shape of his concept of *Scripture*. My language concerning his concepts of divine illumination, inspiration, and election, for instance, serves none other than *occasionally* to highlight just this indication; it does *not* pretend to offer a full account or exhaustive definition of the concepts. And the same rule of delimitation applies to my language of "externality," "creation," "creature," "reader," "theological anthropology," and so on. Moreover, neither is my reading to offer, in addition to exposition of Barth's above-mentioned view of Scripture, any extensive commentary on, or in-depth analysis of, Barth's biblical exposition (or related scriptural texts), reading of European intellectual history, church history, history of dogma, the history of the doctrine of Scripture, or the history of theological and biblical interpretation. In short: as I sketch a picture of Barth's concept of Scripture, my occasional indication of this significant reference to the Spirit is at best *preliminary*—and no more.

In thesis form: Barth was convinced that Holy Scripture is *outside* of itself—it is what it *is*, only by virtue of the saving action of the triune God. Generally put, this formal sounding language of divine action is simply a way of drawing out the theological force of Barth's characterization of the Spirit's unidirectional, gracious employment of Scripture as canonical witness to God's self-revelation in Jesus Christ.[14] Instead of orienting to the Spirit's use of Scripture through "a kind of hermeneutical immediacy,"[15] Barth wrote, "I was and I am an ordinary theologian, who does not have the Word of God at his disposal, but, at best, a 'Doctrine of the Word of God.'"[16] Conversely, if Barth resists any "kind of hermeneutical immediacy," his resistance, I suggest, stems from his belief in God as absolute sovereign over the human person, unbound sovereignty and majesty that are irreducible to human subjects and their self-theorization—including Scripture's own. More closely, Barth's belief suggests that if God's unbound giving of the proper person has a logical priority in proper scripture-reading, our characterization of the proper reader demands more than mere readerly discipline or merely a different way of reading Scripture as Holy Scripture.[17] By indicating the consequence of the contingence *and* necessity of the Spirit's gift of person in the formation, reception, and reading of the biblical canon, Barth could speak confidently *and* self-critically of a logical priority of the history and objectivity of revelation and reconciliation in biblical and theological studies. And this needs a bit of elaboration.

Put slightly differently, if by the miracle of regeneration Scripture points its centre radically away from itself to Christ, it is by the Spirit's electing, sanctifying activity that the unidirectional, unbound relation of his life-giving activity to what Scripture is *comes* to readerly attention.[18] Barth's construal of the proper reader, I suggest, is a corollary of his pneumatological construal of what Scripture is by God's saving act. If Barth stressed that neither Scripture nor the reader is absolute in relation to God,[19] and

14. For more qualified and extensive treatments of the point in its bibliological employment see, for example, Wood, *Barth's Theology of Interpretation*. See also: McCormack, "The Being of Holy Scripture is in Becoming," 55–75; McCormack, "Historical Criticism and Dogmatic Interest in Karl Barth's Theological Exegesis of the New Testament," 322–38; Nimmo, "Exegesis, Ontology and Ethics," 171–87; Schmid, *Verkündigung und Dogmatik in der Theologie Karl Barths*.

15. Lauster, *Prinzip und Methode*, 261. For a classic of the portrayal, see A. Jülicher's criticism of Barth as a "pneumatic," in "A Modern Interpreter of Paul," 72–73.

16. *ChD*, 8.

17. Cf. Briggs, *Words in Action*, 148–53, and Briggs, *The Virtuous Reader*, 66–67; on revelation as a capacity innate to the humanity of the biblical writers and the reader, see Neufeld, *Reconceiving Texts as Speech Acts*, 134–35.

18. *Contra* Smith, *What is Scripture*, 237: "*There is no ontology of scripture.* The concept has no metaphysical, nor logical, reference; there is nothing that scripture finally 'is.'"

19. With the reader principle, Barth's concern was not so much the distracting focus on competing interests in readerly activity as the loss of the self-objectivity of God.

resisted any direct identification of *providentia Dei* with *confusio hominem*, the sort of theological conviction that had made him a life-long stranger to what he called "absolutism" of the human subjecthood,[20] it was not because he was insensitive to the concerns for humanity raised especially in European intellectual history since the Renaissance and by the critics of ontotheology in the church. If he stressed God's absolute freedom, it was rather because he had deeply understood those concerns from the earliest days of his theological career. He was convinced that even in a narcissistic and violent world—in and outside the church—the church, in its intellectual and practical life, must still preach and teach "the pure gospel" as God's mercy and freedom in complete, *concrete* victory over sin; the church can do so, he stressed, only by virtue of the mystery[21] of God's grace and command *in concreto*. In the very least Scripture's primacy of God's gracious action meant for Barth a logical priority of the Spirit's gift of the person in the biblical witness and the reader, and their absent self-entitlement to the gift without exception. If Barth's critics believed that he taught an "abstract, transcendent God who is not concerned with the real men ('God is all, man is nothing!'), abstract eschatological waiting, without significance for the present, and the equally abstract church," all these ideas, Barth declared, were "not in my head."[22]

From the logical priority of the Spirit's giving of the concrete gift of person, it follows that essential to the church's scriptural orientation, Barth argued, is a logical priority of a proper characterization of the person of the

20. *PT*, 19–20 (ET 22–23). For more qualified accounts on Barth's *Protestant Theology in the Nineteenth Century*, see Webster, *Barth's Earlier Theology*, 91–117; see also, Wood's analysis of the anthropological and hermeneutical dimensions of Barth's observations in *Barth's Theology of Interpretation*, 51–99. In a fairly sympathetic reading of the construal of the primacy of the human subject in theological thinking in Leibniz, Kant, Heidegger, and Hegel, Thomson's reading of the same history coincidentally complements Barth's assessment (Thomson, *Heidegger on Ontotheology*, 15–16).

21. Cf. *Anselm*, 73–75. Commenting on Anselm's understanding of God as that "beyond which nothing greater can be conceived," Barth observes, "it does not say—God is the highest that man has in fact conceived, beyond which he can conceive nothing higher, nor does it say—God is the highest that man could conceive. . . . Clearly it is deliberately chosen in such a way that the object which it describes as something completely independent of whether men in actual fact conceive it or can conceive it." God's being is perfect in and of himself, and *not* a consequence of creaturely valuation. "The concept of a 'better' beyond the Creator would imply for the creature an ascent (*ascendere*) to a point where by nature he cannot stand, a judgement (*iudicare*) by a standard of truth or value which by nature he cannot possess" (152–53).

22. For a fuller background of the quote, see Busch, *Karl Barth: His Life*, 290 n. 124.

biblical writers and their readers over epistemic and methodological concerns. It, moreover, follows that, Barth stressed, for instance, human construal of God and humanity—including the Bible's own—is not to be read back into the relation itself, for if the Spirit is free to employ or reject the biblical witnesses, his election of them is his *unqualified*, sovereign freedom absolutely. If Barth resisted any sort of "coinherence of Bible and church"[23] or "divine speech," the scriptural text and "authorized interpretation of the sacred text,"[24] it was in significant part because his self-described identification with the Reformed Scripture Principle, we suggest, had afforded him an immense doctrinal resource to his enduring pneumatological convictions about Scripture.[25] If this reading of the career of his sermons, biblical expositions, and theological writings is plausible, it also reinforces our position on the significance of Barth's self-described Reformed identity as a biblical theologian[26] and the related weight of biblical exegesis in his theological convictions and their maturation.

My account of Barth's concept of the Bible comes to expression here in a study of what is called "Barth's theological ontology of Holy Scripture." Put in its plainest terms, what follows is a sustained argument for certain key aspects of the above-mentioned pneumatological reference in Barth's theological characterization of the person and work of the biblical witnesses as *peccatores iusti*. It is not intended as a simple recommendation of Barth's view of Scripture, or as a comprehensive critique of many theological issues raised in it. Rather, it is a straightforward textual-commentarial account of his more explicitly bibliological material whose adequacy, integrity, and persuasiveness I leave to the judgement of the

---

23. Lindbeck, "Scripture, Consensus, and Community," 78.

24. Cf. Wolterstorff, *Divine Discourse*, 224–25. Whatever he means by "divine discourse" or "divine speech," he posits it in Scripture's human speech-acts to secure a coinherence between a speaking divine being, text, and interpretation (296): "We are able to surmise certain things about God. The conviction that God speaks and that we can interpret that speech presupposes that God is not *ganz anders*" (225). A key problem of his reading of Barth's concept of a biblical witness is a soteriological deficit. (63–74); on the claim of a priority of a general textual ontology as the ground of "God's Word" being "permanently identified with the texts of Scripture," see Ward, *Word and Supplements*, 137.

25. Cf. Marga's perceptive reading of Barth's discussion on the Reformed Scripture Principle, *Karl Barth's Dialogue with Catholicism in Göttingen and Münster*, 86–87.

26. For more qualified, extensive treatments of the point, see, for example, Torrance, *Karl Barth*; Torrance, *Karl Barth, Biblical and Evangelical Theologian*; Wood, *Barth's Theology of Interpretation*. See also, Freudenberg, *Karl Barth und die reformierte Theologie*.

readers—in the hope that this study may open up lines of enquiry serviceable in their own constructive work.

As a theological sketch, moreover, it does not seek or claim to address many issues that, each in its intricacy and integrity, deserves to be considered in a fuller account than what is clearly beyond the specific scope and purpose of this study. In most general terms, such issues include the relation between, for instance, philosophy and theology, metaphysics and hermeneutics, canon and tradition, or biblical and theological studies. Likewise, the sketch is self-consciously delimited in what it attempts to say about the relation of Christian bibliology to the doctrines of God and revelation, christology and pneumatology, along with their extensions: anthropology, ecclesiology, the doctrines of election, reconciliation, sanctification, and so on. Its occasional attempts only scarcely scratch the surface of these concepts and doctrines at best, but do not seek to engage them in any depth.

This sketch, in other words, is only a preliminary study. In it, I argue that his scripture-reading cannot be fully grasped without a proper account of his view of Scripture and his above-mentioned, occasional reference to the Spirit. If our position is plausible and it is possible to read his *magnum opus* on its own terms as a coherent whole, then we suggest that his scriptural orientation in volumes two to four of the *Church Dogmatics* cannot be grasped properly without this specific attention to his explicit doctrine of Scripture in volume one. A complete analysis of the rest of the *Dogmatics* goes beyond the self-consciously delimited scope of my modest sketch that is only a *preliminary* study, and no more.

With all this in mind, I attempted to attend to what Barth meant by "Holy Scripture": about God's relation to the person and work of the biblical writers in the economy of divine self-communication. I have done so by tracing what Barth had to say about the nature, properties and ends of the Bible in God's use of it, through a series of representative writings from his days as a theological student to the publication of the first volume of the *Church Dogmatics*.

Chapter One surveys a set of texts including his sermons, confirmation notes and academic essays from 1906 through 1915, texts arguably representative of his view of Scripture. It traces two prominently concurrent and increasingly competing sets of convictions in Barth's understanding of the relation between Scripture and the reader. The theological force of his convictions about the primacy and priority of God is underscored by tracing the Spirit's activity in and through the scriptural text and the reader. If at first glance he seemed to conflate the Spirit and the reader in his view of Scripture, the material, notably his Safenwil sermons and increasingly forcefully from late 1914 and especially through 1915, affords a different picture. By stressing the primacy and priority of God in the Spirit's relation to Scripture, Barth can, we suggest, begin to rework and describe his scriptural orientation that attends to the text on its own terms as a creaturely free instrument of the Spirit of God.

The gradual process of Barth's reorientation is surveyed in Chapter Two, through a reading of his lectures, both extramural and formal, from 1915 to 1925, and the first two editions of the Romans commentary. I first trace certain bibliological effects of his reorientation by emphasizing Barth's recognition of the eschatological and external character of the relation of the Spirit to the hidden, new creation that the biblical witnesses *are* in the old creation. By referring the hidden, eschatological relation of their new and old person to the unbound course of God's merciful turning towards a sinful humanity, Barth can begin to describe the authors, texts, witness and readers of Scripture as objects of divine mercy for the Spirit's new creation in the passing of an old and broken world.

This soteriological understanding of the biblical witnesses as no more and no less than *peccatores iusti* in "The Righteousness of God" and "The New World in the Bible" lectures is then traced in the prefaces and fourth chapter of *Romans* in the first two editions. By indicating the radical comprehensiveness of Christ in the Pauline eschatological orientation to Scripture, Barth is able to draw out resultant aspects of the person and work of the biblical witnesses and their extrinsic, sanctified solidarity with all humanity. The point is further unpacked through a focused reading of the "Biblical Questions, Insights, and Vistas" lecture. In it I underscore Barth's concept of the externality of the Spirit to the biblical witnesses. His increasingly Reformed articulation of his view of Scripture at Göttingen is the focus of the second part of Chapter Two.

The second part of Chapter Two surveys his increasingly explicitly Reformed view of Scripture through a reading of some of the Göttingen texts. What he lacked in preparation as a novice professor in Reformed theology, he made up with an intense immersion in the field, notably through a series of exegetical, historical and doctrinal lectures from 1921 to 1925. His immersion, especially his self-identification with the Reformed Scripture Principle, was to become formative of the direction in his theological thinking. A focused analysis of the famous public correspondence with Harnack indicates Barth's characteristically Reformed conviction about the pure deity of the Word and Spirit in his polemical, but essentially constructive, critique of Harnack's naturalist and historicist characterizations of revelation, history, the Bible and the reader. By recognizing God's absolute freedom and priority in the Spirit's unbound self-objectivity in Scripture and the reader, Barth can be optimistic about the "'probabilities (Wahrscheinlichkeiten)'" for "the theological task of a pure historical science of the Bible."[27]

The point about the Reformed character of Barth's scripture and doctrinal orientation is argued by way of surveying related, general elements in his pneumatology and concepts of the Trinity, revelation, incarnation, and pure doctrine in his lectures on the Reformed confessions and "The Doctrinal Task of the Reformed church" lecture. The survey underscores the theological force of Barth's increasing emphasis on witness as characteristic of the Reformed soteriological orientation to the majesty and mystery of the freedom of the triune God in the Spirit's electing and sanctifying inspiration and illumination of the biblical witness.

This understanding of Barth's concept of the soteriological primacy of the Spirit in and through Scripture is then unpacked in a focused overview of the Göttingen dogmatics lectures. This section highlights concepts of God's aseity, deity, and life as Barth's theological basis for describing the Spirit's sanctifying use of the scriptural text as canonical witness in trinitarian terms that respect the absolute freedom of the ontological Trinity. This theological basis reinforces Barth's concepts of canon and witness in "The Scripture Principle of the Reformed church" lecture. This crucial lecture helps restate the prominence of the irreducible work of the unbound Spirit in Barth's increasingly magisterial presentation of the Reformed scriptural orientation. By characterizing the person and work of the biblical witnesses in the light of the mystery of God's own life, Barth can stress the primacy and priority of the mystery of the Trinity *ad intra* in the Spirit's external relation to the canon and the church.

Barth's account of the Spirit's work as gratuitous, external, and necessary to the hidden, new person, and work of the biblical witnesses in the old is explored in Chapter Three, through a reading of some of his exegetical and dogmatic writings in Münster. In the reading I suggest that the Johannine indication of the Word's utter distinction from all creation, and

27. "Das Schriftprinzip," 536.

unique, mysterious hypostatic union of subject with Jesus provides Barth a textual basis for his self-identification with the Reformed soteriological primacy of illumination and christological idiom of divine-human dissimilarity in the church's characterization of the extrinsic, unidirectional relation of Jesus Christ to the biblical witnesses and their readers. Barth's trinitarian characterization of God's intramental and extramental freedom in the asymmetrical relation of Jesus as revelation to the biblical witnesses is then traced through a reading of some parts of *Die Christliche Dogmatik im Entwurf*. This material also provides an occasion to refute a general trend of depicting the *Church Dogmatics* as Barth's retraction of his earlier, alleged existential orientation to divine action.

The sketch of his relevant pneumatological language of divine action in the preceding three chapters provides an orientation to a corresponding reading of the first volume in Chapter Four.

In the first part of the reading I sketch key soteriological aspects of Barth's reading of the Protestant Scripture Principle. I emphasize that in Barth's view if God's unbound being or pure deity is characteristic of the Spirit's regeneration of the biblical witnesses as children of God in Christ, the ontological problem of their hidden, new person has a logical priority in the church's undertakings with their written witness over epistemological questions. The second part of the reading explores Barth's characterization of the relation of the Spirit's free animation and self-manifestations to their genuine, human authorship and communication, and considers especially his expositions of 1 Tim and 2 Pet. On his reading, the scriptural text is essentially a genuine, human response of moved, though no less fallible, writers testifying in, through and by a love, freedom, intention, objectivity, and unique ministry that point radically away from theirs to God's own. If this reading is plausible, a key question for the church's consideration of Scripture's *whole* humanity is the sort of genuine or concrete, human person and witness that the writers *are* in their new life through Christ by his Spirit. By *his* Spirit the church, Barth believes, can open up to God's relation to the canon on his own terms. And genuine, spiritual openness to the biblical witness means, in the very least, a readerly willingness—to read, as Barth writes: "Listen to my last piece of advice: exegesis, exegesis and yet more exegesis! Keep to the Word, to the scripture that has been given to us."[28]

---

28. Barth, *Das Evangelium in der Gegenwart*, 17.

I suggest that more than observations of his immediate interactions with the biblical text,[29] which have been pursued to good effects in a number of most recent full-length studies,[30] to capture the theological force of Barth's advice requires a more extensive *theological* mapping of his view of Scripture. Such a sketch, moreover, is more fruitful and accurate by attending to his soteriological concept of externality in what he had to say about what Scripture *is* in the light of and by virtue of the absolute freedom of God.

In my approach to an account of "Barth's theological ontology of Holy Scripture" I am guided by a sense that close—commentarial—attention to what Barth does say in the texts—for example, the immanent features such as a degree of material irregularity and incompleteness in his theological observations and decisions—helps illuminate his thinking on its own terms such as its human character. Moreover, I hope that the result, despite a risk of being repetitive at times in the course of the exposition, may more likely provide a fruitful and serviceable *reading* of him as a reading of *him*, who did, in and prior to the obviously massive first volume of the *CD*, have a great deal to say about what Scripture is.[31]

A few more words about the material orientation of my argument developed in the course of this study: it does not subject the texts to periodization. I am content to let the material itself help illuminate Barth's own relationship to his world and surroundings, asserting no claim on which writing should be considered representative of "the early Barth" or which year or text is the definitive statement of his reorientation from the liberal convictions to postliberal ones. To help avoid misunderstanding, I hope to stress quite plainly that the initial historical-genetic commitments in this study, for example, in the order of appearance of the material, are categorically minimal.

On citations and translations: I have gratefully consulted the standard English translations of Barth where available, and where none existed, I supplied my own. And I have generally cited them, when they reflect my own reading of the original texts. Where a nuance seemed better indicated

29. R. M. Wright notes the problem of absent methodological norm in analysing Barth's exegesis in "Karl Barth's Academic Lectures on Ephesians Göttingen, 1921–1922," xi.

30. The field is vast. For more recent works, see, for example, Wright, "Karl Barth's Academic Lectures on Ephesians Göttingen, 1921–1922"; Bourgine, *L'Herméneutique Théologique de Karl Barth*; Burnett, *Karl Barth's Theological Exegesis*; Kirchstein, *Der souveräne Gott und die Heilige Schrift*; McGlasson, *Jesus and Judas*.

31. Cf. Webster, *Barth's Earlier Theology*, 6–7.

in the original language, I have inscribed it. I have limited English translations to the French and German texts; other languages remain as they appear in the texts cited.

On inclusive language: the majority of the English translations cited as well as some of the secondary literature pre-date contemporary inclusive sensibility. I have left their texts as they are, but have chosen to observe the practices in my own translations. As reality is irreducible to language, none of my measures pretends to be self-sufficient. The gender specific pronouns and the first and third person plurals are used generically, and without intending or implying exclusion.

I

Scripture
Early Convictions

THIS CHAPTER SURVEYS BARTH's view of Scripture, through a reading of some representative texts from 1906 through his pastorate in Safenwil during 1913–15. An important supplement to the survey is a focused, occasional account of his soteriological reference to the work of the Spirit in and through Scripture. Conventional reading of his view of Scripture tends to overlook the reference and its theological force of his enduring characterization of the objectivity of Christ's self-revelation in Scripture as the *Spirit's* sheer miracle.[1] "Miracle" as Barth's central theme in his view of Scripture concerns not merely epistemic or intellectual "wonder," but a new humanity borne to us by God's life-giving presence through the risen Christ. The presupposition that Scripture is borne to us by the Spirit of the risen Christ is one that Barth did not seek (or need) to prove or posit in his view of Scripture. It is, however, true that sometimes in the material he apparently gives an impression to the contrary. In this respect, a stark contrast is arguably equally pronounced between his theological writings and sermons. The contrast, I suggest, is visible between his express confidence in the reliability of trans-personal consciousness as a way to construe revelation's objectivity and his arguably more profound sense of praise and wonder of the majesty of God in Jesus Christ. The contrast, as we shall see in the material, has substantially more to do with Barth's increasingly pointed emphasis on God's asymmetric, soteriological relation to his believers, and with Barth's resistance to two interrelated

---

1. For a most recent example, see Bender, "Scripture and Canon in Karl Barth's Early Theology," 165–80.

errors in Christian theology: the first one is abstracting the humanity and history of the biblical witnesses from the Spirit's saving economy, and the second one is a claim of deification that asserts a coinherence in nature or action between their humanity and the Spirit's pure deity. Although it is true that the language of "Spirit" is not as always explicit or frequent as the references to "God" in Barth's talk of Scripture, the material arguably affords *occasions* for considering the significance of Barth's pneumatological reference alongside his maturing accounts of Scripture's relation to revelation and the reader. A close reading of the material therefore can help open up conversation about Barth's view of Scripture.

The material, moreover, has considerable relevance to the matter of Barth's theological maturation in two aspects. The first aspect is that it helps illuminate a complex mixture of continuity and development of characteristic preoccupations in his concepts of revelation and Scripture. If this reading is plausible, it supports our position that his view of Scripture during his later "break" from a certain liberal Protestant account of this relation was not a wholesale rejection of his earlier convictions about the soteriological character of the primacy, priority, and freedom of God in Scripture. Barth's key conviction was about certain characteristics of the Spirit's activity in and through Scripture. The complexity of mapping Barth's development—and this is the second aspect—I suggest, has, in significant part, to do with his maturing self-critical appreciation for the Spirit's gracious work as unbound, external, and necessary to Scripture's humanity: superficially put, a far-reaching implication of the conviction is a committed resistance to obliging the Godhead to human agency, or reducing their relation to mere noetic issues without due attention to the irreducible, ontological problem of human knowledge of the pure deity of God. By recognizing theological characterization of Scripture essentially as an extension of the church's recognition of the ontological problem of God, Barth was able to begin increasingly to emphasize the mystery of God's deity in the divine employment of the biblical witnesses. One way by which Barth articulated this emphasis was a reference to the work of the Spirit in the economy of revelation and salvation.

More closely, a focus on Barth's pneumatological reference helps illuminate his conviction about the priority of the economy of God's saving work in grasping the anthropological orientation of the biblical witnesses. One implication of acknowledging God's ontological primacy in the knowledge of God and his relation to Scripture is that, instead of merely reading

Scripture differently,[2] Barth had to be a different *person* altogether: not only did he have to repent from faulty convictions, he also had to learn "to be taught"[3] the theme of God anew in his search for a proper understanding of its anthropological orientation, or a "better" understanding. As Barth wrote in retrospect: "better in the sense that in it, God, in his unique position over against man, and especially religious man, might be clearly given the honour we found him to have in the Bible."[4]

On Barth's account, "better" denoted a sometimes incredibly contrite, painful, though no less purposively positive, relation of learning, unlearning and "being taught." The theme of "being taught" does *not* suggest "a kind of hermeneutical immediacy"[5] in Barth. Quite on the contrary! It presupposes Barth's utter rejection of that sort of doctrinal and scriptural orientations as well as their tendency to confuse divine revelation and human faith in the phenomenon of theological learning and teaching. Barth rejected any direct identity between revelation and faith, and the practices of interpretation that asserted it. But Barth did not reject the belief that God did and could command and teach the church by means of the biblical witness. Barth's talk of readerly obedience and openness, I think, needs not be confused as the aforesaid kind of assertion that he clearly rejected. Neither did Barth regard consensus as a measure of the truth of Scripture or readerly receptivity—he saw the danger of Gnosticism was more or less present in the sort of consensus that was unable or unwilling to point beyond itself to God.

What Barth found troubling was not human speech or consensus about God. Instead what was troubling for him was a hamartological deficit in the sort of God-talk that identified God so directly with the world and its affairs that led to absolutization of the human in relation to the divine, a culture identity that was readily dismissive of any concept of a divine "beyond" the human sphere as offensive and (therefore) inconsequential intellectually. This was a trait of an absent divine-human asymmetry, for example, in the concept of authority that Barth already

2. See, for example, Bender, "Scripture and Canon in Karl Barth's Early Theology," 165–66.

3. My notion of "being taught" in the terms of Barth's reading of the Bible, by no means, presupposes any sort of identity between the text and interpretation; instead it suggests that on Barth's reading, the knowledge of God in Scripture points to God's unbound prerogative by virtue of his deity.

4. Barth, "A Thank-You and a Bow—Kiekegaard's Reveille," 97.

5. Lauster, *Prinzip und Methode*, 261.

noticed in modern Protestantism as he saw it present in sixteenth-century Catholicism. And we can see in the early material that Barth was highly critical of it. But perhaps not all good readers of Barth are readily convinced about his explicit resistance to the trait—my point concerns a key to his view of Scripture: his anthropology of the biblical witnesses. Just precisely at this point, it cannot be emphasized enough, I think, the significance of his pneumatological reference, its ontological force and resultant epistemological (and anthropological) implications: the truth about the priority and primacy of the Spirit are irreducible to a mere matter of interpretation of the Bible; neither is the rightness of a reading of Scripture a mere matter of human valuation. Conversely, docetic views of the biblical text and its reader are just as problematic. Succinctly put, for Barth the Bible and its readers are bound to God, but God is unbound to them and their theorizations.[6] Whether or not Barth is seen as a generally careful reader of the scriptural texts, and whether or not his reading is seen as plausible in the eyes of his good readers, "being taught," for instance, is a merely functional theme I occasionally employ to underscore Barth's ontic emphasis on the priority and necessity of divine action in human understanding and acceptance of Scripture's form and content. Once again, the theme does not assume or claim any sort of direct identity or domestication of text and interpretation in Barth's view of Scripture. Instead it is to underscore a pneumatological deficit in depicting Barth's renewed scriptural orientation as none other than a human "discovery of the Bible" or, worse, a sort of reader primacy. The material, however, affords a substantially different picture of Barth's view of what Scripture is.

Second, his renewed concept of Scripture, I suggest, can be seen as an explicit resistance to a certain harmatologically deficient orientation that claims human innate reflexivity or capacity for revelation. As Barth put it: "Everything had always been settled without God. God was always thought to be good enough to put the crowning touch to what men began of their own accord."[7] Similarly, neither was Barth interested in suggesting the Spirit's relation to Scripture as reducible to the church's creed or doctrine.[8] Rather, to speak of the God of Scripture, as Barth reflected, was "a task

---

6. As important as a sketch of Barth's view of interpretation of Scripture is, my reading scarcely touches its surface; more focused, excellent works can be found elsewhere: for example, Wood, *Barth's Theology of Interpretation*; Paddison, *Scripture*.

7. *Der Römerbrief* 1919, cited in Busch, *Karl Barth: His Life*, 99.

8. Bender, "Scripture and Canon in Karl Barth's Early Theology," 167.

beside which all cultural, moral, and patriotic duties, all efforts in 'applied religion,' are child's play."[9]

It is, however, true that Barth's emphasis on God's pure deity and asymmetry to creatures seems more straightforward in his sermons than it does in his theological writings from these early years. In my selection of the Barth-texts, I do not attempt to provide a theory for its apparent inconsistency. Instead, what I wish to indicate in the material is a measure of a reference to the Spirit in his concept of Scripture and certain implications of his pneumatological reference.

In this connexion, his concept of Scripture is traced in this chapter through a survey of his posthumously published "Zwinglis '67 Schlussreden' aus das erste Religionsgespräch zu Zürich 1523"[10] from 1906 and *Konfirmandenunterricht* from 1901–11,[11] and his academic publications "Moderne Theologie und Reichsgottesarbeit"[12] from 1909 and "Der christliche Glaube und die Geschichte"[13] from 1910/2. Read in connection with his later writings that will be examined in subsequent chapters, this survey attempts to offer an orientation to considering Barth's scriptural orientation and a plausible direction of reading him in *CD* I. It aims to open up lines of enquiry, through attending to his early pneumatological convictions in some of the more explicit bibliological material. This material, however, is only a fraction of Barth's work in this period of his career. While its relevance to understanding his bibliology is considerably significant, the weight of the material in relation to his later writings is kept in view. This survey proceeds with these considerations, goals and material difficulties in mind.

"Zwinglis '67 Schlussreden' aus das erste Religionsgespräch zu Zürich 1523"

In his student paper "Zwinglis '67 Schlussreden' aus das erste Religionsgespräch zu Zürich 1523," Barth identifies certain key elements in Zwingli's specification of what Scripture is in light of God's primacy and priority in

9. Barth, "The Righteousness of God," in *WGWM*, 25–26.

10. Barth, "Zwinglis '67 Schlussreden' aus das erste Religionsgespräch zu Zürich 1523," 104–19.

11. Barth, *Konfirmandenunterricht*, 197–206.

12. Barth, "Moderne Theologie und Reichsgottesarbeit," 341–47.

13. Barth, "Der Christliche Glaube und die Geschichte," 149–212.

the community of believers. Written in the WS 1905/6 for his father's course on church history, this paper offers an account of Barth's initial thinking on the nature of revelation and corresponding bibliological implications.[14]

In his sketch of the 1523 Zürich disputation Barth focuses on Zwingli's chief concern: a proper understanding of the relation of God to humanity through Scripture as an irreducible authority.[15] In a sense, what Barth finds attractive is Zwingli's deployment of a concept of God's radical relational superiority in the articulation of the nature of Scripture's self-authenticating authority: if God's relational primacy concerns his ontological force in, over and through Scripture, the church's relation to Scripture is at best noetic, not ontic. By understanding God's ontological force as a theological basis to describe Scripture's relation to the church, Zwingli can rework the dogmatic foundations in church's scriptural orientation. Barth sums up the polemical and constructive goals of this deployment in a provocative slogan: "Away from Rome! Return to the Gospel!"[16]

In Barth's view, by reversing the priority of institutions in favour of the individuals, Zwingli can secure Scripture's priority over tradition in matters of biblical interpretation.[17] Interpretation of Scripture for Zwingli, Barth argues, consists of a community of persons whose capacity or reflexivity for revelation is consistently spontaneous. Whether his cryptic and underdeveloped presentation of Zwingli is plausible, we can identify a relevant set of key themes in his reading of Zwingli's concept of divine-human relation, as follows.

First, in Zwingli Barth recognizes the individual as an irreducible norm in the self-presence of Christ. Crucially, Zwingli's 'Christ,' on Barth's reading, seems to serve as an automatic affirmation of the individual's capacity or spontaneity for revelation in virtue of being human whose grasp of the gospel as present in Scripture, moreover, becomes an irreducible authority *de facto*.

Second, the *de facto* inner authority of the individual refers to an interrelatedness between the themes of Scripture's inspiration and revelation in the pneumatological idiom of divine self-mediation. Divine self-mediation

14. One key implication, in Barth's largely subtle expression, is the import of the work of the Spirit in human knowledge of Christ. Barth, "Zwinglis '67 Schlussreden," 115.

15. Ibid., 107: "das Verhältnis von göttlicher und menschlicher Autorität, d. h. speziell von Schrift und Kirchentum" [the relation between divine and human authorities, that is, especially between Scripture and ecclesiasticism].

16. Ibid., 108.

17. Ibid., 107.

in Zwingli points to the unmediated nature of God's self-communicative presence in individuals on the basis of their humanity in Christ.[18] Christ's community of individual persons as construed in accordance of their relation to Christ, in short, becomes the context and content of the hermeneutical situation of the church's scriptural orientation.

What picture of God's relation to the individual and Scripture emerges in his reading of Zwingli's concept of divine self-mediation? In Barth's reflection on Zwingli's second movement on the gospel, he is identifying two corollaries of Zwingli's account of a trans-individual mediation of Christ. The first corollary is the domestication of Scripture's revelation in the individuals. The individuals can read their self-described relation to Christ back into revelation, a coinherence of God's human relations in soteriological terms that is intrinsic to being human in Christ.

This anthropological orientation reflects Zwingli's humanism that, moreover, has the individual as a legitimate theological norm against institutional abuse and oppression. In Zwingli, Barth recognizes the priority of the human person in God's use of creaturely media. As a medium, Scripture's primary form is God's domestic presence to trans-personal consciousness whose expression in the scriptural text is formally secondary and subordinated to the reader. The reader's primacy or the reader principle in Zwingli is grounded in a pneumatological view of their common humanity of the biblical writers and their readers with Jesus as "the children of God."[19] Succinctly put, the reader's self-described relation to Christ is qualitatively equivalent to, and can be legitimately read back into, God's own relation to Scripture. Scripture's relation to the reader, in short, comes under the determination and theme of the personal experience of trans-individual consciousness.

More closely, the theme of personal consciousness, as we can see, finds itself in the setting of the pneumatological idiom of divine self-mediation. That is also to say, on Barth's reading of Zwingli, only in the economy of divine self-mediation can the common humanity of the reader and the biblical writers and Jesus come to light. The concept of divine priority is a theological basis for the "givenness" of Scripture in Barth's reading of Zwingli: "where was he to find the divine authority to which he appealed? His answer read: In the Holy Scripture, Old and New Testaments."[20] The

18. Ibid., 109.

19. Ibid., 111.

20. Ibid., 112.

seminal point is, in short, Zwingli's domestication of the objectivity of God's use of Scripture in the Christian reader, an objectivity in which if the reader and the biblical writers coinhere in Christ, the scriptural text is to be read in the light of their coinherence.

In light of this understanding of the reader's relation to Scripture, one may ask moreover: What is Zwingli's concept of the biblical *text* in the economy of divine self-communication? Crucially, for Barth Scripture's orientation to God's saving economy suggests the problem of construing Scripture through a general theory of text or history that does not respect the precedence and particularity of the Spirit's *salvific* testimony as the Scripture's origin and referent. The point is pronounced in his contrast of Zwingli's "formal principle of the Reformational proclamation" vis-à-vis two views:

> *Orthodoxy*: the Holy Scripture is in its wording binding for Christianity and the church at all times, and the (ultra-)*history of religion* [school]: the Bible is like other literature of antiquity, a historical mass, and hence has only historical, that is, limited meaning and binding authority.[21]

If Barth is uninterested in reinforcing either of the views, it is in part because he is able to recognize their common dilemma in relating human authority to divine authority. On Barth's reading, the ontological problem of God's use of Scripture precedes its corresponding epistemological issues. What Barth finds attractive in Zwingli is an appreciation of God's self-authenticating dissimilarity from creatures. In this specific sense, our reading can perhaps add to Bender's perceptive observation that "Barth's later understanding of Scripture was an attempt to overcome this dilemma, refusing to side with one position over against the other in what Barth in time came to maintain was a false choice."[22]

If the dilemma entails "a false choice," we suggest that it is because Barth is, at least preliminarily, able to recognize the theological force of Zwlingi's concept of Creator-creature dissimilarity: the concept is so essential to the reformer's understanding of God's deity in the divine employment of

---

21. Ibid., 112–13.

22. Bender, "Scripture and Canon in Karl Barth's Early Theology," 172. Bender's perceptive reading tends distracted by an excessive emphasis on Barth's "dynamic and dialectical view of Scripture," a distraction that undermines the concretely prevailing *ontological* problem of Scripture in favour of the epistemological or the methodological one. Barth's view of Scripture concerns, as we can see, *more* than merely a different *way* of reading Scripture.

Scripture that the concept seeks its basis in this God, but not in itself. A human in Christ is interpreted before they interpret, and their interpretation of who God is and God's relation to creatures is an act of what they already are in the relation: their person is bound to Christ's own communication and the Spirit's regeneration. Their person is therefore not a mere matter of their self-interpretation or self-determination. Neither is their person a result of human consensus. Barth understands that theology's characterization of the nature of the text depends on what Scripture *is* "in its summary (Zusammenfassung) as gospel and in its living authentication through its indwelling Spirit."[23] A net result of Barth's reference to the Spirit is that it points the humanity of Scripture beyond human subjectivity.[24] A case in point is Barth's subordination of the category of "text" to a comprehensive concept of "testimony" as a subset of the outreaching work of the Spirit. The subordination, moreover, does not suggest Barth's interest in deifying human testimony. By contrast, Barth complains that Zwingli lacks a precise *distinction* between the Word and Scripture:

> The . . . question, which the modern theologian who is historically minded theologian imposes immediately: How do we differentiate *"the self-authenticating Word of God from Scripture as such"*? Could and needed Zwingli not position the concept with this sharpness that has become essential for us.[25]

Note that as Barth turns to the question of divine-human dissimilarity on Zwlingi, he is interested in a more precise pneumatological reference in Protestantism's characterization of the relation between Scripture and the church. Barth apparently thinks that this sort of pneumatological precision might sharpen theology's characterization of the relation between the Spirit, Scripture, and the church.

If key issue in the concept of divine-human dissimilarity is a proper characterization of divine and human agencies in Scripture, Barth's reflection on it is still underdeveloped, however: it lacks the conceptual clarity and precision in his theological language regarding the person and work of the biblical writers in their distinction from and relation to the Spirit.

---

23. Barth, "Zwinglis '67 Schlussreden'," 113: "nicht die Schrift als äußeres Lehrgesetz, sondern in ihrer Zusammenfassung als Evangelium und in ihrer lebendigen Beglaubigung durch den ihr innewohnenden Geist." [not Scripture as an external creed, but in its summary as gospel and in its living attestation by the indwelling Spirit.]

24. Williams, "Barth on the Triune God," 161–81.

25. Barth, "Zwinglis '67 Schlussreden'," 113–14.

Neither does Barth discuss the relation between the Spirit and the Word in any substantial detail.

For him God's self-authenticating "unity" in Scripture and the reader is key concept in Zwingli's scriptural orientation, though by "unity" he means not so much coherence in God's own objectivity in and through "Holy Scripture," as an inner coherence *in* the reader. The reader, in effect, operates as the hermeneutical situation of Scripture, revelation, and, finally, the triune God. Of all this, Barth would gradually become aware— much to his horror. For now, we can simply note his initial awareness of a basic, but no less crucial, pneumatological orientation in Zwingli's construal of Holy Scripture.

As Barth construes Zwingli's Reformed scriptural orientation, he is identifying two basic features. The first feature concerns the tension between Reformed Protestantism and sixteenth-century Roman Catholicism, namely, the prevailing priority of God over the church in relation to the Bible.[26] Once again, the Reformed emphasis on divine primacy and priority entails an emphasis on God's distinction from the church, a distinction whose primary ground, moreover, is God's self-communication, not dogma. And this leads to the second feature: the church's proper scriptural orientation concerns the church's attentiveness beyond doctrine but to (the interiority of) the text itself: "The study of the Holy Scripture had led to this understanding which was therefore the basis (Grundlage) of the new proclamation, to which the Reformation position always appealed."[27]

On Barth's reading, however, the scriptural text is relatively passive compared to the reader. If the distinction between God, the scriptural text, and the church does not seem to extend to a sharp distinction between the text and the reader, it is, I suggest, not because Barth wants to do away with the Creator-creature distinction; but because, instead, he is interested in a reference to God in grasping the ground of the relation between the text and the reader in the economy of revelation and salvation. Yet Barth's reading seems to give the impression that the reference to God is in effect no more than a reference to human subjectivity. As Barth refers to Zwingli's view on the sacraments:

> The eternal truths of the Gospel are comprehended, not in outward forms (Formen), but are always understood spiritually (geistig). If,

26. Ibid., 115.
27. Ibid., 114.

> however, we keep such forms, they are to us nothing more than symbols (Sinnbilder) of a spiritual reality.[28]

Scripture relates to individuals as reality relates to the mind. It is a "geistig" reality. If reading Scripture is only a matter of hermeneutics, and hermeneutics is primarily a matter of what goes on cognitively, Barth is convinced that the question of Scripture's pneumatological nature, content and properties is appropriately a question of the being of personal consciousness in the experience of reading Scripture. In short, for Barth a key message from his reading of Zwlingi is the liberation of the individual from institutions as a result of a renewed recognition of God's distinction from the church and of God's revelation as an *internal* gospel after all.[29]

Barth's treatment of Zwingli indicates his initial awareness of pneumatological reference in the reformer's account of what Scripture is, on at least two counts. The first one is Barth's awareness of Zwingli's reference to the Spirit in the distinction between divine agency and human agency in Scripture and the reader.[30] More closely, as he unpacks the distinction however preliminarily, Barth shows a *slight* hint of awareness of a characteristic pneumatological investment in the reformer's concepts of revelation and God and extensional teachings about Scripture, history and the human person. Whether or not Barth rightly perceives these pneumatological teachings, he seems to accept the reference to the Spirit as characteristic of his Protestant bibliological heritage. That said, I stress that given the scarcity of textual evidence Barth's idea about the Spirit is far from obvious.

The second proof is an extension of the first: far from regarding the human person in absolute terms, his point about the individual indicates his concepts of the soteriological primacy and priority of the Spirit in the relation of the reader to Scripture and revelation. His insistence on the distinction between divine and human agency in his discussion of the post-Reformation doctrine of verbal inspiration is a case in point. It is, however, fair to say that Barth's account of pneumatological teachings about Scripture does not enjoy the same level of prominence as his discussion on related christological, bibiological teachings. The absent, formal, doctrinal language such as "illumination" does not suggest that Barth is unaware of the *teaching* about the inner testimony of the Spirit in his reading of Zwingli's (and more briefly Luther's) concept of Scripture. On the contrary, Barth's

28. Ibid., 117.

29. Ibid., 119.

30. Ibid., 117.

appeal to the teaching is explicit in his account of the subordination of the external form of Scripture to the internal.[31] In spite of being subtle when comparing to his christological discussion, his account of pneumatological teachings about Scripture is arguably visible.

Whether or not Barth's treatment of Zwingli is sound or instructive, it is perhaps not too severe to say that in the student paper his language of Spirit is underdeveloped. For instance, it lacks an expressed doctrine of the Trinity, its extensions such as the *hypostasis* of the Spirit in relation to the Son and to the biblical witnesses and their readers. What he lacks in detail and precision about the relation of divine agency to human agency in Scripture, for instance, Barth will, to an extent, make up for with an appeal to a teaching about the necessity and priority of divine renewal of the human person in church work, as we shall see in the "Moderne Theologie und Reichsgottesarbeit" essay.

"Moderne Theologie und Reichsgottesarbeit"

In the essay Barth teaches about the priority and primacy of divine renewal of the human person in the intellectual and practical spheres of church work.[32] Barth perceives that if (1) the source and norm of the inner life of an individual in Christ is none other than God himself who alone gives and absolves her inner life, (2) her inner life is irreducible to her life in church or her certainty in Christ irreducible to her certainty in human norms, and (3) church work inevitably takes place in a sphere of human authority (4) whose talk about God carries, in Barth's view, an inherent risk of losing sight of the need to appeal to God for authority, certainty, and renewal in the Christian life.

31. Ibid., 113: "nicht die Schrift als äußeres Lehrgesetz, sondern in ihrer Zusammenfassung als Evangelium und in ihrer lebendigen Beglaubigung durch den ihr innewohnenden Geist" [not the scripture as external creed, but in its summary as gospel and in its living attestation through its indwelling Spirit].

32. My reading treats the article along with the subsequent published responses between Barth and E. C. Achelis of Marburg and P. Drews of Halle. Achelis, "Noch einmal," 355; Drews, "Zum dritten Mal," 351–54; Barth, "Antwort an D. Achelis und D. Drews," 354–65.

One key issue in church work is a proper account of God's distinction from, and relation to, the individual[33] in the Christ[34] of Scripture,[35] the Christ who is irreducible to tradition and doctrine.[36] If a human person in Christ is irreducible to her relation to the church, the issue presents a concrete, intellectual and practical challenge in church ministry: the challenge of bearing witness to this Christ without losing sight of a proper account of divine agency in human witness. As Barth regards the challenge as a commonplace among graduates from "modern" theological faculties such as Marburg and Heidelberg, he underscores a "reason" for this challenge: "the deepest reason of that fact was found in certain difficulties which arise from our scientific understanding of religion in history and present" (wissenschaftlichen Verständnis der Religion in Geschichte und Gegenwart).[37] The "reason" can be unpacked in at least two aspects.

The first aspect concerns divine agency in faith's proper relation to revelation,[38] and more concretely, the challenge of theological and pastoral work to bear witness (Zeugnis) to the God of Scripture. Barth apparently regards the challenge as one from "modern" schools such as Marburg to the more conservative theological faculties and their graduates: "Can you bear witness to the faith that is in you (1 Pet. 3), as we can?"[39] Although Barth's account of 1 Peter 3.15 is fairly underdeveloped and cryptic and its weight limited, he is indicating what is significant here and would remain so in his overall view of Scripture: the priority of a divine giving of an inner, personal certainty about the scriptural testimony of Jesus Christ in the scriptural and doctrinal orientation of the church.

33. Barth, "Antwort an D. Achelis und D. Drews," 363–64: "Kein Anderer als Gott, und Gott nicht als irgendwelche äußere Norm, sondern als die individuelle innere Gewißheit und Autorität, die ihm in Christus, wie er durch die Geschichte der Völker und Menschen geht, zur Offenbarung wird." [None other than God—God not as some external norm, but God as the inner conscience and authority of the individual in Christ, how revelation comes as he goes through the Geschichte of peoples and humanity.]

34. Barth, "Moderne Theologie und Reichsgottesarbeit," 345. On the theme of "ministry."

35. Ibid., 344. The context of Barth's point on the New Testament's resemblance to other literature is his account of the priority of divine agency—with an emphasis on the constant human need of renewal by God—in the reader's relation to the biblical witnesses, and more importantly, to the Jesus of their testimony.

36. Barth, "Antwort an D. Achelis und D. Drews," 361–62.

37. Barth, "Moderne Theologie und Reichsgottesarbeit," 341.

38. Ibid., 341–42.

39. Ibid., 342.

Awaking of religion is individually conditioned, as we understand it. Where a person has come to the recognition of that, which is carried out through a well-recognized order, is to him actually impossible, there he experiences that a power meets him in the tradition of the Christian church or in its life, a power to which he must submit in obedience and trust totally. But when does he come to the knowledge of the demarcation (Bruch) in his moral will? And which side of the Christian traditions, which signs of life of the present religion (Lebensäußerungen gegenwärtiger Religion) become to him revelation (Offenbarung) which frees and obliges him? To all questions, to which only he himself as such can respond, there is no general ordo salutis, but also no general source of revelation (allgemeingiltige Offenbarungsquelle) that one could demonstrate to the other.

The individual life of a revelation-based religion (das Leben der auf der Offenbarung beruhenden Religion) is finite. Having been mortified (erlegen) by that power, the Christian overcomes the world (see 1 Joh. 5.4). With rising clarity as well as with constant fighting in her inner life, in her willing and thinking through the experience of which the new affects her, she obeys the divine norms (göttlichen Normen), her world becomes God's world that works out for the best for those who love him (see Rom. 8, 28). But none other than faith can supply the yardsticks of this world-overcoming (Aber die Maßstäbe zu dieser Weltüberwindung müssen aus seinem eigenen Glauben hervorgehen, kein Andrer kann sie ihm geben.) Christian morality (christliche Sittlichkeit) knows no single, normative commandments (normativen Einzelgebote), and gives no normative Christian worldview.[40]

If the proper office of theological and pastoral work is to refer to God as the origin and strength of the Christian life—and this is the second aspect—Barth thinks that our referential method and practice carry, for all their careful designs of good intention, an inherent risk, through complacency, error, or omission, in failing to point away from ourselves to God as his own authority, sufficiency and hermeneutical situation of all his works. In this specific sense, put differently, Barth is identifying an inherent danger of losing sight of God's self-determined and self-sufficient relation to us in the intellectual and pastoral spheres of church work: the church's scriptural orientation that does not explicitly respect the priority of God's renewal activity can compromise the integrity of the very spiritual nature, content, ends, and ethical character of Christian bibliology. Although his initial

40. Ibid., 342–43.

articulation of all this finds expression in his confidence in the reliability of trans-personal consciousness, we can see Barth stressing the priority of God's renewal act in believers as a necessary condition of their relation to revelation. Whether his concept of deity is fully developed at this point, Barth does not reduce the act of divine renewal to mere human subjectivity in any form:[41] instead he rejects any "general ordo salutis" or any "general source of revelation."[42]

As he reflects on the divine-human vertical relation Barth is recognizing that revelation delimits personal experience also: the individual is a consequence of revelation, *not* vice versa: in a sense, God's relation and use of Scripture is the ground and hermeneutical situation of the reader's personal awakening.[43] The reader's spiritual awakening is in, by, and through *God's* activity, so that there is "no general source of revelation which one could demonstrate to another."[44] The relation of the readers to God is not to be read back into God's relation to them individually or collectively: there is a formal reserve of God as a mystery of his freedom. That is Barth's seminal point.

What picture of Scripture emerges from Barth's account of revelation and Scripture? First, Scripture is a passive object of God's internal awakening of the readers. In readerly undertakings "Scripture" is construed as passive by derivation. In this construal, Scripture's external form as text is a book like any other.[45] Once again, a net result of all this concerns the precedence of God's quickening and the consequence of the readerly internalization of the unity of Scripture's form and content. The theologian who acknowledges his constant need of God's help can and must, in self-involving terms, recognize and articulate the priority of God's use of the scriptural text in the economy of revelation and salvation: "the same theologian, who owes the strength and peace of his inner life to the New Testament which lifts him up above the world to God, sees also in the New Testament a collection of religious writings like any other."[46] There is, so to speak, no "backdoor" to Scripture's spiritual content. Once again, the reader's relation to the Christ

---

41. Williams, "Barth on the Triune God," 161–81.

42. Barth, "Moderne Theologie und Reichsgottesarbeit," 342–43.

43. Ibid.

44. Ibid.

45. Ibid., 344.

46. Ibid.

of Scripture is construed in terms of the precedence of God's relation to the person of the biblical writers and their work.

That is to say, in reading Scripture the reader becomes aware of his finitude before revelation, and of the constant *human* need for spiritual renewal. In this sense, the reality of the "modern" theologian consists of God's gift of the human freedom of faith and obedience, a gift that neither the theologian nor the church can secure or supply, but that which can be gratefully acknowledged and concretely lived in its graciously established and momentously disclosed *human* reality of which Scripture is a part. As such, the situation of practical work calls for a self-involving and attentive theologian who by the gift of Christ's scriptural testimony becomes genuinely conscious of the constant danger of preaching or teaching what one does not *live* personally. For Barth, faith in revelation cannot live in isolation from its source, namely, God. Speaking of "ministry" from this perspective, Barth writes:

> It is for him a life's work, because this orientation to the thoughts of the past is not to be complete in some semesters, but only drawing on the variety of multifaceted practical experiences, how these thoughts themselves are the products of multifaceted experience. This work is for him not theoretical, it is imposed on his conscience, because the conscience is absolved only in the innermost connection with his own moral-personal development.[47]

Thus Barth on a key *practical* difficulty confronting practitioners in the intellectual or practical life of the church. By understanding Scripture in terms of God's irreducible agency and the resultant, radical responsibility of human agency in Christ, Barth can appreciate the danger of abuse of power in the church and its institutions. Of these dangers, Barth thinks that Protestant pietism and sixteenth-century Roman Catholicism are a case in point, noting that "modern" theology has neither room nor respect for any form of Gnosticism.[48]

But for all its emphasis on God and compassionate ethical concerns, there is a crucial deficiency in his view of Scripture: by placing Scripture's objectivity in mere human objectivity, authentication of the relation of

47. Ibid., 345.

48. Ibid., 346. While Barth does not offer a definition of "Gnosticism," it is not to be confused with an absent human consensus, especially if one is to consider that in the material Barth utterly rejects any personal or institutional privilege as a ground or means to the knowledge of God and its human objectivity.

Christ to Scripture is restricted and reduced to the faith and obedience of the individual in the church. As he writes, "None other than God—God not as some external norm, but God as the inner conscience and authority of the individual in Christ, how revelation comes as he goes through the Geschichte of peoples and humanity."[49] Just at this point, Barth's overemphasis on readerly ethics, for all its legitimate importance, apparently overshadows the interrelated but more formally and materially significant account of the God's saving economy as *external* to human objectivity. Put differently, an implication of Barth's view of Scripture that he himself appears to overlook concerns Scripture's primary objectivity as the objectivity of the ontological Trinity, not Scripture's primary objectivity as creaturely or human objectivity. His talk of God as the cause of human objectivity comes short of being an explicit doctrine of the Trinity—and still less a concept of the Spirit. But for now, we can simply acknowledge his initial awareness of the God's saving economy as Scripture's hermeneutical situation.

For Barth personal experience refers to an objectivity in relation to which individuals are recipients, witnesses and not the origin. In his view, all this suggests that only by orienting to the priority of the spiritual reality of Scripture, can the church begin to be taught and to acknowledge its proper anthropological orientation to being human in Christ. In Gnostic elitism as in pietism's excessive sense of self-responsibility, the heart of both abuses is a narcissistic culture of self-entitlement to the grace of revelation.[50] By contrast, instead of asserting "modern" theology's authority over dissenting views, the "modern" theologians can and must acknowledge modestly, humbly, and gratefully that which God alone can supply, namely, the gift of faith in the Jesus Christ of Scripture.

This article affords an entrée to Barth's soteriological character of his view of Scripture, especially Barth's emphasis on the necessity and priority of God's regenerative act as miracle. But for all its intention to stress the priority of God's saving activity, the article is, on its own terms, deficient in its account of divine-human distinction. Its deficiency is visible at least on two fronts: (a) a lack of a substantial account of God's self-objectivity of the person and work of the biblical witnesses as *writers*, and (b) an absent, corresponding account of the "modern" Christians as *readers*. Talk of Scripture's writers and readers absent a theological account of their distinction begs the question about the primacy and priority of divine agency in

49. Barth, "Antwort an D. Achelis und D. Drews," 363–64.
50. Barth, "Moderne Theologie und Reichsgottesarbeit," 347.

their relation to one another and to God himself. The question concerns therefore a threefold relation over which God is sovereign and free absolutely. More closely, if the threefold relation *is* and comes to our attention by virtue of God's saving activity, and God's economy consequently has a logical priority in and over the church's account of the relation, then an absent account of the text-reader distinction further begs the question about the basis of the church's talk of the unity of God's works in time. Succinctly put, does the church's account of the threefold relation stem from the church's more primary conviction about the primacy and priority of God? In our reading of his confirmation notes, we will see Barth considering Scripture's spiritual character with the question in view.

Konfirmandenunterricht 1909/1911

Barth's emphasis on the spiritual nature of Scripture is visible in his confirmation instruction. As he reflected on bibliology's central theological issue—God's relation to the biblical text—Barth continued to develop his understanding of the nature of work of pastors and theologians as *referential*.

As an assistant pastor in Geneva, Barth taught confirmation classes between 1909 and 1911. The beginning of Barth's career as a *Konfirmator* was rather humbling. When he asked his students for names of Old Testament prophets their reply was "Abraham and Eve."[51] As he reflected on the chief purpose of the lessons, Barth saw that it was "to give young people some coherence and clarity in their inner life."[52] That would mean, once again, indicating the priority and primacy of God's agency in relation to human agency. As he wrote, "We pastors and theologians have neither to administer nor to distribute religion: our task is always only to arouse, to encourage and to shape."[53]

Put simply, the task of the pastors and theologians is *at best* indicative and preparatory of the miraculous divine-human encounter in personal religious experience. The referential emphasis is visible in the confirmation lessons. But the lessons' limitation as material of Barth's view of Scripture needs to be kept in view. Many of the statements are no more than one or two short and severely cryptic, and sometimes incomplete, sentences. Within their limitations, the lessons do offer a basic introduction to the

51. Busch, *Karl Barth: His Life*, 55.

52. Ibid.

53. Ibid., 52.

Protestant biblical canon in light of the relation of revelation to the Bible and the readers. In relation, they afford a basic evidence of Barth's initial awareness of classical issues raised in the history of the doctrine of inspiration. Of the doctrine of inspiration, Barth warns his students against deification of the text, and he does so by deferring to the Word's own activity in theology's characterization of the biblical writers and the readers:[54] "Because God reveals to the people of the Bible internally, we call the Bible God's revelation. When in reading and hearing we can also get their experiences. Self-efficacy of the divine Word." This requires a little bit of elaboration.

As he reflects on reading and hearing as modes of God's self-presence to the reader in and through Scripture, Barth is identifying the economy of the Word as the hermeneutical situation of God's relation to the biblical witnesses and the relation as a theological basis of construing the reader's own relation to the Word. Since the readers, thinks Barth, are bound to the Word's economy of self-communication in and through the Bible, they are not entitled to rely on any arbitrary or artificial distinction between the divine Word and the human word, as he writes, "Where is the border between God's Word and human word? *No border.*"[55] Yet only in light of his emphasis on the priority and primacy of divine agency in human agency, can a key intention in his apparent trivialization of divine-human dissimilarity be understood. His intention, I suggest, concerns the subordination of the theme of the human person of the biblical witnesses to the theme of miracle against a tendency of reducing God's activity to mere expressions of human affairs.[56] By keeping some sort of divine-human distinction, Barth is able to circumscribe the spiritual character of readerly activity by pointing beyond mere human subjectivity to a kind of external objectivity of the text, as he writes about "*Bible reading*": "Regularity! Not slavery but faith. Must be done rationally also: whole Scripture in relation."[57]

---

54. Barth, *Konfirmandenunterricht*, 68–69.

55. Ibid., 69.

56. In his letter to M. Rade on Dec. 31, 1910, Barth expressed his suspicion of a tendency of trivializing the distinction between the "hominum confusione et Dei providential" in relation of political and churchly developments in Germany (Barth, *B-Rade*, 76–79).

57. Barth, *Konfirmandenunterricht*, 69. "Zusammenhang" refers to Scripture's intratextual property, possibly reflecting his differing from Zwingli's notion of Scripture as "Zusammenfassung als Evangelium" by emphasizing inter-textual co-relations (that is, individualities of the texts) over textual unity or canonical coherence—thus pushing textual objectivity of revelation into the cognitive farther away from the external Word or the texts as they were. See also, Barth, "Zwinglis '67 Schlussreden," 113.

The understanding of the theme of "whole Scripture in relation" is christologically grounded. Put in the plain terms of the lesson notes: the revelation of "Jesus Christ" makes Scripture "significant."[58] Scripture's significance is spiritually construed in terms of its place as a miracle in the economy of revelation and salvation; only in light of the priority of God, not in positing Christ's relation to Scripture in the text or its more immediate linguistic features, can Scripture's spiritual nature, content, and properties be grasped properly. However, once again, his view of Scripture does not consist of a qualitative demarcation between the Bible and the reader in moments of divine *autopistia*, moments that are borne to human *persons*, not things. Moreover, by apparently reducing the human person of the biblical witnesses to the human person of the readers, Barth seems to reduce the text to interpretation. Formally put, if God's relation to the reader and the reader's self-described relation to God virtually coinhere, the reader can see the common spiritual reality in all literature among which the scriptural text is just like any other.[59] Once again, the question of the objectivity of the text in the economy of revelation and salvation seems to be a question of readerly consensus.

That is, however, not to suggest that Barth thinks that a general concept of what a text is can have priority over what Scripture is in God's saving economy. On the contrary the economy has logical priority in theology's consideration of what Scripture is. As Barth speaks of a christologically grounded referential character of the "whole Scripture" as *holy*:

> The Christian certainty and therefore our instruction [are] also based on God's revelation in the Holy Scripture, especially the New Testament. For there we find the oldest messages and thoughts about Jesus, written down by people, who themselves have vividly experienced the majesty of the Christian certainty. We shall, of course, let the good people, who have lived later, show us the way to Jesus and from Jesus to God. We call the Bible Holy Scripture, not because we would apply to its letter (Buchstaben) or its individual thoughts a special holiness, but because Scripture speaks of that which is holy.[60]

In summary, although his account of the relation of revelation to Scripture is severely compressed here two themes are prominent in the

---

58. Barth, *Konfirmandenunterricht*, 69.

59. Ibid.

60. Ibid., 67.

confirmation instruction notes, namely, Scripture's spiritual character and the priority and primacy of the economy of God's saving activity. In light of Barth's emphasis on the priority of the human person, some questions should be raised, once again, about the lack of a *hypostasis* between Scripture and the reader. The central issue concerns whether in God's economy of revelation and salvation, there *is* "Holy Scripture"—more than mere human cognition or valuation. If Barth thinks that the reader is Scripture's hermeneutical situation, he has to show, on one hand, how human cognition can carry the weight of the unity of God's saving work in time, and on the other hand, how the Christ of Scripture is identical with the Christ in the reader without trivializing the hypostasis of the biblical witnesses. My points are not raised as criticisms, especially given the obvious limitations of the confirmation notes. What Barth lacks in depth and detail in these notes he will make up with lengthy reflections on the forms of revelation by way of his Neutchatel lecture "Der christliche Glaube und die Geschichte."[61] It is to this lecture that we now turn.

"Der christliche Glaube und die Geschichte"

This article helps illuminate his convictions about the essential, spiritual character of the objectivity and instrumentality of Christ's biblical witnesses to the church.[62] His lengthy argument can be summarized briefly as follows, in two parts. First, on his reading, the church's proper grasp and articulation of the correlation of faith, history and revelation concerns the precedence of God's determination of faith and the consequence of faith conforming its own "essential presupposition and theoretical basis" and proper ends to its given nature. In a broad stroke, Barth sketches a major problem in theology, namely, theology's characterization of the hermeneutical situation of its relation to revelation.[63] Revelation, Barth stresses, is more objective than as construed by the *Bewußtseinstheologie* of the Erlangen school.

According to Barth, the "one-sidedness" of the Erlangen school was countered by Ritschl's theory of "historical revelation" (geschichtlichen Offenbarung). Strangely, while the theory was a way of emphasizing revelation's objectivity in history,[64] the historian *qua* historian in the school

61. Barth, "Der Christliche Glaube und die Geschichte," 149–212.

62. Ibid., 165–66.

63. Ibid., 157.

64. Ibid., 158.

of the history of religions school became unable or unwilling to understand revelation as a miracle. Instead, the historian preferred to construe revelation and the Bible as no more than *human* affairs: As a result, "*God disappeared from history.*"[65]

The historian's construal of the history of revelation of Jesus Christ in Scripture, Barth observes, inhabited a convention of epistemic avoidance of the theme of miracle in favour of the concept of "scientific knowing of causes and effect" and of the Kantian theme of intellectual "truthfulness."[66] Unlike Kant, Barth distinguishes God's objectivity from human subjectivity and natural phenomena. Barth does this by a formal reserve for divine agency as a mystery in the divine employment of human agency. The notion of an asymmetry between divine and human agencies is Barth's seminal point. Succinctly put, a key problem that Protestant scriptural orientation faces, in Barth's view, concerns the church's proper recognition of theology's relation to revelation amidst the prevailing theological culture in which the theme of miracle is lost in its concepts of God and revelation. The revelation of the historical Jesus' relation to faith, Barth contends, can and must be construed on its own terms in theology: generally put, its construal of the relation concerns revelation's self-determined presence to faith's correspondingly relatively passive nature as "experience of God" (Gotteserlebnis).[67] Faith's relation to God, for Barth, finds its norm *in* Scripture's Jesus, crucially, by virtue of divine agency.[68] The unity of God in his works, in short, is faith's hermeneutical situation.

More closely—second—the hermeneutical situation of faith concerns the *objectivity* of the miracle of Scripture's testimony to Christ. If Christ of Scripture is a miraculous *anthropological* objectivity, and Scripture's anthropological objectivity is derived from God's self-objectivity, then the former is unbound to human cognition, but bound entirely to its divine deployment.[69] If Scripture's divine deployment is an event in God's saving economy, human recognition of Scripture's Christ is an experience of God's transformative supply of a "regulative, heuristic, limit-conceptual moment of faith" to faith itself as a "concrete reality."[70] The precedence of God's sav-

65. Ibid., 159.
66. Ibid., 159–60.
67. Ibid., 161.
68. Ibid., 165–66, 169.
69. Ibid., 165–66.
70. Ibid., 161.

ing activity in the consequence of faith and obedience is what Barth calls "the Realitätsprinzip."[71] The relation between divine and human agencies in the saving economy is as concrete as it is asymmetric. In short, reality of faith is *concrete* or concretely *is*: it calls for human response not as a capacity natural to being human, but human response as a moment of concrete personal obedience to God.

The soteriological emphasis in Barth's account of the human objectivity of the biblical writers is visible in his general discussion of the Pauline epistles. In relation, Barth sees a problem in the canonization of the letters. Their canonization, Barth criticizes, was a way to turn the miraculous presence of God into "a safe, that is, visible and controllable fact, that is, in the elements of the church," namely, "holy institutions, teachings and persons."[72] Succinctly put, Barth thinks that the problem of construing Scripture in terms of mere ecclesiality concerns the loss of concrete contingence of the objectivity of Scripture as a sheer miracle. By positing itself permanently as Christ's *visible* presence, the church becomes a *de facto* object of faith. Construal of Scripture becomes essentially construal of no more than tradition and human decision. Talk of the biblical canon becomes just another way of emphasizing church authority as the rule or norm of faith.[73] Faith in the "elements of the church," however, is not identical to faith in Christ, Barth reckons; neither is faith as faith of the biblical writers a subset of a general concept of *Kulturbewußtsein*. By contrast, Barth thinks that only by God's saving activity can Scripture's anthropological objectivity be grasped not as the objectivity merely of the powerful and privileged groups or persons in the church, but Scripture's anthropological objectivity as the objectivity of Christ to all the Spirit's faithful in all ages.

Put in terms of Barth's concept of inspiration in this article, Barth seems to struggle to come to terms with the historicity and objectivity of the biblical writers as *writers* and more crucially the unidirectional relational concreteness of their readers as mere *readers*. In this sense, the problem of his treatment of the Bible concerns not so much his concept of text as his apparent direct identity between text and interpretation, and between faith and revelation. Equally crucial perhaps is his construal of biblical canonicity in terms of ecclesiality: his articulation of God's self-objectivity in the Bible by way of readerly objectivity is symptomatic of his struggle to

71. Ibid., 165–66.
72. Ibid., 166–67.
73. Ibid., 167–71.

describe the canon as having a significance, freedom and uniqueness that correspond to revelation's own.

Moreover, although he recognizes the priority of God's regenerative self-mediating use of Scripture—Scripture not as text but Scripture as a moment of faith—Barth struggles to distinguish the writer from the reader because, I suggest, he is not explicit about the priority and externality of Christ to Scripture and to Scripture's reader. Once again, the notion of externality concerns the deity of God as the basis of his primacy and priority in and over Scripture's human agency. The reader's relation to Scripture, once again, is construed directly in the reader's self-described relation to God; in this construal of a theology of "supreme confidence" of the Christian,[74] Scripture is consistently available and bound to the reader's undertakings.

That is not to suggest, however, that Barth thinks that Scripture's nature, content, and ends are merely a matter of interpretation. Neither is God's use of Scripture a merely interpretive event. Recognition of Christ's relation to Scripture is more than a matter of interpretation. As Barth states, "We see what he has seen, we experience what he has experienced, we believe henceforth not for the sake of what he says, but because we ourselves have heard and understood that Christ is truly Saviour of the world."[75]

In relation to the priority and concreteness of God's saving economy, moreover, Barth's construes Scripture as revelation's "effectiveness" (Wirkenden) and the reader as a corresponding "effectuation" (Bewirkenden).[76] The primary-secondary distinction recognizes an epistemic order of revelation-Scripture-reader, but, as we can see, he construes the order as a hermeneutical *circle* of some sort that appears to be enclosed *in* the reader or anthropological objectivity. Thus I suggest that in this article Barth's recognition of the externality and self-objectivity of God's pure deity in relation to Scripture's humanity, for all his talk of miracle, appears superficial. It does so in part because he seems to posit revelation in faith; for example, his statement: "the methodology of the Christian faith knows only Christ outside of us. It actually does not know Christ. It knows only Christ in us."[77] Although in this article it is unclear if Barth is fully aware of the risks involved in his identification of faith and revelation for theology, we can

---

74. McCormack, *Karl Barth's Critically Realistic Dialectical Theology*, 76.

75. Barth, "Der Christliche Glaube und die Geschichte," 168. McCormack's translation, *Karl Barth's Critically Realistic Dialectical Theology*, 76.

76. Barth, "Der Christliche Glaube und die Geschichte," 203.

77. Ibid., 194.

simply note that the priority of God's relation to the faithful in the latter's relation to revelation, Scripture and the church is Barth's seminal point.

What picture of Scripture emerges in this lecture? In Barth's view the text of Scripture is subservient to the reader, though the former is "somehow" indispensable by virtue of its divine employment as a means of revelation. Though he does not say much on this "somehow," we can see that the text is significant for him because of his affirmation of God's relation to Scripture, and that the basis of the unity of Scripture's content and textual form is none other than revelation. Under this theological construal, Scripture's content as revelation is at once inexhaustible, passive and, paradoxically, subservient to the reader's undertakings whose responsibility is not to the text, or to the church, but to their conscience that only God in Christ can judge.

Although Barth wants to ground the recognition of the text's authority exclusively in God's self-revelatory activity, he construes the objectivity of the latter as mere anthropology objectivity and *apparently* no more. This shortcoming can perhaps help illuminate why he grounds the history of the formation of the biblical canon in *human* affairs—especially in their philosophical and socio-political dimensions—but not beyond.[78] On his account here, the illuminated readers' ideas of God, revelation, and Scripture appear consistently to coincide with their reality in the economy of revelation and salvation. Although he stresses the noetic capacity of faith, he appears to acknowledge the notion of the externality of Christ to the creaturely realm on the one hand. On the other hand he gives the impression that the notion is just another way of stressing the latency of truth in trans-personal consciousness. If my reading is plausible, all this suggests that in one sense that there are two competing sets of convictions in his view of Scripture: one set tends to emphasize the prominence of the concept of trans-personal consciousness as a way of construing Scripture's anthropological objectivity, while the other set tends to underscore the greater self-objectivity of the pure deity of God. The stark contrast of the two sets of convictions is especially pronounced in light of his sermons. For all their material significance for his view of Scripture, they are rarely accounted for in recent readings on the topic. It is to the sermons that we now turn.

78. Ibid., 164–74.

1913–15 Sermons

In contrast to his view of Scripture highlighted in his theological writings, Barth's sermons afford a somewhat more sober picture of God's relation to Scripture. What follows is a focused survey of the bibliological significance in his biblical exposition through a reading of his sermons from 1913 to 1915.[79] As a student and preacher of the Bible Barth speaks with a profoundly moving conviction about God's majesty that is yet seen as lucid and powerful in his theological writings surveyed. The apparent difference may, perhaps, be a matter of language and style, but his theological deference to divine activity as qualitatively different from human activity is clearly more substantial in his biblical expositions in the homilies, as observes W. H. Willimon:

> Barth's preaching eventually convinced him that he needed to find another way, a way that was more rigorously and attentively biblical, more objectively tied to the biblical text and less linked to human subjectivity, more peculiarly theological and more particularly Christian.[80]

On Barth's account in a sermon in January 1913, for example, the Bible speaks of God as "boundlessly holy and righteous" and of whose "Light" shines on "the sinners" not only in time abut also in "all eternity" for God is a God of the living, not of the dead.[81] On his account, the Spirit's illuminating and life-giving work is described in terms of God's loving majesty that towers over time and dwarfs the sinfulness of humanity. By understanding the sheer greatness of God's own holiness and righteousness as the essence of the divine Light in the Bible, Barth can at least suggest Scripture's relation to the saints in terms of the christological ground and soteriological significance of the scriptural terms "sinner," "holiness," and "righteousness."

The understanding of the relation of the Spirit's illumination and vivification to the Bible is attested again in a sermon less than a month later.[82] In it, Barth describes the Spirit's relation of the Bible in terms of the Spirit's

---

79. For a comprehensive introduction to Barth's sermons, see Genest, *Karl Barth und die Predigt*. J. Fähler's concise study of Barth's sermons from 1913–15 focuses on their relation to the development of the First World War, without substantial attention to his concept of Scripture (*Der Ausbruch des 1. Weltkrieges in Karl Barths Predigten 1913–1915*).

80. Willimon, *The Early Preaching of Karl Barth*, ix–xviii (esp. x–xi).

81. 26 Jan 1913 (152), Jn 2.23–25, 39–50.

82. 16 Feb 1913 (153), Mk 11.27–33, 51–64.

use of it as "his witness."[83] Crucially, as the Spirit's witness, the Bible's spirit is "not our own"; nor does the Spirit speak to us in our spirits without the witness of the Bible.[84] By understanding the Bible in terms of the Spirit's distinctiveness to our spirits, Barth can describe the scriptural witness to Jesus in terms of a confrontational nature whose essence, in his view, is "the witness of God in antiquity" (das Gotteszeugnis der Vorzeit).[85] On his reading of the grounds of "Protestantism,"

> the Spirit of God speaks to us through none other than the mouths of his witnesses. Not our own spirit (Geist), but the Bible testifies to us that we are in the right. We have Paul and John on our side and Jesus himself and Moses and the prophets! That was the evidence that they opposed their opponents. There like Jesus they said: Do believe you in the Bible? yes or no! . . . They joined themselves in the chain of God's witnesses of foretime now known: he who rejects the first must reject the rest.[86]

Thus Barth on Scripture's pneumatologically specified primacy and uniqueness and christologically grounded instrumentality in a theological language pointing in the direction of a divine-human asymmetry from an understanding of divine precedence (in time and beyond) and the consequence of the Spirit's employment of the scriptures as his witness in the church.

The problem of the Bible's divine-human asymmetric relation draws his attention in a sermon on Amos 5.4.[87] On Barth's reading, Scripture describes that in the "Light of the truth" (Wahrheit) there appears "obviously and undeniably the eternal contrast between God and humanity" (Da erscheint ihnen offenkundig und unleugbar der ewige Gegensatz zwischen Gott und Mensch).[88] In the light of this contrast, Barth can speak of Scripture in terms of its "prophetic work" (prophetisichen Dienst) that makes the Bible utterly unlike any other book, a work that disturbs our "human" understanding of its content to undertake "ever new searches."[89]

---

83. Ibid., 60.

84. Ibid.

85. Ibid.

86. Ibid.

87. 25 Mar 1914, Amos 5.4 (211), 249–61.

88. Ibid., 252.

89. Ibid.

Human words! Human thoughts! Human work! So we learn to think of our supposed piety, as did Amos cry out to the Israelites there and then. And only then does it awake in us the living deep longing to know God as he is, and to be obedient to him according to his will and not ours. Where we read the Bible rightly, we hear the prophetic voice which calls out to us: It is not enough! Seek! Cosiness (Behaglichkeit) and self-sufficiency (Selbstgenügsamkeit) cannot achieve it, which, instead, lead to the death of our inner life, as we are told time and again: God is wholly different, and so is the real life wholly different from what you are imagining now![90]

Notice, crucially, here, by understanding Scripture's "prophetic voice" in terms of God's "otherness," Barth can stress a qualitative difference between Scripture's God and the reader's idea of "God," between divine will and human will, and between divine command and human obedience.[91] He can, moreover, affirm Scripture's human elements without surrendering their divine determination to the reader's determination. Constructively, this provides him a theological basis to describe Scripture in terms of the asymmetrical and disruptive nature of God's life-giving power and covenantal purpose.[92]

Barth's emphasis on the primacy, uniqueness and righteousness of God vis-à-vis fallen humanity comes to expression with a great deal of urgency in his Reformation Day sermon in 1914.[93] In it, Barth stresses Scripture as God's "old eternal truth" uttered to his parishioners "in a wholly new way" even as much of Europe is at war, reminding them that, the Johannine emphasis on the distinctiveness of the Spirit's light from which Jesus Christ shines "in the dark world" helps illuminate for him that God has the Bible open to us so that "Moses and the prophets are beginning to speak again,

---

90. Ibid.

91. The point of divine-human asymmetry is obvious in a sermon from June 1914: "Gott ist natürlich kein Mann, der mit den Menschen körperlich kämpfen kann." [God is naturally not human, but can battle with humanity corporally.] 28. Jun 1914, Gen 32. 23–32 (227), 338–48 (esp. 339–40).

92. The point of the priority, primacy and distinctiveness of Scripture's God to the reader's "God" is also emphatic in a February sermon in the same year. 1 Feb 1914, Rom. 1. 16 (204), 48–61 (esp. 55–56). The contrast of God and humanity is made between God's Word and Scripture and preaching.

93. 1 Nov 1914, Jn 17.20–21 (244), 544–52.

as if they were in our midst."[94] The "confusing time" in which they might find themselves therefore is nevertheless "a time of grace" (Gnadenzeit).[95]

The problem of the "confusing time" overshadowed by "a time of grace" is identified under a set of stark contrasts between the "dark world" and "the world of God"[96] which is laid open for us in the Bible.[97] What is the "Bible"? Barth asks.[98] He confesses an "anxiety before the true Bible, before the Bible of God, before the Bible, which the living Word is, revelation of divine judgments and divine grace, before the Bible, which is a sword that which penetrates our thoughts (cf. Heb 4.12), a hammer that smashes the rock (Jer. 23.29), a source (Quelle) from which flows the water of life for which the Bible genuinely thirsts (cf. Acts 22.16)."[99] By understanding "the true Bible" in terms of God's uses of it in accordance with the Word's relation to us in the revelation of Jesus Christ as divine judgment and grace "in *a world that does not believe*" him,[100] Barth can speak of Scripture in the light of the grace and work of Christ's Spirit as God's reign,[101] "the gospel which is the truth of the strength of God."[102] The stark contrasts between the "dark world" and the "world of God" in the Bible therefore are ordered to the divine "redemption of the world."[103]

More closely, by understanding "the true Bible" in the light of "the power of *prayers*" as antithetical to the triumphalism of the world, and indeed, to a world that does not believe in Jesus or listen to his prayer in Jn 17.20–21,[104] Barth can identify the nature of the truth of the Bible with the christologically grounded and soteriologically manifested "help" that comes and can only come from the Father answering the prayer of whose own Son.[105] Barth can, moreover, describe Scripture in terms of a

---

94. Ibid., 545.

95. Ibid., 544–45.

96. Ibid., 545.

97. Ibid.

98. Ibid.

99. Ibid.

100. Ibid., 547.

101. Ibid.

102. Ibid., 547–48.

103. Ibid.

104. Ibid., 550.

105. Ibid. For biblical references, Barth also cites Pss 121 and 130.

theologically specified expectancy of "a better future"[106] shared by all "in the dark world," Roman Catholics and Protestants alike, who respond in "gratitude" as one "world of God" in "the pure flame of God's love" to "the call of Jesus."[107] In this connexion to his christological orientation, only in the light of Barth's soteriological emphasis on prayer can the theological force of his view of Scripture—his mortifying humility before "the true Bible"—be grasped properly. Succinctly put, Scripture is the Spirit's means of drawing us into "the river of life" in the world of God whose will, reign, power, and love, moreover, are antithetical to that of the "dark world." The church can therefore expect no unity outside of Christ, nor can it know the "true Bible" apart from God's redemptive help which and through which it is summoned to seek and obey—in prayer.

This understanding of the problem of God's free use of the Bible as substantially distinct in origin, purpose and end is increasingly empathic through late 1914 and 1915. For example, on Barth's account in a sermon in March 1915,[108] because God speaks to us in Scripture as none other than himself and originally from himself as "righteousness and truth, love and peace," "the whole Bible speaks (sagt) to us, if we let it address (rede) us, instead of making up our own pious thoughts about God."[109]

By understanding "the whole Bible" as oriented and sent to us in accordance with God's "righteousness and truth, love and peace," Barth can, as it were, begin to shake his theology off of the pneumatology of self-justification from his liberal Protestant heritage. Crucially, for him, Christian bibliology does not speak out of a self-congratulatory spirit of triumphant human discovery, merit or self-entitlement—it needs not puff up or despair, if God, "to whom the Bible points (zeigt), is a God who helps, saves, redeems, relieves."[110]

More formally put, only because God shows himself as Scripture's referent, that is, in virtue of his own activity in accordance with his identity, not in virtue of Scripture's or readerly activity and regardless of our own ideas about deity, humanity, society and personal self-identity, that "the whole Scripture speaks to us." In a sense, by understanding the precedence, primacy, and finality of divine initiative in Scripture's human elements,

---

106. 1 Nov 1914 (244), 551.

107. Ibid., 551–52.

108. 14 March 1915, Isa 53.4–5a (263), 100–110.

109. Ibid., 107.

110. Ibid.

Barth can begin to describe "the whole Bible" as a new order of human agency bound to God in his unbound redemptive activity.

Some of the characteristic features of this bibliological understanding of the ontological primacy of God's use of Scripture are especially visible in a significant sermon on 2 Pet 1.19 on 25 April 1915.[111] On Barth's reading, the Petrine emphasis on the soteriological comprehensiveness of "the prophetic word" provides him a textual basis to describe the scriptural text (Bibelbuch) in terms of the christologically grounded soteriological activity of "the living Word of God" in fulfilling his promises, stressing that, the biblical word is and belongs to a "new order of being" (neuen Daseinsordnungen), "the truth-world."[112]

> The *truth-world*, the world of real lives, stands outside and wants to enter. I should be ripped out of lie and out of pretence. I should be placed in the strength and joy of the heavenly reign, that actuality is in being (das Eigentliche ist im Dasein). I shall experience what the prophets and apostles have experienced and become what they have become. The truth should break forward from its hidden cornice, being known to me so long ago. And I shall rejoice: at last I have found myself, my better, higher "I"! As a brother of Jesus Christ I should be illuminated and should illuminate myself for the other.[113]

Thus Barth describes the being of the prophets and apostles in active terms that denote a new human order of agent and subject whose activity, moreover, has a preceding determined ontological specificity that is independent of readerly determination: "out of the new ground grows a new being with a new order of being."[114]

111. 25 April 1915, 2 Pet 1.19 (269), 161–71.

112. Ibid., 162–65.

113. Ibid.

114. Ibid., 165. Barth's description of the "new order of being" seems to emphasize the soteriological significance of the priority of divine action and a lack of direct and static objectivity in human perception of this order in Scripture. In his analysis of the ontology in Barth's early sermons, T. Schlegel likens his ontology with philosophical epistemology, and thus overlooking the magnitude of the theological force of Barth's term "new" in its christological and pneumatological reference to the radical antecedence and transcendence of divine action in this new order. *Theologie als unmögliche Notwendigkeit*, 38–39. The point of God's action as the origin of the being of this new created order was reaffirmed explicitly in his response to a question on the issue of the ontological basis of the divine-human relation of analogy in the knowledge of God, in a speech at Princeton on 2 May 1962. His point was that the human claim of this relation has no ontological force. Barth, *Gespräche 1959–1962*, 293–97.

The relation of the Bible to this ontological order can be described in at least three ways. First, on *origin*: it is this order, not the order of "our human word," that is the origin of the biblical prophets and apostles whose activity is, moreover, bound to their being in this ontological order.[115] Second, on *relation*: it is on the basis of the relation of this order to "our human world" that Scripture is understood and heard as a word whose humanity is categorically different from ours.[116] From this it also follows that their word is the textual ingredient of their humanity whose nature (in relation to us) is bound to their activity and ends that correspond to the Word's own. Third, on *distinction*: the biblical word as a part of this order is not identical with the order itself whose being is bound to the Word, not to the biblical word. By understanding Scripture's origin, nature and ends as grounded in divine activity, not human activity, Barth can begin to describe the hidden nature of Scripture's being.

> In the Bible lies dormant (verborgen schlummert) *the truth*: the truth (Wahrheit) about life and the world, the truth about you and I, the truth about the past and the future, about God's beginnings, ways and ends. A world of truth. The whole living relation from that which is real actually (Der ganze lebendige Zusammenhang von dem, was eigentlich, wirklich ist.). The prophets and apostles have discovered this new world and have witnessed from it, and with their words have placed a piece of it in our human world.[117]

It is a revealing statement, illuminating Barth's description of Scripture's origin, nature, and ends as grounded in the latency of truth whose own world, which resembles "our human world," is substantially different on christological ground: "He has embodied this new world with his own person as the Son of the Father full of grace and truth."[118] And because "the new world" receives its being from Christ, it also follows that its difference "from our human world" is categorically ontological and its ontological category is antecedently determined by the preceding relation, *not* first between the world and Jesus, but first between the Father and Son. By understanding the precedence of the triune God as the living relation of the Word to the biblical text, Barth can begin to describe our relation to Scripture in terms of *waiting*:

115. 25 April 1915 (269), 162–63.
116. Ibid.
117. Ibid.
118. Ibid., 163.

> And see, now *wait* on the living Word of God; wait in the biblical text; wait in the history (Geschichte) of humanity, in which the Word has entered as the most hidden and yet the most tremendous strength; wait in illuminated people (erleuchteten Menschen) who live inconspicuously near others and are truly none other than his witnesses and prophets, spring-source (Brunnquelle) of truth as the Bible itself; wait in our own lives. In all our lives somewhere there is a cornice (Ecklein) where the Word of the truth-world is already set up and lets itself be heard (wo das Wort von der Wahrheitswelt bereits aufgerichtet ist und sich vernehmen läßt)— waiting for our souls, for us ourselves, in order to address us. That is something miraculous (Wunderbares), if the Word of the truth-world has now begun to address us.[119]

Thus Barth on the precedence of the divine illumination of the Word and the consequence of the determined origin, nature and ends of what Scripture is.[120]

This understanding of divine activity of promise and fulfilment as the essence of the biblical word is unpacked with significant hamartiological and soteriological references as essential to the Petrine eschatology in a sermon on 2 Pet 3.13 in August in the same year.[121] On Barth's account, the Petrine ontological orientation to God's activity of radical renewal is an evidence of the futuristic, expectant and deferential character of the Bible, indicating the promise and fulfilment of the biblical word as essentially a matter of God's righteousness.[122] By understanding God's righteousness as the origin, authority, and ends of the biblical word, Barth can describe Scripture's relation to us in terms of divine self-determination, instead of human self-determination: "again and again the righteousness, the righteousness of God, which must come and will come from him to the people one day."[123]

For Barth, in the Bible, "God promises us righteousness. The righteousness belongs to the future. How could it be otherwise? God himself is

---

119. Ibid., 163.

120. On the point of the formal and material precedence and primacy of the work of the Holy Spirit in relation to Scripture's being, more specifically, to the human nature of Scripture's language as a result of the Spirit's movement, see also, 30 May 1915, Acts 2.5–11 (275), 217–37 (esp. 230).

121. 8 Aug 1915, 2 Pet 3.13 (284), 313–24.

122. Ibid., 315–16f.

123. Ibid.

pure righteousness."[124] By identifying Scripture with God's active confrontation to unrighteousness, Barth can begin to describe God's righteous use of Scripture as "*the command*" for the people of the Old and New Testaments in ways that point beyond human affairs and the realm of creation—their decays, failures, and lies—and confidently indicate that humanity and history can be understood as God makes himself known to us in the witness of Christ's Spirit in us.[125]

By understanding humanity and history in the light of the work of the Spirit of Christ, Barth can recognize a certain logical feature of the Petrine scriptural orientation: "There is no knowledge of God without hope. Knowledge of God is nothing other than pure hope."[126] And this "hope" is entirely *open* to God's supreme ontological force in his economy of revelation and salvation: "We read: As *God* appeared to Moses in the desert, he named himself: I am who I shall be (Ex. 3.14)."[127] Once again: "God is, who he will be, and will be who he is. He is the A and the O, the beginning and the end (Rev. 1.8)."[128]

On Barth's reading, because the future is bound to the righteousness of God's own holy name, knowledge of God in Scripture is not and cannot be reduced and restricted to reception: "For us humanity the future is something invisible, dubious."[129] By recognizing God's self-pronouncement of his holy name as a formally and materially irreducible human delimitation to the Bible that in bearing witness to this God reaches to us beyond itself and capacity as a creature, Scripture, then, is best described in terms of God's purposive prevenience: "The future is his like the present."[130]

Once again, on Barth's reading, the Petrine text summons the reader—to wait. This "waiting" is a "waiting-on-God" (Auf-Gott-Warten), "[n]ot a waiting-for-later-time, but a waiting-on-eternity" which is straightforwardly the here and now as it will be one day."[131] By recognizing God's self-announced purposive presence as the hermeneutical situation of Scripture's relation to us, Barth can begin to speak of the nature of

124. Ibid., 318.
125. Ibid., 316–17.
126. Ibid., 317.
127. Ibid.
128. Ibid.
129. Ibid.
130. Ibid.
131. Ibid., 323.

the biblical text in terms of christologically ground and soteriologically oriented expectancy on the basis of that which is formally and materially self-authenticating in its human acknowledgement and yet radically beyond human determination, namely, God's use of Scripture as a witness of his righteousness through the future that he has for the whole humankind for the sake of his holy name.

For Barth, because Scripture's God speaks as one who has "whole abundance of mercy and goodness ready for you and all creation," it also follows that because Scripture is bound to God's holy name, it is also bound to the abundance and comprehensiveness of the unbound mercy and goodness of God as the Creator.[132] In Scripture, the "waiting" is confident in the Creator, not in the creature, asking (bittet) for God's abundant mercy in unceasing repentance in the light of God's righteousness and goodness.[133] For Barth, it is therefore "we as a new people and new Christians" that we wait and ask for that which "he has promised us" in the Bible and for the Bible of his promise made good.[134] "We belong to God, so we must hope."[135]

By understanding the soteriological significance of the precedence of divine mercy in what Scripture is in God's use, Barth can begin to stress the essential dissimilarity between human action and divine action in the "knowledge of God" in Scripture as the sheer mercy of Spirit whose light all new humanity can only await.[136] He can also describe this waiting as characteristic of Scripture in God's use of it as his witness whose activity is, in all its actuality, humanity, and intention, delimited by its nature as a new creation of God's mercy for the sake of God's own name. In this specific sense, even though he is yet able to speak clearly of the ontological distinctiveness of God's self-communicative presence as the Spirit's Word but refers the voice of the Bible still in the language of conscience,[137] Barth

132. Ibid., 323–24.

133. Ibid.

134. Ibid., 324.

135. Ibid., 318.

136. Ibid., 324.

137. Cf. 7 Nov 1915, Matt 9.14–17 (296), 442–53. In this Reformation Day sermon, Barth stresses the disruptive and uncompromising character of "conscience of God, the holiness of God" as the medium in which Scripture addresses us. While the direction of his reorientation is to sketch God's being, instead of creaturely being, as the basis for the doctrine of the *testimonium Spiritus sancti internum*, here Barth is on his way, and just so is his help: his biblical expositions and later immersion in the Reformed tradition would prove radically formative of his unlearning and learning of a proper concepts of God and Scripture.

sees that Scripture is radically bound to the future that God has for us, a future whose order is one of a new being "according to God's promise in which righteousness dwells."[138]

Summary

To summarize: I began this chapter by suggesting that there was a contrast between his express confidence in the reliability of trans-personal consciousness for revelation and his increasingly pointed criticism of that confidence in the light of a profound sense of the unbound sovereignty and majesty of God in Christ. In addition, I suggested that there was a limited but significant presence of references to the work of the Spirit in Barth's concept of Scripture. In relation, I showed that Barth's confidence in the reader's principle did in fact sometimes appear to be excessive early on in his career, but that his earlier confidence was not a denial of his deeper and more comprehensive enduring convictions about the deity and uniqueness of God. Instead, I suggested that the convictions appeared to anchor Barth's thinking and helped shape his anthropological reorientation expressed in his earlier theological reflections on the origin, nature, content and ends of Scripture as a sheer miracle. But I noted that it was true that Barth's discussion of the Trinity in his pneumatological reference was problematically minimal; it was problematic because Barth's apparent lack of clarity on the Spirit's hypostasis in the Godhead suggested some conceptual difficulty in clearly articulating a distinction between divine transcendence and divine immanence on one hand and the freedom of Scripture's human agency from and for the reader on the other.

To indicate how all this was so in Barth, we read his posthumously published paper and confirmation lesson notes, two of his academic publications, some of his sermons between 1913 and 1915, and some of Barth's correspondence and autobiographical materials.

We have indicated that this chapter is an attempt of introducing and orienting our subsequent reading and fuller discussion of Barth's view of

---

138. 8 Aug 1915 (284), 316. "Nun soll uns heute wieder *ein* Bibelwort *Alles* sagen, was uns die Bibel von unserer Hoffnung und Zukunft zu sagen hat: Wir warten eines neuen Himmels und einer neuen Erde, nach Gottes Verheißung, in welchen Gerechtigkeit wohnet." [*Everything* should say to us again *one* biblical word only, what the Bible of our hope and future has to say to us: We await a new heaven and a new earth according to God's promise in which righteousness dwells.]

Scripture as presented in some of his writings from 1915 onward and in the first volume of the *Church Dogmatics*.

I have done so by introducing a series of bibliological themes: Scripture *is* by virtue of God's free, renewal activity and command. This command summons Scripture's waiting on and pointing to this God through his mercy and future that he has for all creation in Christ. In Christ prayer is the essence of this human waiting in scriptural reading.

In the next chapter I will trace these themes in Barth's thoughts on Scripture, and, in particular, his maturing account of God's pure deity and sheer majesty of love and freedom in and through the Spirit's economy of Scripture as a miraculous human witness to Christ. It is to this material we now turn.

2

Being Taught
The Bible and the Reformed Scripture Principle

THIS CHAPTER SKETCHES A set of key aspects of Barth's gradually renewed view of the Bible between 1915–1925. In a nutshell it sketches the view in the light of Barth's increasingly forceful account of the pure deity of God. To show how this is so, I develop the sketch through a focused reading of selected materials including his lectures, both extramural and formal, correspondence, sermons, and the first two editions of the Romans commentary.

If common misconstrual of his renewed view of Scripture tends to suffer from inattentativeness to his emphasis on God's pure deity, we suggest that the sketch can perhaps open up conversation. The sketch might help show that it is crucially Scripture *not* first as mere human "valuation or construction"[1] of the biblical witnesses or the reader,[2] but Scripture *first* as a created object of God's saving action, that Barth speaks of the biblical canon and its reception in the light of the priority of regeneration.[3] More closely, the material suggests an insurmountable difficulty against a widespread view of Barth's scriptural orientation as "a kind of hermeneutical

---

1. Pannenberg, "The Crisis of the Scripture Principle," in *Basic Question in Theology*, 1:1–14 (esp. 8–9). A similar problem is visible in R. Burnett's emphasis on faith or its affectation as the center of Barth's scriptural orientation (*Kark Barth's Theological Exegesis*, 95–100, 111, 125–27, 192–97).

2. Whatever Bender means by "the theological sense of Scripture" he tends to downplay Scripture's essential externality in relation to "the grammatical, historical and literary elements of Scripture" ("Scripture and Canon in Karl Barth's Early Theology," 170–71).

3. For a more extensive, excellent account of the point on Barth's *eschatological* anthropological orientation in his Göttingen theology, see Asprey, *Eschatological Presence in Karl Barth's Göttingen Theology*, 24ff.

immediacy,"[4] or an "antihistorische Revolution,"[5] or mere "antiliberal polemics."[6] Likewise, just as it is problematic to portray Barth's construal of the Bible's historicity as a kind of coinherence between the spheres of *providentia Dei* and *confusio hominem*,[7] or between the history of the miracle of Spirit's scriptural testimony and the history of the church as a reader,[8] just so it is problematic to overlook the derived significance of the human in Barth's maturing view of Scripture.

What picture of Scripture emerges from the material? On Barth's reading, Christ's scriptural self-presence by the Spirit cannot be ontologically posited and henceforth hermeneutically applied.[9] Put differently, if the problem of Scripture is christologically grounded, it follows that it concerns the *soteriological* character of God's "positive relation" to the biblical writers. This "positive relation," as Barth construes it in his 1922 Romans commentary, concerns especially "the righteousness of God."[10] In this connexion, if common portrayals of Barth tend to construe his view of divine-human relation in sheer negativity or direct identity, we suggest that it is because they overlook the pneumatological primacy of his scriptural orientation. As Barth writes,

> We can no longer hear the No under which we stand apart from the divine Yes from which it proceeds. This means that the marks of human unrighteousness and ungodliness are crossed by the deeper marks of the divine forgiveness; that the discord of human defiance is penetrated by the undertones of the divine melody "Nevertheless."[11]

---

4. Lauster, *Prinzip und Methode*, 261; Jülicher, "A Modern Interpretor of Paul," 72–73.

5. Lauster, *Prinzip und Methode*, 259–64. See also, Graf, "Die antihistorische Revolution," 377–405.

6. Dorrien, *The Barthian Revolt*, 10–11. Common portrayals of Barth's view of Scripture tend to isolate his polemics from his pneumatological orientation. For a recent example, see, van der Wall, "Ways of Polemicizing" 401–14; in the same volume, Stegeman, "Ethics or Dogmatics?," 415–32.

7. Kirchstein, *Der souveräne Gott und die heilige Schrift*, 30–31. Cf. Barth's direct criticism of the tendency as characteristic of German theological culture of the day. Barth to Rade on 31 August 1914. *B-Rade*, 95–99.

8. Plasger, "Du sollst Vater und Mutter ehren!," 404.

9. *GD*, 160.

10. *Römerbrief 1922*, 69 (ET 94–96).

11. Ibid.

Thus Barth on the primacy of divine mercy in biblical and theological studies. As he puts it in "The Righteousness of God" lecture: "For now something real has happened—the only real thing that can happen: God has now taken his own work in hand."[12] If in God's "hand" Scripture as "his own work" can have an objectivity and freedom that correspond to God's own in keeping with God's own patience with us,[13] "we shall then," Barth stresses confidently, "enjoy the freedom of saying now Yes and now No, and of saying both not as a result of outward chance or of inward caprice but because we are so moved by the will of God, which has been abundantly proved 'good, and acceptable, and perfect' (Rom. 12:2)."[14] If my reading is plausible, we suggest that the *theological* character of Barth's account of the *eschatological* problem of Scripture is *optimistic*.

In a sense, the eschatological optimism emerges from his view of Scripture concerns hope and witness as characteristic of the church's scriptural and doctrinal orientation to the Spirit's unbound regeneration of the biblical witnesses *in* the salvific drama of the first and second advents of Christ. It concerns the sheer miracle of the church being taught afresh by God in his relation to the biblical writers as his witnesses to the church in this drama. In this specific sense, the theme of 'being taught,' once again, does *not* in any sense suggest Barth's reading of Scripture as unquestionable, in significant part because the theme is a way of stressing his convictions about the external and soteriological character of God's use of Scripture. It serves, moreover, to underscore related significance of his intense immersion in the Bible and the Reformed Scripture Principle. The Principle affords him a resourceful doctrine of the being of God as a way of underscoring Barth's convictions about divine-human dissimilarity and the logical priority of the ontic to the noetic in the church's undertakings with the biblical canon.

In this connexion, Barth's gradually renewed and increasingly Reformed view of the Bible as miracle are traced in this chapter in two parts. The first part offers a focused reading of "The Righteousness of God," "The New World in the Bible," "Biblical Questions, Insights, and Vistas," and the fourth chapter of his *Romans* commentary in the first two editions. The second part examines his increasingly Reformed articulation of

12. Barth, "The Righteousness of God," 26.

13. For the fuller development of the point on the hermeneutical significance of the theme of divine patience, see Wood, *Barth's Theology of Interpretation*, 7f.

14. *TCPS*, 325–26.

certain aspects of his view surveyed in Part one, through a focused reading of his published correspondence with Harnack, "The Doctrinal Task of the Reformed Church" lecture, and parts of the lecture cycles on the Reformed confessional writings and his Göttingen dogmatics. The material highlighted in our exposition, moreover, is only a fraction of his prolific career from 1915 to 1925. Within these material limitations, however, they afford a significant account of certain relevant aspects of his scriptural orientation, aspects that are often overlooked in conventional reading of Barth. If our reading is plausible, we suggest that it can at least reinforce our position concerning his identity as a Reformed biblical theologian, and can offer a constructive orientation to *CD* I. Read in connection with his later material, this survey attempts to sketch the ontological force of certain pneumatological aspects of his renewed relation to the Bible and that of his self-identification with the Reformed Scripture Principle. It is the material that to which we now turn.

"The Righteousness of God"

Barth's conviction about divine-human dissimilarity is emphatic in his view of Scripture in the 1916 lecture "The Righteousness of God." In it, Barth stresses the primacy and priority of God's loving act of fellowship with the biblical witnesses, a fellowship that is inaccessible by mere human work such as 'thoughts,' for Scripture bears witness to "a fundamentally different way to come into relation with the righteousness of God."[15] "This *other* way," he writes, "we enter not by speech nor reflection nor reason, but by being still, by listening to and not silencing the conscience when we have hardly begun to hear its voice."[16] The "voice" is construed by way of two significant features.

The first feature is the increasingly prominent theme of divine-human dissimilarity in Barth's pneumatological construal of God's relation to Scripture, a relation in which, moreover, God is heard and spoken of "as a Wholly Other."[17] Only as a "Wholly Other" to the biblical human witnesses is God known as the referent of their "voice" and "conscience." "When we let conscience speak to the end, its tells us not only that there is something else, a righteousness above unrighteousness, but also—and more important—that

15. Barth, "The Righteousness of God," 23.

16. Ibid.

17. Ibid., 24.

this something else . . . is God."[18] The theme of God's wholly otherness in Scripture is Barth's way of indicating the dissimilarity of Christ to the biblical writers and their readers. "Christ" in Scripture, Barth writes, is he who is a "greater than Moses and a greater than John the Baptist."[19] In view of "John the Baptist," for instance, Barth construes Christ's superiority not as a mere human relativity between the incarnate and the Baptist, but Christ's superiority as the absolute majesty of God's pure deity. Constructively put, the theme of God as their "Wholly Other" concerns a subordination of their person and work *in* the freedom and love that God has for them in Christ. In Christ, the relation of their new humanity to the old is construed not as their human possibility in this world or in the one to come, for the relation has its centre in Christ and radically beyond their being human. Their being human by virtue of their being in Christ means in one sense that they *are* human only in virtue of God's express love through Christ— that is, in virtue of God's capacity for humanity, and *not* humanity's capacity for God. Of "the way of Christ," writes Barth, "[a] greater than Moses and a greater than John the Baptist is here. He is the love of God glorified before the world was and forever glorified. Can one say that humanity has exhausted the possibilities of his way?"[20] In short, Barth's renewed view of Scripture stresses a *soteriological* concept of divine-human dissimilarity in God's loving relation to the biblical witnesses through Christ.

Christ's love for the biblical witnesses is a soteriological theme—and this is the second feature—of the externality of their humanity. Their humanity concerns a miraculous gift of sheer grace, not "the Babel of our human righteousness, human consequence, human significance"[21] or "tower-building of various sorts."[22] But essential to their being human as moved by God is "the deepest need" and "longing" for God *to act*: "oh that Thou wouldest rend the heavens, that thou wouldest come down! Oppressed and afflicted by his own unrighteousness and the unrighteousness of others, man—every man—lifts up from the depths of his nature the cry for righteousness, the righteousness of God."[23] "God's righteousness" is a soteriological theme of the externality of Christ's Spirit. The Spirit's capacity

18. Ibid., 23.
19. Ibid., 26.
20. Ibid.
21. Ibid., 15.
22. Ibid., 24.
23. Ibid., 13.

to move the biblical witnesses to pray "from the depths of" their "nature" concerns the externality of their own "righteousness" for its construal is subordinated wholly to the self-objectivity of "the righteousness of God" as God-for-us. "God himself, the real, the living God, and his love which comes in glory!"[24] Only in the light of the logical priority of their being in Christ, does Barth speak of God as the object, referent, and content of the testimony of Scripture. Scripture's readerly reception, moreover, is a theme that comes under the theme of the priority of Spirit's gift of person in the reader. Thus Barth writes,

> It will then be, above all, a matter of our recognizing God once more as God. . . . For here one must give himself up in order to give himself over to God, that God's will may be done. To do his will, however, means to begin with him anew. His will is not a corrected continuation of our own. It approaches ours as a Wholly Other. There is nothing for our will except a basic re-creation. Not a reformation but a re-creation and re-growth. For the will to which the conscience points is purity, goodness, truth, and brotherhood as the perfect will of God. It is a will which knows no subterfuges, reservations, nor preliminary compromises. It is a will with character, a will blessed and holy through and through. It is the righteousness of God. . . . For now something real has happened—the only real thing that can happen: God has now taken his own work in hand.[25]

In the preface of *The Word of God and the Word of Man*, Barth speaks self-critically of his initial language of anthropological interiority in his construal of God's self-objectivity for Scripture: "naturally I would no longer speak of "the voice of him that crieth in the wilderness," as I have done here on the first page, as 'the voice of conscience.'"[26] If he is uninterested in construing the objectivity of Scripture as a mere anthropological objectivity of the biblical writers or their readers, we suggest that it is in part because he is increasingly aware of the problem of trivializing the pure deity and externality of Christ to humanity. More closely, the problem concerns a widespread inattentiveness to the unidirectional character of the sheer grace of the self-presence of Christ of Scripture. Put differently, the problem of this widespread inattentiveness tends to abstract or isolate Scripture's humanity

24. Ibid., 22.
25. Ibid., 25–26.
26. Ibid., 7.

from God's saving economy not as mere human interiority but God's saving economy as essentially God's self-objectivity as God-for-us.

In this connexion, we can quickly see Barth's renewed emphasis on the externality of divine presence and revelation in his use of the old language of his liberal Protestant heritage of interiority, a renewed emphasis that is fundamentally foreign and offensive to "our idealism, our principles, and our Christianity"[27] in which God is not "far, strange, and high,"[28] but God is construed rather as "a god in our own image"[29] under our "own management."[30] But Barth's insistence on God's externality and freedom is clear to the point of being, in his word, "violent,"[31] we can easily see his needs to clarify the sense in which the new world that brings forward prophets like "Moses and John the Baptist" is different from "the old world" and how their textual witness to Christ is a consequence of God's prior unidirectional activity, but not a consequence of the history of religion or that of cultural progress.[32] My points are raised not as so much criticisms of Barth who is apparently conscious of the conceptual deficiency in his stammering articulation of all this and is not pretending that his thinking has no room for improvement, as we can see in his reflections on some aspects of his maturing view of Scripture in the 1916 lecture.

"The New World in the Bible"

Barth's maturing construal of God's primacy in Scripture is visible in the famous lecture "The New World in the Bible."[33] In it, he sketches Scripture's nature, properties and purposiveness by way of an optimistic vision of God's establishment and manifestations of the "house," "nation," and "new world" of Christ amidst an old and broken humanity and creation.[34] Although not prominent in the lecture, "creature" or "creatureliness" is, we suggest, an appropriate theological language to draw out two constructive

27. Ibid., 25.

28. Ibid., 26.

29. Ibid., 22.

30. Ibid., 16.

31. Ibid., 27.

32. Ibid., 26.

33. Instead of "The Strange New World in the Bible," we refer the lecture as "The New World in the Bible" to better reflect the German title.

34. Barth, "The New World in the Bible," 28.

aspects of his vision of Scripture's anthropological and creaturely orientation, as follows.

The first aspect concerns God's outpouring love as the hermeneutical situation of the anthropological orientation in Scripture. Scripture, Barth thinks, is a consequence of God's prior "outpouring of eternal love," crucially, "of love as God understands it."[35] The deceptively simple concept of divine love is Barth's way of stressing the Spirit's purposive use of Scripture as an instrument of God's own righteousness. "The Holy Spirit establishes the righteousness of heaven in the midst of the unrighteousness of earth and will not stop nor stay until all that is dead has brought to life and a new *world* has come into being": "This is within the Bible. It is within the Bible for us. For it we were baptized."[36] The concept of divine love speaks of God's confrontation with sin and God's regeneration of a new humanity for his love; the love of God in Scripture points us to the comprehensiveness of the primacy and priority of God: "The whole Bible authoritatively announces that God must be all in all; and the events of the Bible are the beginning, the glorious beginning of a new *world*."[37]

By stressing the mysterious economy of the outpouring love of the Spirit, Barth can describe the ends of the biblical witness as corresponding to God's own purposive action and "patience"[38] in Christ's unidirectional relation to his new creation in the old one. Only in the outpouring love of Christ's Spirit, can their longing and waiting for God be grasped in a *concrete* self-involving expectancy of the Spirit making good of his unbound faithfulness towards them. Only in God's love can the reading church hope to be "met, guided, drawn on, and made to grow by the grace of God" as "the Bible unfolds to us" through this love.[39] Hence Barth's emotional construal of the purposive mystery of the relation of God's light to the biblical witnesses:

> We remember . . . how Isaiah and Jeremiah wished not to speak but had to speak the secrets of divine judgement and divine blessings upon a sinful people—how, later, during the deepest humiliation of this people there stood up strange and solitary "servants of

35. Ibid., 40.

36. Ibid., 50.

37. Ibid., 49.

38. Wood, *Barth's Theology of Interpretation*, 7; see also, Wood, "'Ich sah mit Staunen,'" 186.

39. Barth, "The New World in the Bible," 34.

God" who struggled ever more fiercely with the question, Where is now thy God? and forever gave the answer, Israel hath yet God for consolation!—how in the midst of all the wrongdoing and misery of the people they could but blare out, as it were, the announcement: Arise, shine, for thy light is come, and the glory of the Lord is risen upon thee! What does it mean? Why do these men speak so? Whence is kindled all the indignation, all the pity, all the joy, all the hope and the unbounded confidence which even today we see flaring up like fire from every page of the prophets and the psalms?[40]

If only in and through God's light that "is come" upon the biblical witnesses can theology begin to grasp the external character of their "whence," it also follows—and this is the second aspect—that an essential aspect of Barth's concept of divine-human dissimilarity is the theme of the *mystery* of God's self-objectivity in Scripture. The theme, more closely, concerns in one sense the prevailing priority of God's self-objectivity in and above Scripture's humanity. As a consequence of God's self-giving presence, the gift of Scripture's creaturely and anthropological orientation, moreover, has "its own distinct grounds, possibilities, and hypotheses"; as memory of the manifestations of the new world in the old, the gift is "'history' far beyond what is elsewhere called history."[41] The historicity and humanity of Scripture, in Barth's view, are corollaries of the theme of the self-objectivity of the Spirit's saving economy. And in this specific sense, his theme of "far beyond" denotes the *eschatological* essence of the Spirit's gift of the person, work, and ends of the biblical writers as a gratuitous extension of the mystery of the self-objectivity of God in Christ by the Spirit.

In this connexion, Barth stresses the contingence and externality of the unity of the biblical canon, as he asks, "What is the significance of the remarkable line from Abraham to Christ?" Barth can begin to stammer in awe about the "significance" of the self-objectivity of Christ's Spirit—God's "marvelous light"—as God's capacity for humanity, but the self-objectivity of Christ's Spirit, not as humanity's capacity for God, a joyful and moving recognition that we suggest would remain entirely characteristic of his pneumatological view of the ontological problem of the historicity and humanity of the biblical witness:

40. Ibid., 30.
41. Ibid., 37.

> We have found in the Bible, a new world, God's sovereignty, God's glory, God's incomprehensible love. Not the history of man but the history of God! Not the virtues of men but the virtues of him who hath called us out of darkness into his marvelous light! Not human standpoints but the standpoint of God![42]

Once again: "The contents of the Bible are 'God.' But what is the content of the contents? Something 'new' breaks forth! But what is the new?"[43] Succinctly put, the ever-newness of "the content" of Scripture's "contents" concerns the pure deity of God standing "before us as he really is"[44] or "the fullness of the Godhead,"[45] "contents" that the Spirit deploys to command our attention "away from ourselves"[46] to attend to the pure deity of God.

> Can one read or hear read even as much as two chapters from the Bible and still with good conscience say, God's word went forth to humanity, his mandate guided history from Abraham to Christ, the Holy Spirit descended in tongues of fire upon the apostles at Pentecost, a Saul became a Paul and travelled over land and sea . . . Is *that* all? Is *that* all of God and his new world, of the meaning of the Bible, of the content of the contents? The power forces which come to expression in the Bible, the movements of peoples, the battles, and the convulsions which take place before us there, the miracles and revelations which constantly occur there, the immeasurable promises for the future which are unceasingly repeated to us there—do not all these things stand in a rather strange relation to so small a result—if that is really the only result they have? Is not God—greater than that?[47]

Thus Barth on the fearsome, purifying gift of the human person for recognizing God as God on whom we can only wait:[48] "What is within the Bible?

---

42. Ibid., 45.

43. Ibid., 46.

44. Ibid., 47.

45. Ibid., 48.

46. Ibid., 34. "There is a spirit in the Bible that allows us to stop awhile and play among secondary things as is our wont—but presently it begins to press us on; and however we may object that we are only weak, imperfect, and most average folk, it presses us on to the primary fact, whether we will or no. There is a river in the Bible that carries us away, once we have entrusted our destiny to it—away from ourselves to the sea."

47. Ibid., 46–47.

48. The point on the priority of divine action and the consequence of human waiting in theology's relation to Scripture is visible in his sermon on 2 Pet 3:12 on April 29 1917. See also, Barth and Willimon, *The Early Preaching of Karl Barth*, 25–35.

has a mortifying way of converting itself into the opposing question, Well, what are you looking for, and who are you, pray, who make bold to look?"[49] If God communicates himself by means of Scripture, Barth seems to think that the theme of human communication in Scripture is effectively a subset of the themes of the loving and purifying self-communication of God. As Barth writes, "The Holy Scriptures will interpret themselves in spite of all our human limitations."[50]

Our reading of this lecture considers the soteriological theme of God's love as the context of Barth's polemics, and the related themes of the externality and mystery of God's self-objectivity in Scripture. Barth's language of Spirit is relatively prominent, but still seems to lack consistency and focus. Yet one thing can be said about his pneumatological reference: Barth occasionally speaks of Scripture's creaturely and anthropological orientation in terms of the Spirit's creative, saving economy as God's love for us; stresses God's confrontation with sin as characteristic of the economy. By virtue of that activity, human subjectivity is created and purified *for* recognition of God's deity in Christ: the gift of the human is subservient to, and is known only through, the greater objectivity of God.

The relation of divine giving to human receiving is asymmetric: recognition of God as God remains a sheer miracle for Barth. Although his reflections on these themes are compressed and underdeveloped as compared to his subsequent writings, we can easily see their more conceptually matured and masterful expressions in his Göttingen lectures. For now, we can simply note that the soteriological theme of the Spirit's purifying use of the biblical witness lacks, for instance, detail about the eschatological and historical character of Christ's relation to Scripture's place in the economy of revelation and salvation; more closely, a fuller anthropology of the biblical witnesses as *peccatores iusti*. By way of anticipation, Barth will address some of these issues and discuss others forcefully especially in the fourth

---

Willimon's commentary on the sermon is more interested in Barth's relation to his theological teachers, notably W. Herrman, and does not explicitly attend to the pneumatological orientation of Barth's view of Scripture in the opening of the sermon. "A Word spoken as if straight from the heart of the Bible! . . . A Word spoken out of the Spirit of God. And therefore, dear friends, the Spirit, the Holy Spirit of God, must open our ears so that we may hear what the Word has to say to us" (25). Cf. Barth's emphasis on divine action in a sermon on confirmation day in 1918. 29 March 1918, 1 Sam 20. 23 (419), 106–12 (esp. 108).

49. Barth, "The New Word in the Bible," 32.

50. Ibid., 34.

chapter in the two editions of the *Römerbrief*. It is the first edition of the famous commentary that to which we now turn.

1919 Der Römerbrief

Barth's maturing, christologically grounded soteriological anthropology of the biblical witnesses is visible in his reading of Rom 4. While Barth's pneumatological reference is at best implicit in his reading, and it is *not* a primary theme in our reading, the choice of the text serves to underscore a broader, christological context, and resultant soteriological emphasis of Barth's understanding of Scripture's anthropological orientation. In Rom 4, as he traces Paul's understanding of God's work of binding humanity and history to Christ's self-concealment as God's "No," Barth is able to construe God's "No" in the light of God's immeasurably deeper "Yes."[51] God's deeper "Yes," stresses Barth, is borne to us by God's use of Scripture not as the "Yes" without the "No," but God's use of Scripture always as God's reconciliatory "Nevertheless!"[52]

God's reconciliatory "Nevertheless" is a crucial soteriological theme to underscore God's use of Scripture as being irreducible to mere epistemic issues or merely a different way of reading the Bible. Salvation is not merely interpretive for Barth. Put differently, if Barth is uninterested in mere polemics, it is because only in the light of God's immeasurably loving "Nevertheless" can the ontological force of God's saving relation to Scripture be grasped properly. Thus in his reading of Rom 4, by construing Scripture in the "light of the days of God" that "shines backwards and forwards"[53] amidst the crushing "night of the divine wrath,"[54] Barth can cheerfully devise that "we *can* participate in Christ, therefore we *can* understand history."[55] I suggest that Barth's optimism concerns, in short, God's agency in human participation in Christ in at least two ways.

The first way concerns the self-objectivity of Christ as the hermeneutical situation of the person, work, and ends of the biblical witnesses. On his reading, Scripture's anthropological orientation can be illustrated by the Pauline theme of the biblical Abraham as "*simul justus et peccator*" in

51. *Römerbrief 1919*, 91.
52. Ibid., 91–94f.
53. Ibid., 106.
54. Ibid., 94.
55. Ibid., 144.

Rom 4.[56] The soteriological theme helps illustrate in one sense that only by the sheer grace of Christ's self-revelation, can the relation between the biblical witnesses be understood as a unity and their unity as essentially external to their being human. Their anthropological orientation to Christ can therefore be construed as *external* to itself. As Barth observes:

> Historical individuals are a unified whole (eine solidarische Einheit), a family in one and the same house. They are, admittedly, gradated and differentiated as forerunners, contemporaries, and descendants of the Messiah, according to their special relationship to the great course of prophecy, fulfilment, and completion. But (what is more important than this variation!) they are bound together through their commonality—that in the Messiah the kingdom of God has come near them.[57]

Thus Barth on the soteriological primacy and priority of God in Scripture's anthropological orientation including human objectivity in creaturely history. We may, moreover, understand *him* as a member of "the timelessly, historically and psychologically unbound community of the Spirit."[58] Succinctly put, the Spirit's self-objectivity in the consequence of Scripture's objectivity of Abraham's solidarity with the saints concerns not first historical construction or human valuation, but it concerns first God's employment of them in the salvific economy of revelation.

If the gift of the witness of Abraham can be understood as a consequence of divine action in the saving economy of revelation it follows that the biblical witnesses are being genuinely human not as "Heroes," but each being genuinely human as "only a fellow sinner and fellow redeemed."[59] If their human fellowship with all saints is borne to us only by virtue of the saving economy of God, the "history" and "voice" of their witness, Barth thinks, are borne to us *in* the "history" and "voice" of God.

> The voice of the Bible in any event, if we want to hear it and speak not from a different past than the one in Christ's present and our own future, is nowhere of the part of the ruins of truth, but always

---

56. The point is thoroughly demonstrated by Wood in *Barth's Theology of Interpretation*, 12–18.

57. *Römerbrief 1919*, 106. Cited and translated by Wood in *Barth's Theology of Interpretation*, 15.

58. *Römerbrief 1919*, 106f; 3.

59. Ibid., 117.

> from the momentous sphere of truth, never of the history of reli-
> gion, but always of the history of God.[60]

Thus Barth on the externality of Scripture's human origin and history as immeasurably deeper and broader than church history and the history of religion.[61] By subordinating the objectivity of Scripture's human orienta-tion to the self-objectivity of Christ's deity, Barth can begin to construe the primacy of divine-human dissimilarity in the objectivity of Christ's relation to Scripture under the soteriological theme of "the mercy of God":[62] "God *must* show us his faithfulness, not because we give him a cause, but because he is *God*."[63] Once again: "In Christ the truth of God has once again become free in history, so it begins with him the new, the history of freedom."[64]

If God's reckoning has its centre in Christ, and radically away from the "reckoned" creature, the biblical account of Abraham, thinks Barth, concerns, not first human self-valuation of our relation (or significance or non-significance) to God, but first "God's free, sovereign, new act, so free so sovereign, so new as the divine 'Let there be!' (Gen. 1.3)."[65] Put differ-ently, only in the eschatological comprehensiveness of Christ's free mercy in his ever-fresh use of Scripture can the externality of the relation of the biblical witnesses to their readers be understood. A case in point is Paul, whom Barth describes as one who "speaks as a prophet and apostle of God's kingdom to all people of all ages."[66] To "all people of all ages," Paul can speak only crucially as a new creature pointing radically away from himself to the sovereign freedom of Christ, as Barth writes:

> Instead of reckoning with *God* over against humanity, he *reckons*
> with God in the name of humanity. That is the presupposition un-
> der which he looks at *Geschichte* and writes *Historie*. He searches
> for the real or supposed high points of history so that by means of
> the great and small heroes which he finds there he might protect
> himself against the realism of the curse and salvation and against
> the universalism of judgement and grace as they arise from the

60. Ibid., 107.
61. Ibid., 118.
62. Ibid., 92; 137f.
63. Ibid., 94.
64. Ibid., 95.
65. Ibid., 113.
66. Ibid., 3.

invasion of revelation. For now there is only the question whether the Bible, whose contents he also refers to, shares this presupposition or whether precisely in the Bible the heroes of the past are not portrayed in the light of the divine new creation in Christ.[67]

Thus Barth on the externality of God's sanctifying gift of making real the eschatological person and work of the biblical witnesses, and on their *real* anthropological need of the "absolute miracle of the being of God."[68] More closely, all this comes under the optimistic theme of the absolute freedom of God.

> God's faithfulness can always come to confess this witness. But they are no more than that. They are a consequence of a cause, sign of the subject-matter, form of the content, so already with Abraham. God's decisive action goes before them, and God's own intentions go beyond them. They are a means. That they are, but no more than that, and beware when this is forgotten.[69]

The biblical witnesses are a consequence and object of God's merciful reckoning. When "this is forgotten," when they are more than the means of mercy that they *are*, the reader's construal of their relation to God tends to get read back into God's self-described "reckoned" relation to them. As a result, the unidirectionality of grace is lost in view.

> Now Abraham himself is no scholar, no teacher, but stands outside any "circle" and "movement" and "businesses" as one of the far too many, and is as such a blessed [man] of God (4.10). The content of his promise is the real (reale), not merely intellectual, programmatic basis (Grundlegung) of history in the righteousness of God, and the ground on which he stands is none other than the faithfulness of God, which lets the law be fulfilled. So is not only the barrier of the impossibility (4.14), but also the imprisonment of the specific idea that the divine is locked up under the law is blown up. Yes, *even* those who "are known by the law," and *even* the scholars and teachers, *can* participate in the fulfilment of the promise with their Father Abraham who is *its* father, God be blessed. Even within Judaism and Christianity the new history of humankind can rise. God is *also* the God of the Jews (3.29). But even outside such circle Abraham has his descendent, his "seed," his house (Geschlecht), legitimate heirs in the sense of the promise

---

67. Ibid., 108, cited and translated by Wood in *Barth's Theology of Interpretation*, 17.
68. *Römerbrief 1919*, 136.
69. Ibid., 121.

under where, indifferent in terms of the historical-psychological context, does God's faithfulness genuinely do him justice, where the miracle of the foundation in righteousness takes place, where the Messiah will also appear, where it comes also to the faith to affirm this divine creative act (4.11–12). *The* word, which Abraham heard, which replaces the old presuppositions of history with new ones, is the word of blessings directed to *all* humanity without the particular mediation of the law.

Thus stands the biblical Abraham before us; his faith is not the knowledge of moral, but the foundation (Gegründetsein) in righteousness, his promise not idealist and therefore particularistic, but a real and therefore universal, his descendants not humanly restricted, but a power of the faithfulness of God embraces all humankind.[70]

Thus Barth on the precedence of God's faithfulness and mercy towards the biblical witnesses and the consequence of their being created objects and instruments of God's love.

All this suggests that Barth's maturing, bibliological account of the primacy and priority of God. Further, their human relation to the Spirit is best construed as a radical deference to God's unidirectional acts of *reconciliation*. In this sense, "the history with us and let us to speak of us with history from the singular theme of the commanding reign of God. This place is the Bible's: 'Historia vitae magistra.'"[71] Just as Barth's understanding of history and Scripture cannot be understood properly apart from his logical priority of the gift of person, so can his critique of the historical-critical method not be grasped properly apart from his confidence in the eschatological comprehensiveness of the saving economy of God.

On Barth's reading, moreover, the self-involving bibliological theme of God's gift of human solidarity is prominent. If Paul is to be trusted, he does not so much pray to be read intellectually as to be genuinely understood (and believed!) as a fellow human; seeing the genuine ever-new humanity of the apostle is to stand alongside him on the same free ground as made possible and understood by God in Christ.[72] That is also to say, standing with the apostle is to understand history in light of the ever-new gift of his-

---

70. Ibid., 134–35.

71. Ibid., 143.

72. The point on the necessity of divine action in Paul's self-understanding as a creaturely object of God's mercy in Christ is visible in a sermon in Barth's Ephesians series (no. 468–85) in the same year. 11 May 1919, Eph 1.1–23 (469), 181–88 (esp. 185).

tory's soteriological instrumentality as sign and witness of Christ whose capacity for humanity, moreover, is not to be construed as humanity's (or the historian's) capacity for God. In this sense, the divine-human dissimilarity in being and act, once again, is Barth's seminal point: "The revelation in Christ is not a "historical" (*historisches*) event, but the breakthrough of the power which *was* and *will be* the exposure of the restlessness, the necessity, the actual longitude of time."[73]

In Rom 4 Barth indicates his exegetical orientation of his grasp of Scripture's anthropological orientation. Hidden in Christ, the orientation, however invisible and beyond our control, can be made believable and intelligible through the freedom of the God's creative acts. In virtue of God's acts, Scripture has been and can again be reckoned and confirmed as His true sign and witness in the patience of God who did and will, in his free mercy, again show himself faithful.

1922 Der Römerbrief

As we continue to sketch Barth's maturing anthropology of Scripture, we shall do so simply by tracing his exegetical observations and theological explications from his reading of Rom 4 with other chapters from the Epistle in view. Once again, Barth's pneumatology is *not* part of my account of his reading. His view of Scripture, not pneumatology, is my primary concern. And it is true that Barth's more obvious pneumatological reference lies beyond Rom 4.[74] The selection of the text serves to underscore the *soteriological* character of Barth's christologically grounded anthropology of Scripture, in two ways.

The first way concerns Barth's emphasis of God's utter dissimilarity with the biblical witnesses and their readers in his theme of divine mercy.

---

73. *Römerbrief 1919*, 106.

74. Cf. *Römerbrief 1922*, chapters 5–8. There is an indirect reference to "uncreated light" in Barth's account of human comprehension of the faith of Abraham (v. 22), an arguably indirect pneumatological theme that comes under the larger theme of divine reckoning; but it can also be taken as a reference to the Word: "Because Abraham's faith is *faith before God* (iv. 17b); because faith is not one element in his character, but forms the absolute limitation which marks his behaviour and dissolves it, the absolute Miracle, the pure Beginning, and the Primal Creation. Because his faith is not comprehended in an historical happening, but is the negation of all occurrence and non–occurrence, it is defined by God as righteousness; and in God, and by God only, Abraham participates in the negation of all negation and in the death of all death. And so in his faith, being unimpeded by historical occurrence, shines forth as light from light uncreated."

The theme of divine mercy is a way of emphasizing the unidirectional character of God's prior turn to all creation and humanity. Creation's renewed relation to God, moreover, is bound to his unbound faithfulness, and is reckoned to him by himself as his righteousness in Christ. If God's absolute righteousness for his *new* creation is his free mercy, Barth writes, "We can no longer hear the No under which we stand apart from the divine Yes from which it proceeds."[75]

> The mercy of God triumphs! It has been given to us. The positive relation between God and man, which is the absolute paradox, veritably exists. This is the theme of the Gospel, proclaimed in fear and trembling, but under pressure of a necessity from which there is no escape. It proclaims eternity as an event. We declare the knowledge of the Unknown God, the Lord of heaven and earth, who dwelleth not in temples made with hands, who needeth not anything, seeing that He himself giveth to all life and breath and all things. We set forth everything given by God to men, as given in order that they may seek Him who is not far from each one of us, in whom we live and move and have our being, who is beyond all our life and movement and existence, and whose nature is to remain faithful, in spite of human depravity.[76]

Although Barth speaks of the relation as a "given," note his emphasis on the ends of this divine giving: "in order that they may seek Him." The relation is by no means intrinsic to creature; instead, Barth emphasizes the relation as a result of God's capacity for mercy, not as a result of our capacity for God. Knowledge of divine mercy therefore points beyond us to God. Put differently and superficially with an anticipation of his more mature thoughts on the subject in his later writings, sanctified human knowledge of God points to God as the origin and agent and means of his relation and revelation to us. In short, a key in Barth's notion of divine-human dissimilarity is the demarcation and correlation between divine and human agencies in the economy of revelation and salvation: "We proclaim that, because it is His nature to remain faithful, the Godhead cannot be graven into any likeness of the skill and device of men."[77]

---

75. Ibid., 69 (ET 94–96).

76. Ibid.

77. Ibid., 69 (ET 94–95).

More closely, Barth's reading of God's utter dissimilarity from creation concerns the soteriological theme of the "righteousness of God."[78] God's judgement of theological and biblical studies, Barth writes, "is peculiarly visible when the world stands under the negation of judgement."[79] Barth's theme of divine judgement is, I suggest, best construed in the light of its soteriological character. A prominent example is Barth's critique of the historicist concept of history: if only in the light of the pure deity of Christ's Spirit can we grasp "the meaning of history, and especially of the complaint of history against its own inadequacy," it is because it "is the redemption of all creation, and most particularly when the creature knows itself to be no more than a creature, and so points beyond itself."[80] Just as the creature's relation to God *is* outside of creation, just so *is* creaturely history outside of itself: "The righteousness of God," which "is righteousness from outside— justitia forensis, justitia aliena"—"is His forgiveness, the radical alteration of the relation between God and man."[81] In short, the absolute freedom and precedence of God is Barth's seminal point.

The point about Barth's view of the priority and primacy of God in the relation of Jesus to Scripture concerns—and this is the second way—the absolute freedom of God in revelation, in Christ's relation to creation.[82] "The revelation of which is in Jesus, because it is the revelation of the righteousness of God, must be the most complete veiling of His incomprehensibility."[83] An essential point in Barth's paradoxical polemics is that revelation of God is also revelation of the righteousness of God. Revelation of God is concrete, not abstract; concerns God as an acting agent, not as a mere idea. Once again, a focus on divine agency may be a helpful way forward in grasping Barth's complex language of divine righteousness.

> God's righteousness is revealed "through his faithfulness in Jesus Christ." The faithfulness of God is that divine persistence by virtue of which he again and again provides, at many scattered points in history, possibilities, opportunities, and witnesses to the knowledge of his righteousness. Jesus of Nazareth is the one among these many other points in which they can all be perceived in their

---

78. Ibid.
79. Ibid.
80. Ibid.
81. Ibid., 68–69 (ET 93).
82. Ibid., 70 (ET 96).
83. Ibid., 71–72 (ET 98).

> coherent meaning as a line, as the true central theme of history
> (der eigentliche rote Faden der Geschichte). Christ is the content
> of this perception: the righteousness of God himself.[84]

Note that Barth perceives the righteousness of God in christological terms, in terms of Jesus of Nazareth as a witness in time, a witness and time that God provided for the knowledge of God's righteousness in creation. It is against God's righteousness, the absolute freedom of his agency in his revelation that the witness of God is measured—judged: to bear witness to God is to come under his judgement. As Barth writes, Jesus "sets Himself wholly under the judgement under which the world is set" and "sacrifices to the incomparably Greater and to the invisibly Other every claim to genius and every human heroic or aesthetic or psychic possibility, because there is no conceivable human possibility of which He did not rid Himself."[85] God's agency is absolute and unbound in Jesus; and for Barth this notion of divine freedom and primacy in the relation between the divine and human in agency characterizes the biblical witnesses and their relation to Jesus Christ. In short, God's relation to them through Jesus Christ is unidirectional.

More closely, Barth's point is the freedom and precedence of the whole Godhead in and through Scripture. Scripture as the witness of Jesus Christ by virtue of revelation is irreducible to faith; it is not a possession of faith; for Scripture is borne to us by none other than by God himself, that is, the entire Godhead. On our parts, so Barth writes, "There is no such thing as mature and assured possession of faith": "What I heard yesterday I must hear again today; and if I am to hear it afresh to-morrow, it must be revealed by the Father of Jesus, who is in heaven, and by Him only."[86] God is unbound to Scripture, and Scripture is unbound to us because God is free. Once again: "He speaks where law is, not because law is there, but because he willeth to speak. God is free."[87] Put differently, all this is just a way of underscoring Barth's view of Scripture as an extension of the soteriological theme of "miracle": "He who says 'God,' says 'miracle.'"[88]

Crucially, "miracle" is an essential theme of his critique of a naturalist anthropological orientation in biblical and theological studies. Under the

84. Ibid., cited and translated by Wood in *Barth's Theology of Interpretation*, 19.
85. Ibid., 70–71 (ET 97).
86. Ibid., 71–72 (ET 98).
87. Ibid., 67–68 (ET 92).
88. Ibid., 96 (ET 120–21).

theme Barth construes Abraham's perception (Einsicht) as "the miracle of perception" while avoiding Gnosticism and Pelagianism[89]—by stressing the primacy and priority of divine agency in his anthropology of Abraham as a "believer" judged by God, the absolute agent of miracle: "In what [Abraham] is—seer, spiritual and moral hero—his faith—that is to say, what he is not—miracle, the new world, God—is made manifest."[90] If Barth is uninterested in viewing Abraham's agency in sheer negativity, it is in part, I suggest, because Barth believes that in our thinking about miracle a proper account of divine agency demands a proper account of the resultant human agency. One way of that sort of proper accounting is what he calls the "method of reckoning," a "method" that, crucially, "is not preoccupied with what may be *reckoned* to men *as of debt*, but with that which is *of grace*."[91] Put differently, human agency is a un-necessity to divine agency; divine employment of human agents is his grace; and his grace is unidirectional. Like all witnesses, the biblical witness "sees their createdness bearing witness to the Creator, and what is visible in them as void and deprivation, as longing and hope for that which is invisible."[92] However, it may be fair for one to wonder if Barth *apparently* overrates human consciousness in Christian vocation and places excessive responsibility on creaturely self-knowledge as a consequence of creaturely knowledge of God. But does the former necessarily follow the latter, and what is the proper manner of accounting for that sort of apparent correspondence? Does one who knows God know himself necessarily and simultaneously? To these questions Barth's emphasis on human silence and waiting before God is instructive. I suggest that for Barth the Bible's knowledge of God sometimes comes to expression as a relative *silence* before God who must himself speak. "All flesh must be silent before the inconspicuousness of God, in order that all flesh may see His salvation."[93] The silence is an act of human waiting, an act that Barth regards as a consequence of grace from the God whose waiting precedes all human waiting. "By the knowledge of Jesus Christ all human waiting is guaranteed, authorised, and established; for He makes it known

89. Ibid.

90. Ibid.

91. Ibid., 96–97 (ET 121–22).

92. Ibid.

93. Ibid., 74–75 (ET 100). In this connection, Barth's emphasis on the precedence of divine action and decision and the consequence of humility and waiting in human determination is central to a sermon on 1 Pet in 1921. 9 Oct 1921, 1 Pet 1.24–25 (578), 190–96.

that it is not men who wait, but God—in His faithfulness."[94] The notion of Einsicht may be appreciated by way of Barth's emphasis on gratitude, humility, and prayer, as we shall see in his lectures on the Gospel of John.

If our reading is plausible, we suggest that it at least reinforces my emphasis on the soteriological character of Barth's anthropology of the biblical witnesses as *peccatores iusti*, and of his exegetical and doctrinal orientation. For him, God's agency is external, unbound and necessary to the human agency of Scripture, and the relation of the former to the latter is unidirectional and optimistic. His optimism is christologically grounded and is arguably hamartologically robust, though the above-described bibliological themes would become increasingly more sophisticated through his intense immense in the Reformed tradition. In the lecture, "Biblical Questions, Insights, and Vistas," for example, Barth offers some focused reflections on the relation and demarcation between divine agency and human agency in Scripture. It is the material that to which we now turn.

"Biblical Questions, Insights, and Vistas"

In an important lecture, "Biblical Questions, Insights, and Vistas," one of the key themes Barth reflects on is the theme of divine agency in Scripture. The lecture is important, in part because it helps illuminate Barth's characteristic emphasis on the pure deity of God in God's relation to the biblical witnesses; an implication of the emphasis is Barth's increasingly refined notion of the priority of God's saving economy in Scripture's self-understanding as God's new creation. Moreover, it is important, in part because Barth is arguably careful *not* to give the impression that Scripture provides a metaphysic of creation; in his view Scripture has none of that to offer. The question of what Scripture offers does not begin or end with what Scripture has in itself: for if what Scripture *is* in God is *external* to itself, its self-understanding does neither begin nor end within itself, but it begins and finds rest in God. The sovereign priority of God in, through and above what Scripture offers is Barth's seminal point in the lecture.

In one way, the presupposition of God's relation to Scripture is not one that we can ontologically posit and hereafter hermeneutically applied: "we are far from being equal to that knowledge. If we were, we should not

94. *Römerbrief 1922*, 70 (ET 96).

be asking what the Bible offers."[95] My notion of Scripture's externality is just another way to draw out Barth's emphasis on God being free, external, and necessary to Scripture's human agency. As Barth introduces the subject of the lecture,

> What the Bible has to offer us, above all, is insight to the effect that the knowledge of God is the eternal problem of our profoundest personal existence, that it is the starting-point at which we begin and yet do not begin, from which we are separated and yet not separated. From the Bible we may learn to soften the affirmations of our belief or unbelief, and perhaps to keep silence, until we perceive the true relation between God and ourselves.[96]

That is also to suggest that on the part of its readers, what Scripture is or what it offers is not always immediately clear. For Barth, Scripture's clarity has first to do with *God*—with its divine employment as the decision and action of God merciful turning, not with human valuation including Scripture's own. Put differently the clarity or unity of God's action is irreducible to human cognition, since the latter is an object of his action, not the subject. From this it also follows that Scripture's first interest or concern is not itself. Rather, God commands "their *complete* attention,"[97] as Barth writes: in them, "there is the same seeing of the invisible, the same hearing of the inaudible, the same incomprehensible but no less undeniable epidemic of standing still and looking up" and "among whom attention to a Wholly Other seems never wholly to have lapsed."[98] Note that Barth carefully avoids suggesting human agency as the origin, power and guarantee of "their *complete* attention, their *entire* obedience" to God.[99] Barth admits that Scripture is "[a] human document like any other, it can lay no *a priori* dogmatic claim to special attention and consideration."[100] Put simply, it is not the biblical witnesses or their writings that command attention and consideration, Barth argues; it is not they who *cause* conversion and repentance to God; it is rather God to whom they owe their faith, life, and vocation. So instead Barth speaks of their self-conscious "limits" and "rela-

95. Barth, "Biblical Questions, Insights, and Vistas," 52.

96. Ibid., 59.

97. Ibid., 74.

98. Ibid., 64.

99. Ibid., 74.

100. Ibid., 60ff. In the very least a net effect of this position is a displacement of confession and doctrine as an ontic basis of Scripture.

tivity" in their relation to God: "Bible piety is conscious of its own limits, of its relativity. In its essence it is humility, fear of the Lord."[101] Barth goes on to stress divine transcendence in and through their agency, an important feature of his concept of Scripture: "It points beyond the world, and points at the same time and above all beyond itself. It lives absolutely by virtue of its Object and for its Object."[102] In the very least Barth suggests that God's agency is free, external, and yet necessary to their human agency and ends. The notion of divine transcendence means in one sense that God is the sovereign subject of his gratuitous help and saving presence to the biblical witnesses: divine agency is irreducible to human agency. If this reading of his reflections on the theme of divine agency in Scripture is plausible, I suggest it can at least help open up conversation about his characterization of Scripture's human agency and his resultant doctrinal and exegetical orientation to the scriptural text, in two ways.

The first way is that as he sketches knowledge of God as a human impossibility in Scripture, Barth is able to indicate the resurrection as an overarching theme for his understanding of the miraculous nature of the human agency of the biblical witnesses.[103] In them the distinction between their new and old humanity points beyond the distinction to the utter uniqueness of God as the "*totaliter aliter*."[104] From this it also follows that if the new humanity in Scripture relates to its old humanity by virtue of God's regeneration and forgiveness, then only in the light of God's sovereign priority and unbound agency, theology may begin to grasp Scripture's sanctified humanity as *simul justus et peccator*.

> When we ask the Bible what it has to offer, it answers by putting to us the fact of *election*. What we call religion and culture may be available to everybody, but the belief, simple and comprehensive, which is offered in the Bible, is not available to everybody: not at any time nor in any respect can any who will, reach out and take it. . . . The knowledge which the Bible offers and commands us to accept forces us out upon a narrow ridge of rock upon which

101. Ibid., 69.

102. Ibid.

103. Ibid., 86. "The only real way to *name* the theme of the Bible, which is the Easter message, is to have it, to show it, to live it. . . . Let us be satisfied that all Biblical questions, insights, and vistas focus upon this common theme." As important as the theme of the resurrection in Barth, it goes much beyond the scope of my reading. I focus on only one element of the theme, namely, divine agency.

104. Ibid., 92.

we must balance between Yes and No, between life and death, between heaven and earth. "Work out your own salvation with fear and trembling. For it is God which worketh in you both to will and to do of his good pleasure."[105]

If God's working is necessary to our grasp of the distinction between the new and the old, between the divine and human, it follows that, as Barth writes, to "the fact of election" "our responses cannot be determined once and for all: they are constantly to be made anew. Indeed opposite responses are awakened *simultaneously* in a single individual."[106] Contrary to a widespread view that claims he reduces the objectivity of God's saving economy to mere human subjectivity,[107] Barth puts it rather boldly, "The only eternal election is God's: the dispositions of history and of the individual mind are secondary and temporal."[108] That is also to suggest that if Barth is uninterested in reducing divine election to religion,[109] confession or doctrine, it is in part because he insists on divine *action* as the condition of the renewal and freedom of human relation to, and recognition and proclamation of, God in Scripture. This is Barth's formal reserve for divine agency in Scripture. This formal reserve is Barth's preface to his (apparently occasional) exegetical orientation, as he goes on to say, "With this conscious reservation, that we are saying something that we do not know, that *is* true on when it *becomes* true, let the page now be turned, and the Bible's final suggestion be taken up (as a suggestion!)."[110] A net effect of all this is that as Barth describes God's agency, Barth is able to sketch Scripture's respect for and recognition of the freedom, priority, sovereignty and necessity of the action of God in and through its human agency. This respect is characteristic of their new humanity; it refers their newness beyond themselves to the doing and turning of *God*.

> Resurrection means the *new world*, the world of a new quality and kind. Our discovery of the significance of the world we live in, that its life comes from death, our knowledge that *its* origin

---

105. Ibid., 58.

106. Ibid., 58–59.

107. Williams, "Barth on the Triune God," 161–81.

108. Barth, "Biblical Questions, Insights, and Vistas," 58.

109. Ibid., 86–87. "Religion's blind and vicious habit of asserting eternally that it possesses something, feasts upon it, and distributes it, must sometime cease, if we are ever to have an honest, a fierce, seeking, asking, and knocking."

110. Ibid., 87.

is in God because our *own* is in God, is not a continuation of anything that has been or is, either in the spiritual or the natural realm, but comes to our mind spontaneously as a new creation. Reality as we have known it, even if it be understood in the optimistic way of the reformers as a process of growth, is neither verified nor explained by this new truth; but in the light of this truth, it is seen to be clothed upon with new reality. *Qualiter? Totaliter aliter!* "That which is born of the flesh is flesh; and that which is born of the [S]pirit is spirit." There are no transitions, intermixings, or intermediate stages. There is only crisis, finality, new insight. What the Bible brings us from beyond the grave is the perfect, the absolute miracle. . . . The Bible without the *absolute* miracle is simply *not* the Bible.[111]

Crucially by speaking of resurrection as Scripture's common theme—and this is the second way—Barth can underscore the soteriological character of his account of divine agency. "The highest expression of the *totaliter aliter* which the Bible utters is the teaching of the forgiveness of sins."[112] Put slightly differently, the soteriological emphasis is another way of underscoring reconciliation as the context of Scripture's human agency through Christ:

To me—let me say incidentally—this fact of 'forgiveness' is even more astonishing than the raising of Lazarus. It is a new and unprecedented factor in the practical reckoning of life. In the midst of the field of moral and political reality the moral subject is constituted anew by virtue of his interconnection with the order of the kingdom of heaven, by virtue of his being counted unto God; the beginning of good is perceived in the midst of bad; the royal freedom of man is established by virtue of the royal freedom of God; the possibility is given of understanding all things in the light of God, of doing the greatest and the smallest deeds to the glory of God, of prizing the good man not too much and damning the bad man not too much, but seeing both as brothers united in the reconciling light of God.[113]

In one sense the priority of "the reconciling light of God" in Barth's account of Scripture's human agency means, in the very least, the priority

111. Ibid., 91. Wherever appropriate in this text, I changed "spirit" to "Spirit" in S.A. Weston's excellent translation to better reflect Barth's references to the third person of the Trinity in his account of the resurrection of Jesus Christ.

112. Ibid., 92.

113. Ibid., 92.

of God's ever-fresh, redemptive-creative act of animation of the human person. It means, moreover, that only by this act can the reader begin to understand the biblical witnesses as they understand themselves. Scripture "desires not to be accepted but understood, πνευματικοῖς πνευματικά, spirit by spirit."[114] Crucially—although it is by no means prominent or consistent in the text—Barth considers briefly the redemption of "the subject" that is "born anew" in the terms of the power of the Spirit of the risen Christ: "The Spirit is the Creator and the Redeemer in one. It was in the power of the Spirit that Christ rose from the dead. It was on account of the Spirit, on account of the unity of God, that the Bible speaks of the corporeality of the resurrection and the new world."[115] As Barth speaks of the Spirit, he is considering at the same time the *whole* Godhead at work in redemption: the brief reference to the Spirit therefore does not suggest a doctrine of appropriations. Instead, Barth speaks of "the unity of God" in the reference to the *comprehensiveness* of the redemptive work of the Spirit. It is by virtue of the reconciling and redemptive work of the entire Godhead in the power of the Spirit that Scripture speaks as what it *is* in God's saving economy. In *one* sense, the reference to the Spirit affords Barth a *preliminary* sketch of God's deployment of the biblical witness before the parousia, the biblical witness whose act is interpreted in the light of their new person. As Barth reflects on the new and old human subject as a whole, following immediately his cryptic, pneumatological reference to the agency of the entire Godhead:

> A change of predicates takes place between the sowing in corruption and the raising in incorruption . . . . The subject remains the same. But since the subject is born anew, that is, "from above," ἄνωθεν, and is conscious of itself in God, ultimately there can remain in it no "below" whatever. Everything awaits in eternity. . . .
>
> The dependence of our *whole* existence upon God, our ultimate understanding of the meaning of breadth and length and depth and height, our acceptance of appearances not as mere appearances but as appearances of the idea, as works of the Creator who will sustain what he has made—the whole again being understood as intelligence in motion, consciousness at work, faith in action—this is the meaning of Easter.[116]

114. Ibid., 73.
115. Ibid., 93.
116. Ibid., 93–94.

In one sense, the soteriological account of Barth's account of divine agency in relation to the human agency of Scripture helps underscore the logical priority of the new person, and clarifies, to an extent, the primacy and irreducibility of the ontic over the noetic in theology's characterization of the biblical witness as God's work and new creature. In Barth's words, in short: "We *are* known before we *know*."[117]

From all this it is at least plausible to argue that by displacing human agency and subjectivity as the referent, context, and content of Scripture, and that instead by recognizing God's priority, objectivity, transcendence, and freedom, Barth appears consistent in his anti-Gnostic stance displayed in his earlier writings. Yet in his effort of displacing the human as the measure of all things Barth is *not* docetic. He is rather thoroughly committed to speak of the human; but does so in the terms of "the reconciling light of God," and the human as the creative work of the Redeemer. The displacement of the human as the absolute is therefore a recognition of the human, a recognition that is an extension of the recognition of God as God-for-us. The two-fold recognition is in one sense an exercise of interpretation with respect to God's agency in the miracle of the birth and support of the new person "from above." Just as the electing God's creative animation precedes faith and obedience, so contrition like conversion precedes interpretation. The ontic precedes and is irreducible to the noetic, not because of some arbitrary metaphysics by which theology is bound, but because Scripture and theology are bound to an unbound God who is beyond and above his works. The human is only apparently immediate: understanding of appearances of humanity and our history require interpretation. For Barth the humanity and history of the Bible is a case in point.

> Biblical history is natural history, spiritual history, and world history only in so far as it is first and foremost the history of *man*. God is the subject of this history and he alone; but it is a God beyond and above *man*, who is the element in which *man* originally lives, moves, and has his being, who is to be sought and found by *man*, who will lend to *man* the first fruits of the Spirit. In Christ as the Son of *man* all things, the heavenly and the earthly, are comprehended. . . . Observers of God there are none, as surely as there are no officious collaborators with God. There may, however, be children of God who are what they are by his grace. There our God-given selves, which do *not yet* appear what they shall be, this

---

117. Ibid., 95–96.

our experience, yours and mine, which may always *become* the experience of God—this is the meaning of Easter.[118]

For Barth an account of Scripture's humanity is only as robust as its account of God's deity. That is, however, not to suggest that Barth thinks that an account of God's deity can be derived from an account of Scripture's humanity, in part because the relation of the Redeemer to the redeemed is unidirectional, and in part because the interpretation of the human and their phenomena may have no understanding of the whole until the parousia. If what can be said about Scripture's humanity is bound by what can be said about God's deity, for Barth, then there is a logical demand in an anthropology of Scripture for an account of God's agency as electing, creative and sanctifying subject that is external, unbound, and necessary to Scripture's human agency. Whether or not Barth himself succeeds in meeting that demand, his above-described accounts appear cryptic given his absent discussion on the doctrine of the triune God or the relation between the Word and the Spirit. A more substantial and constructive account of divine agency in his concept of God is necessary. By way of anticipation: Barth's maturing concepts of God and Scripture will gain increasing precision and grandeur in his immersion in the Reformed tradition at Göttingen. It is the material that to which we now turn.

Barth, Göttingen, and the Reformed Scripture Principle

Appreciation of Barth's immersion in the Reformed tradition in Göttingen is important for understanding his view of Scripture. A common inattentiveness to Barth's Reformed orientation tends to overlook his reading of the Scripture Principle,[119] and mischaracterize his scriptural orientation

---

118. Ibid., 94–95.

119. See, for example, Thompson, "Witness to the Word," 189f. "Barth himself has been accused (quite reasonably in my view) of having collapsed the Spirit's illumination into the concept of revelation." Similarly, C. Trueman, who thinks "Barth's theology . . . as a radical break with the trajectories of Reformed Orthodoxy" (24), argues that to overcome "the radical discontinuity that exists between the infinite nature of God and the finite nature of doctrinal formulation" Barth focuses "on revelation as Christ, and on scripture as witness to that revelation, and thus pressing the non-identity of human statements about God and God's own revelation of himself" (22). With respect to Barth's view of Scripture, our contention here is quite simply that had Thompson and Trueman considered Barth's writings on the Scripture Principle such as the 1925 article and

as "devotion to the church."[120] By contrast, we stress Barth's soteriological orientation to the absolute freedom, precedence, and deity of God in and through Scripture.

All this is just another way to suggest his continual, and often painstaking, preoccupation with the Bible. In late September, 1921, "fourteen days after the second edition of *Romans* was ready," Barth began as chair of Reformed theology at Göttingen.[121] Between his acceptance of the appointment in mid-February of the same year and his relocation to "the distant city of Albrecht Ritschl,"[122] Barth was once again occupied with his continual study of the Epistle, reached only Rom 6.9 by May 18, and lamented, "Unfortunately, most unfortunately, still no manuscript" and concluded of the slow progress, "Evil times!"[123] Even by early August, the situation apparently did not improve: "I amble like a drunk man back and forth between writing desk, dining table, and bed, traveling each kilometer with my eye already on the next one."[124] When the manuscript was finally completed in the fall of the same year, biblical exposition remained a prominent preoccupation in his writings and maturation at Göttingen.[125] As E. Thurneysen illustrates the point:

> Karl Barth stands before us already in this early period as a reader and expositor of Scripture. The tablets of Holy Scripture are erected before him and the books of the expositors from Calvin through the biblicists and all the way to the modern critical biblical interpretation lie open in his hands. Both then and now this has been

---

more widely at the exegetical lectures such as those on the Gospel of John, their reading of Barth's concepts of revelation, witness, and scripture would need to be abandoned. Trueman, "Calvin, Barth, and Reformed Theology: Historical Prolegomena," (3–26). For an insightful study of Barth's relation to Calvin, see Chung, *Admiration and Challenge*. On Barth's Reformed scriptural orientation and understanding of Calvin's pneumatology and christology of divine-human dissimilarity, Chung argues that "it would not be an overstatement that Calvin would approve of Barth's appeal to him for a reformulation of Scripture-principle."

120. Dorrien, *The Barthian Revolt*, 71–72, 89–90, 144–45.

121. *B-Bultmann*, 156.

122. Ibid.

123. *RevT*, 58–59.

124. Ibid., 59.

125. Each semester between 1921–25, except for Summer 1922, Barth offered exegetical lectures on the New Testament: Ephesians (WS 1921/22), James (WS 1922/23), 1 Corinthians 15 (SS 1923), 1 John (WS 1923/24), Philippians (SS 1924), Colossians (WS 1924/25), and Sermon on the Mount (SS 1925).

the source from which his whole theology has come. It has grown out of the work of preaching, and it serves the proclamation of the church. And so it has remained. That the springs of the Bible should flow afresh in our time is the great concern that here is central, and indeed the sole concern. Barth is no abstract thinker, as will be very clear from these beginnings, and abstract here would mean liberated from the Scriptures. He does not project theological speculations out of his own mind; he is not concerned about a system; he is and he remains student and teacher of the Holy Scriptures. Whoever tries to understand him as other than this will not understand him at all.[126]

In this connexion, we suggest that the continuity of his preoccupation with the Bible and the maturation in his pneumatological convictions were two complementary aspects of his increasing self-described identification with the Reformed scriptural orientation whose theological commitments he was able to teach at Göttingen, in short, "with pleasure and a good conscience."[127]

The increasing profile of the Reformed Scripture Principle is visible in his lectures on the Reformed confessional writings (SS 1923), his 1923 Emden lecture "The Doctrinal Task of the Reformed churches," the prolegomena in his first dogmatics lectures (WS 1924/25), and a significant 1925 article "Das Schriftprinzip der reformierten Kirche" stressing the pneumatological primacy in the Reformed scriptural orientation. The article then appeared to be almost *verbatim* in *ChD* and slightly revised in *CD* I. If our reading is plausible, the material at least reinforces our position that Barth's self-described Reformed scriptural orientation cannot be grasped properly apart from the ontological force of his pneumatological emphasis. It is the material that to which we now turn, beginning with a famous public correspondence between Barth and Harnack in 1923.

Barth-Harnack Correspondence

In 1923 *Die Christliche Welt* published a significant series of correspondence between Barth and A. von Harnack.[128] With Harnack Barth arguably

---

126. *RevT*, 12–13.

127. *B-Bultmann*, 156. For a more qualified account of Barth's relation to German Reformed churches, see Freudenberg, *Karl Barth und die reformierte Theologie*, 38–83.

128. Harnack, "Fünfzehn Fragen an die Varächter der wissenschaftlichen Theologie unter den Theologen," in Barth, *Offene Briefe 1909–1935*, 59–62 (ET 85–87);

shares a common concern for the theological task of a proper construal of Scripture's objectivity,[129] though just as visible is a fundamental difference in their anthropological orientations to the task. Barth sees the task as a consequence of God's ever-prior turning to us: it concerns divine-human relation in God's self-objectivity, not mere anthropological objectivity.[130] In relation to the task, a proper anthropological objectivity is one that points beyond itself as a "coincidence" in the Spirit's outgoing economy.[131] On Rumscheidt's reading, Harnack is worried about the *theological* character of Barth's construal of the task, a character that appears to be "at worse, narrow in scope and sectarian."[132] In a sense, Harnack's worry concerns the intellectual respectability of Barth's vision of biblical and theological studies of Scripture. In this vision, as Harnack writes,

> What seems to be lost completely is its link between theology and the *universitas litterarum* and culture. There are rather new links between this evangelical theology and Catholicism and Romanticism. But let us hope we have here no more than the cocoon-stage of something that some day will turn out to be a genuinely evangelical butterfly.[133]

Barth, "Sechzehn Antworten an Herrn Professor von Harnack," 62–67 (ET 87–91); cf. 67–87. Harnack, "Open letter to Professor Karl Barth," 91–93. Harnack, *Offene Briefe 1909–1935*, 87–88 (ET 105–6). For a more extensive analysis of the correspondence, see, Rumscheidt, *Adolf von Harnack*, 29–53. See also Hunsinger, *Disruptive Grace*, 319–37.

129. Rumscheidt, *Adolf von Harnack*, 29–30.

130. Harnack's publication coincided with Barth's third Göttingen semester working through Zwingli, having just lectured on Calvin in the previous semester. In the Zwlingi and Calvin lectures, the soteriological character of "biblical history," we suggest, is essential to Barth's pneumatological construal of the Reformed scriptural orientation. Barth, *The Theology of John Calvin*, 1. "[S]harply differently from secular history," "biblical history" which *overshadows* it, "is not something given," but is borne to us in the event of divine turning. In this connexion, "biblical history" in its own "sphere" is "instructive as regards our regards our relation to God, or, more accurately, our relation to the salvation that comes from God": "biblical history only proclaims the sacred history, salvation history, the history of God" which is "the meaning and content of all history, and that seeks to speak in and above and beyond all so-called secular history" (2).

131. Barth, *Harnack*, 102. Barth, *Offene Briefe 1909–1935*, 83. "daß also die Sache mit dem Zeichen und *damit* das Zeichen mit der Sache zusammenfällt . . ." Cf. Webster, *Barth*, 41–43; for a fuller development on the theological difference between Barth and Harnack on historical method and biblical exegesis, see Webster, *Barth's Earlier Theology*, 74–75f.

132. Rumscheidt, *Adolf von Harnack*, 31.

133. Zahn-Harnack, *Adolf von Harnack*, 417–18. As with all quotes cited from the work, the quote is Rumscheidt's translation: *Adolf von Harnack*, 31. If Rumscheidt's view is plausible, Bender's reading of Harnack likening Barth's theology with "the dangers of

More closely, what concerns Harnack, argues Rumscheidt, is the obstacle that Barth's theological vision of Scripture is to liberal theology's progress of de-theologizing "the question of the person of Jesus and of his place in the creeds," a progress whose end, crucially, is "a broad consensus in which the individual Christian conscience could then decide freely how to view Christ's being."[134] If what is essential to Harnack's scepticism is the ontological question of the objectivity of Jesus Christ,[135] our reading suggests that their fundamental difference cannot be properly grasped apart from the theological force of Barth's soteriological concept of divine agency in and through Scripture.[136] As Barth declares before Harnack in the lecture, "Biblical Questions, Insights, and Vistas":

> Biblical history in the Old and New Testaments is not really history at all, but seem from above is a series of free divine acts and seen from below a series of fruitless attempts to undertake something in itself impossible. From the viewpoint of ordered development in particular and in general it is quite incomprehensible—as every religious teacher who is worth his salt knows only too well.[137]

Harnack was "deeply shaken"[138] by the lecture whose "effect" on him was, in his word, "staggering": "The severity of the charges made in that address is still vivid in my mind. Instead of any of its force, it appears to me more and more hazardous, and yes, in a way even scandalous."[139] What Harnack found "scandalous," suggests Rumscheidt, was in one sense, Barth's emphasis on the ontic in the problem of the unbound freedom

---

fanaticism and a resurgent Gnosticism" seems problematic ("Christ and Canon, Theology and History," 5).

134. Rumscheidt, *Adolf von Harnack*, 31.

135. Ibid., 32.

136. Bender's reading tends to overlook Barth's soteriological externality of the illumination and revelation: "What becomes clear in Barth's responses to Harnack is Barth's insistence that it is not historical knowledge and critical reflection, but the power of the Spirit and the corresponding faith it establishes, that provides the true understanding of the content of Scripture, which is God's own Self-revelation in Christ" ("Christ and Canon, Theology and History," 6). The point on God's illuminating and merciful turning as the organizing agent and subject of Scripture's content and unity is visible in a 1922 sermon on Isa 60.19–20, entitled "The Eternal Light," 7 May 1922, 8–17 (ET 57–66).

137. Barth, "Bibilical Questions, Insights, and Vistas," 72.

138. Rumscheidt, *Adolf von Harnack*, 30.

139. Zahn-Harnack, *Adolf von Harnack*, 415 (ET 30–31).

and precedence of the self-objectivity of God.[140] By contrast, "the issue for liberal theology is, in fact, the noetic *ratio* (method), rather than the ontic *ratio* (the limiting substance of faith) and that, secondly, that limiting substance is quietly taken for granted," continues Rumscheidt: "To claim that it is the freedom of God, precisely as the freedom which sets absolute limits, which establishes and guarantees human freedom towards God and neighbor, freedom in scholarship and politics, was to Harnack sheer speculation."[141] Succinctly put, Barth insists that theological objectivity as a *creaturely* objectivity points radically beyond itself to the unidirectional and immeasurably greater self-objectivity of God's being as pure deity. It is this construal of God's absolute freedom in theological objectivity that Harnack finds offensive, for in it, liberal theology's self-entitled "freedom always to be able to remain the judge in a superior vantage-position was utterly rejected and that that means nothing less than a wholly other theology, a wholly other noetic *and* ontic *ratio*."[142] In one crucial sense, all this suggests that Harnack's critique in the subsequent correspondence cannot be grasped properly apart from the ontological force of Barth's emphasis on the unbound freedom and precedence of God.

God's objectivity as the hermeneutical situation of the Bible, on Harnack's reading, concerns primarily an anthropological objectivity through "historical knowledge and critical reflection."[143] The issue concerns not so much whether God's self-objectivity is the objectivity of his relation to humanity. Divine-human relation, in Harnack's construal, appears to be a sort of coinherence in thought or reason. Put differently, by construing a direct identity between the Spirit's illumination and academic research, he is able to ask Barth rhetorically, "[Are the revelations of the Bible] so incomprehensible and indescribable that one must simply wait until they radiate out in man's heart because no faculty of man's soul or mind can grasp them?"[144] For Harnack, if Barth's assumption of human incapacity for "revelations" is "false," he asks: "Do we not need, for an understanding of the Bible, next to an inner openness, historical knowledge and critical reflection?"[145] One way to construe Harnack's rhetoric concerns his Kantian construal of human

---

140. Rumscheidt, *Adolf von Harnack*, 36–38.

141. Ibid.

142. Ibid., 38.

143. Ibid., 85–86.

144. Ibid.

145. Ibid.

activity as categorically "good" being "equivalent" or in "close union" with divine activity.[146] All this is visible in his question to Barth, quoting Phil 4.8:

> "Whatever is true, honourable, just, gracious, if there is any excellence, anything worthy of praise, think on these things"—if this is liberating admonition still stands, how can one erect barriers between the experience of God and the good, and the true and the beautiful, instead of relating them with the experience of God by means of historical knowledge and critical reflection?[147]

Thus Harnack on the objectivity of the deity of Jesus Christ as a matter of human consensus in "historical knowledge and critical reflection." The net effect of the construal is to reduce the prevailing ontological problem of God to its epistemological and hermeneutical concerns, and God's objectivity to human perception.

By contrast, human perception of God, in Barth's view, can only be a consequence of God's illumination of Jesus Christ as Scripture's self-announced content. "[O]nly through an act of this 'content' itself" God who "*was once subject*" "must become that again and again," for "the communication of" Scripture can take place "only through an act of this 'content' itself."[148] The "content" of Scripture, on Barth's reading, is a soteriological theme of the ontological problem of Christ's deity over the consequence of noetic issues concerning objectivity of human perception.[149] Human perception of the God's use of Scripture as a witness to revelation is no more than a consequence of the precedence of "an act of this 'content' itself." Succinctly put, in the light of its soteriological setting, this act takes place in virtue of the life of the triune God as one being, *not* in virtue of "the power of the Spirit *and* the corresponding faith it establishes."[150] What is at stake is Barth's concept of the ontological Trinity in the problematic "*and*" whose net effect, moreover, amounts to a domestication of divine action in human action or their apparent coinherence in the concept of divine-human correspondence. By contrast, Barth's soteriological emphasis on the unidirectionality and externality of revelation is visible in his response to Harnack's reading of Phil 4.8:

---

146. Ibid., 87.
147. Ibid., 86–87.
148. Ibid., 88.
149. Bender, "Christ and Canon, Theology and History," 5–13.
150. Ibid., 6; my emphasis.

> "The peace of God which is *higher* than our understanding." ("Der Friede Gottes, welcher *höher* ist als alle Vernunft.") The "barrier" of this "higher" is a basic and insurmountable (unübersteigbar) one. If he does "keep our hearts and minds in Christ Jesus" and thus makes *possible* the admonition of Phil. 4.8. . . . then *as such* he is *higher* than our understanding. There is a relation between him and what *we* call good, true and beautiful, but this relation is precisely the "barrier," the divine *crisis*, on the basis of which alone one may first speak seriously about the good, the true and the beautiful.[151]

Thus Barth on the unidirectional relation of Christ's to Scripture, and on the soteriological theme of divine-human *asymmetrical* relation in Scripture's witness to revelation.[152]

If conventional reading tends to portray Barth's anthropological orientation as sheer negativity, it is in part because it overlooks his *positive* vision of the unidirectional relation of the consequence of the pure human elements to the prior goodness of God towards creation. God's absolute precedence in the consequence of theology's orientation to Scripture's human elements and objectivity is a soteriological theme of God's deployment of the new humanity of the biblical writers and their readers as Christ's witnesses, as Barth stresses:

> the point is not to keep the historical-critical method of biblical and historical research developed in the last centuries away from the work of theology, but rather to fit that method, and its refinement of the way questions are asked, into that work in a meaningful way.[153]

Thus Barth on scripture-reading and theological work as interrelated, human response to God's prior electing, inspiring, and illuminating activity.[154] Only by the Spirit can theology begin to orient to the human elements in the witness of Scripture. That is, only through the Spirit's gift

---

151. Barth, *Harnack*, 90; Barth, *Offene Briefe 1909–1935*, 65.

152. The point on the unidirectional character of the relation of divine action to human knowledge of God in a 1922 sermon on Prov 18.10, entitled "The Name of the Lord." In it, Barth also repeats his argument in Rom 4 on the precedence of divine election of Abraham and the consequence of the biblical witness to divine self-revelation (19 Nov 1922, 24–38 (ET 24–35)).

153. Barth, *Harnack*, 96.

154. Ibid., 89.

of a new humanity can readers become proper readers of Scripture in "a meaningful way."[155]

> If theology were to regain the courage to face up to concrete objectivity (Sachlichkeit), the courage to bear witness to the *Word* of revelation, of judgement and of *God's* love, the outcome might well be that "science in general" would have to seek "strong ties and a blood relationship" with theology instead of the other way around. . . . Or should the present fortuitous *opinio communis* of others really be the instance through which we have to let our work be judged as to its "persuasiveness and value"?[156]

Thus Barth on a distinction of God's objectivity from human objectivity; the former as the soteriological—ontic and noetic—context of the latter; and on the corresponding asymmetric and unidirectional relation of God's objectivity to human objectivity.

The point on the asymmetrical relation of God's objectivity to human objectivity in Scripture is prominent in the subsequent exchanges and the postscript. In them, Harnack finds Barth's emphasis on the "utter contrast"[157] between God and humanity in the Spirit's illumination of revelation "incomprehensible,"[158] indicating Barth's "concept of revelation" as "the very reason" why "the opposition between us has become all the clearer."[159] The primacy of divine agency in Barth's response is clear: "[i]f there is a way to this 'content,' then the content itself must be the way."[160]

One way to grasp Barth's point concerns his protest against Harnack's construal of theological objectivity as a direct identity between God and humanity, especially against the "conclusiveness" of "historical criticism" about the historian's capacity for "a direct perception" of Christ as Scripture's content and unity.[161] A net effect of Harnack's construal is the trivialization of the extrinsic character of the relation of Christ to Scripture. On Barth's reading, Scripture testifies that "God himself has said and done something,

---

155. Lauster's reading of the correspondence recognizes some traces of Barth's pneumatology but strangely overlooks Barth's constructive proposal to Harnack and its Reformed orientation that prevents any trivialization of the creaturely specificity and historical contingency of the biblical witnesses (Lauster, *Prinzip und Methode*, 262–63).

156. Barth, *Harnack*, 90–91.

157. Ibid., 92, 89.

158. Rumscheidt, *Adolf von Harnack*, 92.

159. Ibid., 91, 93. Barth, *Offene Briefe 1909–1935*, 70.

160. Barth, *Harnack*, 98. Barth, *Offene Briefe 1909–1935*, 76.

161. Barth, *Harnack*, 97–99.

something new in fact, outside of the correlation of all human words and things, but which as this new thing he has injected into that correlation, a word and a thing next to others but this word and this thing."[162] A key word is "outside." Thus Barth on the external and unidirectional relation of the precedence of God's use of Scripture's human elements to their resultant witness to God's self-revelation as God's self-revelation.

If Barth is interested neither in positing in theological or historical study of Scripture an intrinsic objectivity concerning the relation of Christ to Scripture, nor in asserting the superiority of theology over historical science,[163] it is in part because in both disciplines what Barth champions for is the church's openness to the absolute freedom of God's self-objectivity in and through Scripture. Succinctly put, only through God's agency can God's self-revelation in the Jesus Christ of Scripture be understood, as Barth writes, "I doubt whether it is possible at any cogent point to separate one word or one deed of Jesus from the background of this reality, even considered only historically."[164] For once again: "[t]he object of the testimony" of Scripture "has been made known by the apostles and evangelists to such an extent as revelation, as the action of God himself," and thus, in short: "there can be no question of speaking here of a direct historical comprehensibility of this 'historical reality (revelation)."[165]

Put differently, revelation in Scripture is God's capacity for humanity, not humanity's capacity for God. One might ask whether or not Scripture's human elements are in themselves able to reveal Jesus as the Christ. Barth's response is a clear "NO," for "precisely in this NO, which can be uttered in its full severity only in the faith in revelation, the creature recognizes itself as the work and possession of the Creator. Precisely in this NO God is known as God."[166] Precisely as a genuine human witness to revelation, Scripture "is not without 'the deep, secret YES under and above the NO."[167] That is, "as the work and possession of the Creator," Scripture stands or falls

---

162. Ibid., 98.

163. Whatever Bender means by "the proper objectivity of theology" his reading tends to downplay Barth's soteriological emphasis on the extrinsic and contingent nature of human objectivity concerning the Spirit's relation to Scripture (Bender, "Christ and Canon, Theology and History," 10–13).

164. Barth, *Harnack*, 99.

165. Ibid., 99.

166. Ibid., 103.

167. Ibid., 104.

on God's self-revelation as the "deep, secret YES" that God must himself speak as God's Word.[168]

In his postscript, Harnack admits that on his reading, "[r]evelation is not a scientific concept" but expresses a deep pessimism towards Barth's concept of the pure deity of the objectivity of "the Word":[169] "There is no future . . . in the attempt to grasp a 'Word' of this kind as something so purely 'objective' that human speaking, hearing, grasping, and understanding can be eliminated from its operation."[170] If Harnack's worry is Barth's apparent isolation or trivialization of Scripture's human elements from the action of divine self-communication, Barth thinks that Harnack "must really misunderstand" him "precisely at this point."[171] Barth's seminal point is that Scripture's human elements in divine employment are Scripture's human elements in divine employment, if Scripture is—unidirectionally—"the possibility of God" who "has acted in the form of a human possibility."[172] That is also to say, it is Scripture not first as "an object of human-historical cognition,"[173] but Scripture first as a created object of the activity of the Word that Barth construes Scripture's anthropological orientation in its terms as an immeasurably positive event of divine action. What Harnack seems to fail to grasp is the constructive character of Barth's soteriological-pneumatological view of Scripture as "the deep, secret YES under and above the NO."[174] As Barth concludes: "This is how it is with that NO: 'nothing but YES in it.'"[175] All this is illustrated in a passage from "The Need and Promise of Christian Preaching" of 1922:

> The person who says the Bible leads us to where finally we hear only a great No or see a great void, proves only that he has not yet been led thither. *This* No is really Yes. *This* judgement is grace. *This* hell is heaven. *This* fearful God is a loving father who takes the prodigal in his arms. The crucified is the one raised form the dead. . . . This equation is the essence of the whole Bible, but by what truth, what fact, can it be proved? I know no other than the

---

168. Ibid., 103.
169. Ibid., 106.
170. Ibid.
171. Barth, *Harnack*, 104.
172. Ibid., 99.
173. Ibid.
174. Ibid., 104.
175. Ibid.

> reality of the living God, who *is* what he is, who is self-proved. The Bible disclaims all proofs of God. . . . God is the Yes in its fullness: it is only in order that we may *understand* him as *God* that we must pass through his No. The strait gate leads to life; it is only because it is this gate that it must be so narrow. "I will give you rest." "My yoke is easy, and my burden is light." It is only in order that we may know this to be *true* that we must take the yoke and burden upon us. "When ye shall *search* for me with all your heart, I will be *found* of you, saith the Lord." Only the *Lord* can speak so: only he can reduce seeking and finding, question and answer, to one. But the Bible is witness that he *does* so.[176]

Note Barth's crucial word "only" in his deceptively simple concluding statement about the unidirectional and gracious relation of God's saving self-communication to the purposive contingency of Scripture's human communication. Although it is true that Barth's responses to Harnack are at times rather compressed and cryptic, what Barth lacks in detail in his language of divine action he will make up for with a more extensive and sophisticated account of God's use of Scripture in the lectures on the Reformed confessional writings (SS 1923) and the Emden lecture, "The Doctrinal Task of the Reformed Churches." It is this material that to which we now turn.

The Theology of the Reformed Confessions

Barth's emphasis on the primacy and deity of the agency of God in his characterization of the relation of the incarnate Word to Scripture is prominent in his lectures on the Reformed confessional writings. Moreover, the confessional writings afford him an intense immersion in the pneumatology of the Reformed soteriological orientation to the precedence of "the *revelation of God* as a *sovereign* act"[177] and the consequence of the Reformed emphasis on "the isolatedness of God"[178] in the church's acknowledgement that "the scripture principle . . . is grounded in God alone."[179] God's "isolatedness" is a crucial concept by which Barth stresses the *pure deity* of the Word and Spirit, a concept that is, moreover, essential to Barth's notion of the externality of the unity and witness of the Bible. In contrast to a recent reading

176. Barth, "The Need and Promise of Christian Preaching," 120–21.

177. *TRC*, 41.

178. Ibid., 48.

179. Ibid., 56–57.

of Barth's Reformed view of Scripture, it is not the Bible first as a human light concerning the Spirit's relation to the Bible,[180] but the Bible first as the Spirit's own light of God's "*new* relation with humans created by God, special, direct, unique, actual, conquering the chasm of the fall"[181] that Barth perceives that "the Scripture principle is the death of the concept of symbol."[182] Succinctly put, Barth stresses that human construal of the Spirit is not to be read back into the Spirit's relation to the Bible, a relation that in the light of God's pure deity, is, crucially, *unidirectional.* "Unidirectional" is a word that Barth does not deploy in the lectures but underscores the ontological force of his point, in two parts.

The first part concerns Barth's construal of the concrete, unidirectional relation of Christ to Scripture's testimony to Jesus. Just as Christ's relation to his flesh is a knowledge borne to us by the Spirit's illumination, so is the relation of Scripture's human elements to Jesus borne to us "as participants in his life-giving *body through the power of his Spirit.*"[183] More closely, it is the Spirit of "the *whole* Christ," "the body and blood—of the Lord," not the Spirit of "a mere intellectual Christ, a Christ *idea,*" that Barth construes the Spirit of Scripture.[184] If our reading is plausible, it reinforces our objection to construing Barth's scriptural orientation as any sort of domestication of Christ's self-presence in Scripture or in the reader, for such a construal trivializes Barth's soteriological emphasis on the "concretissimum" of the Spirit's electing, inspiring and illuminating work; as Barth writes, "we cannot carry the humanity of Christ around in our heart"; once again: "a mere intellectual Christ, a Christ *idea, is* not Christ."[185]

More closely, Barth's construal of the radical demarcation between Christ and the biblical prophets and apostles cannot be grasped apart from its primacy of illumination. The demarcation in one crucial sense concerns *witness* as characteristic of Scripture, for succinctly put, in the light of the pure deity of the Spirit, Christ's relation to the Bible is "*witnessed* to not as

---

180. Bender, "Scripture and Canon in Karl Barth's Early Theology," 183–85. Bender's thoughtful reading of Barth's view of the "internal testimony of the Holy Spirit" downplays the externality of the illumination to Scripture and to theology's own construal of "the means of God's revelation."

181. Ibid., 46.

182. Ibid., 39.

183. Ibid., 169.

184. Ibid., 171.

185. Ibid.

the truth in our mouth but as the truth in God's mouth":[186] "The prophets and apostles do not boast of perspicacity, they claim no credibility for themselves."[187] Put differently, "[t]here is no equation of divine doing and human having, but rather God remains God."[188] God's use of Scripture as a witness to Jesus Christ is his sheer grace. Only in virtue of the witness of the Spirit to the incarnate one, can Scripture be recognized as God's Word. "The Word of God to us who are neither prophets nor apostles is the witness of the old and new covenant of this Jesus Christ, the Holy Scripture."[189] Witness is characteristic of Scripture's human elements created by the Spirit to point radically beyond "the truth in our mouth" to "the truth in God's mouth,"[190] "the truth" that "*Christ acts.*"[191] "*The highest proof of Scripture derives, in general, from the fact that God in person speaks in it.*"[192] In this connexion, witness is characteristic of the Reformed scriptural orientation confessing that the "knowledge of God is not mediated but is only unmediated, that is, God is known through God himself."[193] All this suggests Barth's placement of the concept of divine self-mediation under the theme of God's "isolatedness" or pure deity; only by the witness of the Spirit of Jesus Christ himself, is Scripture his "legitimate witness" and does it bear witness to God's self-*revelation* as God's *self*-revelation.[194] Succinctly put, just as God is unbound to Scripture or to the reader, so is Scripture unbound to the reader, but the reader and Scripture are altogether bound to God in the economy of revelation and salvation. "For the Reformed, the word 'God' was a concept of superiority, majesty, and freedom": it

> characterized their entire theology, comprehended for them both God's revelation and the *witness* to God's revelation. For them, the isolatedness of God generates the isolatedness of his revelation. *Revelation* is not this and that, not everything and anything, but rather this definitive, incomparable one thing. Therefore, legitimate witness to revelation cannot be any random human word

186. Ibid., 39.

187. Ibid., 59.

188. Ibid., 172.

189. Ibid., 46.

190. Ibid., 39.

191. Ibid., 172.

192. Ibid., 59.

193. Ibid., 48.

194. Ibid., 48–49.

about God but rather this definite human word about God, which the prophets and apostles were called by God and equipped to say. It is the word of Scripture.[195]

Thus Barth on the unidirectional relation of the deity of Christ's Spirit to Scripture's humanity, and on witness as characteristic of the biblical "prophets and apostles" and "the word of Scripture."

A crucial corollary of all this is the Reformed demarcation between the Spirit's illumination as God's own light and *all* created lights especially the church's own. Instead of reading itself back into the Spirit's relation to Scripture, the church's construal strives to indicate the relation on its own terms as a sheer miracle of divine illumination. As Barth writes, "the essence of the Reformed confession" is that it "never was the light, and it never wanted to be, because it knows that it cannot and may not be the light, but rather *testifies* to the light like the Baptist of the New Testament, in whom the Reformed church has had of necessity to recognize its most profound and most authentic being": "The Reformed confession points *beyond* itself." "*Faith* confesses. But it does not confess itself, but what is *written*."[196] Thus Barth on "the clear *distinction* between Scripture and the confession of Scripture, between God's Word and . . . Christian human words."[197] On Barth's reading, the Reformed pneumatological emphasis on the unidirectional relation of the Spirit's self-manifestation to "what is *written*" cannot be grasped apart from its ontological force:

> It is foundational that there can be no talk of man's pathway to God but only of God's way to man. The *Lord* is the subject of the *participatio* that takes place. Not our faith but the Spirit from above overcomes the difference of the spaces, making that which is far into something near, uniting us with the humanity of Christ, setting us in relation to the contingent revelation whose local presence we could under no circumstances ever assert . . .[198]

Barth's pneumatological concept of the contingence of God's self-presence—and this is the second part—concerns the Reformed concept of the primacy of the unidirectional activity of "the Spirit from above" "setting us in relation to the contingent revelation." Barth's concept of "contingent

195. Ibid.
196. Ibid., 38.
197. Ibid., 82.
198. Ibid., 171.

revelation" concerns, in a sense, the *one* economy of the Spirit's work (a) in the Word's "*finite*, temporal revelation taking place in the incarnation"[199] and now (b) in the parousia of the same Jesus.

More closely, in this economy "*Christ the Revealer* is in another space from ours, absolutely separated from the valley of mortality in which we are on pilgrimage,"[200] for "the contingent revelation itself is at the right hand of God, concealed to the physical eye until the end of all things."[201] Succinctly put, "we are *here* and the humanity of Christ is *there*, and therefore the Spirit and only the Spirit is the 'bond of participation.'"[202] Crucially, the Reformed construal of the event of the incarnation in its trinitarian setting helps illuminate for Barth the real, objective content of the precedence of the Spirit's regenerative work and the consequence of the *new* human elements. In this connexion, more than just a different construal or reading of Scripture,[203] and no less than a self-involving recognition of Scripture's *new* humanity in the old one, Barth's self-identification with the Reformed Scripture Principle points *beyond* itself and all creation to the sheer miracle of the self-manifestations of "the identity of the Holy Spirit."[204] The self-presence of Spirit of *Jesus Christ* in and through Scripture "is not fleshly but spiritual, not earthly but heavenly."[205] The ontological force of the Spirit's illumination of the asymmetry in Scripture between God and humanity, between the Creator and creature, between the Redeemer and the redeemed, is Barth's seminal point by way of the concept of contingent revelation. The Reformed "fear . . . that, by accepting the direct givenness and presence of contingent revelation, ultimately that revelation will merge with contingent reality, so that the Creator might no longer be distinguished from the creature."[206]

All this suggests that the Reformed, pneumatological concept of contingent revelation helps illuminate for Barth the absolute freedom and pure deity of the Spirit in the crucial concept of *autopistia*. *Autopistia* is a soteriological concept of the unity of the Spirit's electing, inspiring and

199. Ibid., 158.
200. Ibid., 171.
201. Ibid., 169.
202. Ibid., 171.
203. Bender, "Scripture and Canon in Karl Barth's Early Theology," 166.
204. Freudenberg, *Karl Barth und die reformierte Theologie*, 242–43.
205. Ibid., 168.
206. Ibid., 184.

illuminating activity in and through the Scripture's human elements that
he generates. It is the Spirit's regenerative activity as external, gratuitous,
and necessary to Scripture, not the Spirit's regenerative activity as intrinsic and bound to Scripture, that Barth construes the absolute freedom of
Christ's use of the Bible. In this specific connexion, the church's recognition
of Scripture is "itself the work of the Holy Spirit, for the Spirit can only be
recognized through the Spirit, God only through God. This is the genuine answer of the Reformed church to the question of the grounding of its
Scripture principle."[207] As Barth writes, "only one thing can be meant when
we speak of autopistia and the Spirit's witness: the *revelation of God* as a
sovereign act, grounded solely in God, and emerging from God in freedom.
At this point the dogma of *inspiration* flows into that of *predestination*."[208]

> Inspiration or revelation is conceived of as one single timeless,
> or better, simultaneous act of God upon the biblical authors *and*
> upon us. What appears to be questioning and answering between
> us and the biblical authors, as though they were standing inside
> and we outside, so to speak, is in reality a monologue of the Holy
> Spirit in them and in us. What *cannot* be differentiated with relation to the holiness of Scripture is the real grounds and the cognitive grounds; what *cannot* be differentiated is the fact that there are
> canonical books and the fact that we acknowledge them as such;
> what *cannot* be differentiated is the light that shines from the Bible
> and the eye that perceives this light.[209]

Thus Barth, once again, on the unidirectional objectivity and externality of
the God's electing, inspiring and illuminating act in "the biblical authors"
and their readers whose objectivity, moreover, is bound to the *unbound*
"monologue of the Holy Spirit."

> All respectful genuflections before the "Holy Scriptures of the Old
> and New Testaments," whether orthodox or liberal, do not change
> the fact that the ground of this principle, upon which *everything*
> related to its application depends, its radical and paradoxical
> grounding through non-grounding, through faith in revelation as
> it was once taught in Zürich and Bern with intuitive certainty and
> as it was classically formulated by Calvin, is regarded today as a
> risk that simply evokes anxiety. Any other grounding than this has
> *not* emerged through two centuries of historical biblical study. We

207. Ibid., 57.
208. Ibid., 63.
209. Ibid.

know better than Calvin that there are no "rationes" for the divinity of Scripture, there is no God in history and no God in us. Whether we will again come to know as well as Calvin did that God desires to be and is his own witness in history and in us, and whether we will then risk his prescription, which is not just a prescription but health itself: to read the Bible "as if the living words of God were heard"—that it is the fateful question whose answer will decide the future of Reformed (and not only Reformed) Protestantism.[210]

From all this it is clear that Barth's pneumatological primacy is prominent in his initial account of the Reformed Scripture Principle, and that on Barth's reading, witness to Jesus Christ acting and speaking in person *by the Spirit* is characteristic of Scripture's human elements and of the distinctively Reformed demarcation between the divine Light and created lights especially the church's own. More closely, the Reformed soteriological emphasis on the pure deity and absolute freedom of God in Scripture is visible in Barth's concept of contingent revelation. The concept helps illuminate and secure for Barth, we have suggested, the externality of the unidirectional, concrete relation of the Spirit and the incarnate Word to the biblical prophets and apostles and their readers: "the Spirit can only be recognized through the Spirit, God only through God."[211] Although his concept of the Word is not yet fully developed and even though his related trinitarian language of divine action exceeds the scope of our reading, we can easily see that his construal of Scripture as God's Word cannot be grasped apart from the pneumatological-soteriological orientation in the Reformed concepts of God, contingent revelation, creaturely witness and doctrine. The point is visible in our next material, the Emden lecture "The Doctrinal Task of the Reformed churches."

"The Doctrinal Task of the Reformed Churches"

Barth's pneumatological emphasis on witness as characteristic of the Reformed scriptural and doctrinal orientation is prominent in the Emden lecture. The lecture illuminates that, more than merely to church history or its history of doctrine and interpretation,[212] Barth's orientation to the objectivity

210. Ibid., 64.

211. Ibid., 57.

212. Plasger, *Die relative Autorität des Bekenntnisses bei Karl Barth*, 37–38. Although

of the relationship between the Reformed Scripture Principle and the Bible is soteriological. More closely, his pneumatological concept of human witness concerns the Reformed soteriological emphasis on the absolute freedom and pure deity of the Spirit of Scripture. In this connexion, "[t]he appeal to this principle . . . was meant rather as a simple submission to God's manifestation of himself: *Summa scripturae probatio passim a Dei loquentis persona sumitur*":[213] the older Reformers "refer all doctrine away from itself to the one Object." "To them *truth* is God—not their *thought* about God but God *himself* and God *alone*, as he speaks his own *word* in Scripture and in Spirit."[214] If our reading is plausible, it reinforces our view that more than just a different way of construing and reading the Bible,[215] Barth's self-identification with the Reformed Scripture Principle and concept of doctrine cannot be grasped apart from its ontological force, in at least two ways.

The first way concerns Barth's Reformed asymmetry between doctrine and Scripture. The Scripture's distinction from doctrine, more closely, is a soteriological concept concerning the Spirit's unidirectional use of the biblical witness vis-à-vis the church's construal and use of the Bible. The Bible and the Spirit are unbound to the church, but through the Spirit the church is bound to Scripture. Scripture, on Barth's reading, is borne to us by the Spirit from a sphere that is immeasurably broader and deeper than the spheres of the world and the church. Barth is uninterested "to make revelation a kind of miracle that began and ended on earth, a piece of direct information, a religious fact; whereas, when it is genuine, revelation is always in part concealment."[216] That is also to say, the reading church points beyond its own light to the light of the Spirit of *God*. "The Reformed churches simply do *not* know the word dogma, in its rigid hierarchical sense." Barth continues, "[i]n those churches Christian history has no doctrinal *authority* whatever; the authority lies rather in the *Scriptures* and in the *Spirit*, both of which (even the Scriptures!) are beyond Christian history."[217] Once again: "in the truest sense there is no such thing as Reformed doctrine,

---

he is right about Barth stressing the "reference- and witness- character of Scripture," Plasger tends to downplay Barth's emphasis on the externality and contingency of Spirit's illumination of Scripture in the church.

213. Barth, "The Doctrinal Task," 243.

214. Ibid., 235.

215. Bender, "Scripture and Canon in Karl Barth's Early Theology," 166.

216. Barth, "The Doctrinal Task," 257.

217. Ibid., 230.

except the timeless appeal to the open Bible and to the Spirit which from it speaks to our spirit."[218] Thus Barth on the asymmetric *and* external relation of Scripture and the Spirit to doctrine.

In this connexion—and this is the second way—Barth stresses the Reformed concept of witness as a corollary of their radical respect for the Spirit's pure deity. This respect is an overarching theme of the scriptural orientation of the early Reformers, Barth observes: their distinction between text and commentary is characteristic of their "attention to the will and way of *God* with man"[219] and openness to the Spirit's commanding relation to "the open Bible." Their respect for God's absolute freedom and lordship "which, as a revelation witnessed to and perceived in the Scriptures," moreover, "is itself no idea, no principle, no doctrine, but true origin of all doctrine and the standard by which all doctrine is and forever be measured."[220] Crucially, Barth recognizes the primacy of the Spirit's illumination. "*God's* witness to himself in Holy Scripture was certainly not 'only form' to our fathers; 'form' is precisely what it was not."[221] Only in virtue of God's self-witness in Scripture, does Scripture have a form; only through the Spirit's illumination, can Scripture's form be known. In this sense, it is Scripture as witness *by* "the significant word of the Spirit,"[222] not Scripture as a mere text or human word, that Barth construes *Scripture* as *Holy* Scripture.

That is also to say, Barth's construal of witness as characteristic of the "form" *and* "content" of the scriptural text cannot be grasped apart from his soteriological emphasis. "*God's* witness to himself in Holy Scripture," Barth writes, "was a content immeasurable and inimitable, unalterable and inexhaustible; and as such it was too great to be identical with the content of this or that particular viewpoint or experience."[223] On the early Reformers' discussion on the "form" of Scripture, Barth writes: "It is clear that even theoretically the fathers had no idea of attempting to establish it in advance, for it was a basic thing that needed no basing: spirit is recognized only by spirit, God only by God."[224] Only on the basis of the Spirit's witnessing to

218. Ibid., 229.

219. Ibid., 252.

220. Ibid., 235.

221. Ibid., 242.

222. Ibid., 241.

223. Ibid., 242.

224. Ibid., 243.

Christ's use of Scripture, did the early Reformers speak of Scripture as *Holy* Scripture, as Barth writes,

> The essential characteristic of their genius was not any special insight or type of godliness but their clear understanding of the basis of the things: they knew that that basis was God and God alone. In other words, they had the courage to allow so accidental, contingent, and human a thing as the Bible to become a serious witness of the revelation of God, to allow a book which was in itself profane to become *Holy* Scripture.[225]

Thus Barth on "*Holy* Scripture" as an early Reformed shorthand of the absolute freedom and precedence of the Spirit's self-witness in Scripture.[226]

In the light of the priority of "God's witness to himself," moreover, the soteriological theme of biblical witness comes wholly under the trinitarian themes of the absolute freedom, precedence and deity of the Holy Spirit in his external and internal relations as one being with the Father and the Son. In this specific sense, neither does God's being and act coinhere with Scripture's created elements, nor does Scripture consubstantiate with God. The concepts of God's primacy and priority are corollaries of the concept of the being of his pure deity. In one crucial way, the utter dissimilarity between God and creatures is an essential theme of the Reformed "renewed awareness of the word of God as the word of *God*, a consciousness of a Majesty to which," moreover, "in joy or fear [the saints] may only listen and pray expectantly, ready to believe and ready to obey: Speak, Lord, for thy servant heareth!"[227] Put differently, the trinitarian theme of the absolute freedom of the speaking God in Scripture concerns the ontological problem of the self-communicative *being* of "God" who "refuses to be possessed and from the beginning and end remains the Possessor."[228] It is under the soteriological concept of the absolute freedom of God's self-communicative being that Barth construes the witness character of Reformed scriptural orientation as

---

225. Ibid., 245.

226. Ibid. See his point about a growing inattentiveness to the Spirit's scriptural primacy in certain Reformed churches underlined the loss of the *pneumatological* understanding of the biblical text as *witness*: "the written page, coming to be considered lifeless and no longer a witness, was left in isolation."

227. Ibid., 248.

228. Ibid., 250–51.

essentially "a belief in divine providence and eternal election,"[229] a belief in "an act of free grace by which [God] *himself* makes the proof."[230]

> The relation of this belief to the "scripture principle" understood in terms of its positive content -*God is speaking!*—is evident. The old Reformed churchmen heard the voice of very God in the Scriptures—the voice of a God jealous in the Old Testament sense, who will not give his glory to another, the one, only, unique, almighty and all-glorious God who governs in unconditioned freedom, grants no hearings, but dispenses grace to man in perfect sovereignty—and their passionate appeal to truth and authority and salvation as they were exclusively contained in this one book was simply a confession of *this* God.[231]

Thus Barth on witness as characteristic of the Reformed Scripture Principle appealing to "the voice of very God" speaking in Scripture with "unconditioned freedom." Respect for Scripture, for Barth, is a corollary of respect for the absolute freedom of God: "it is God who both gives and conceals himself in the Scriptures"[232] so that the Bible's human elements "must finally stand subordinate in a creaturehood which may not be relinquished and may not be disregarded."[233] In short, as Barth tells his audience at the lecture:

> The teaching of the Reformed doctrine of the Holy Spirit will become for us a commanding task. . . . Until we do that we can hardly hope to attack our task with power, and the Reformed doctrine of the Spirit must remain what it now is: a corpse, say rather, a ghost.[234]

All this suggests the significance of Barth's recognition of the Reformed respect for the pure deity of the Spirit in Scripture. It is a respect underlying, moreover, Barth's emphasis on the external and contingent character of the Spirit's self-witness in Scripture and the reader. What Barth lacks in detail he will make up in his first dogmatic lecture cycles, the Göttingen dogmatics, and the landmark lecture, "Das Schriftprinzip der reformierten Kirche" of 1925. To reserve space for and to help orient our reading of his view of

229. Ibid., 252.
230. Ibid., 244.
231. Ibid., 252.
232. Ibid., 258.
233. Ibid., 262.
234. Ibid., 271.

canonical witness in the lecture, our treatment of the *GD* focuses instead on three key themes in his construal of the God of Scripture, namely, the absolute freedom, aseity and life of the triune God.

The Göttingen Dogmatics

In the foregoing, I emphasized Barth's convictions about the primacy and priority and pure deity of God's unbound agency, and occasionally addressed a widespread pneumatological deficit in common construal of Barth's scriptural orientation. I have done so in significant part by way of a focused reading of his self-identification with the Reformed Scripture Principle. The Principle affords Barth, we have seen, a way of securing his soteriological emphasis on the utter divine-human dissimilarity in Scripture. In the *GD* lectures, the same emphasis finds more sophisticated expression in Barth's expansive trinitarian construal of the ontic and noetic relation of Christ's Spirit to Scripture. In this connexion, we can demonstrate how it is so, simply by highlighting relevant materials from the prolegomenal and second cycles of the *GD* lectures.

The first theme concerns the *soteriological* setting of the primacy of God in and through the created and human elements of Holy Scripture. "Holy Scripture," on Barth's reading of Calvin, is a theological shorthand denoting no less than the absolute freedom of God: for just as "God is not tied to such aids or such inferior means," so "God's work is not tied to ours."[235] Nor can the concept of God's unbound freedom in Scripture be grasped apart from its soteriological orientation to the Spirit, as Barth writes, "the Holy Spirit is neither a magic quality of some ancient text nor an inner sentiment"[236] nor impersonal "power or potency,"[237] but the "Holy Spirit is God speaking to us, making us his children and servants, giving us mouths and ears and eyes for God's revelation. For he himself is God."[238] God's absolute freedom in and through Scripture means that his relation to Scripture is "not anything that we can reach or achieve or possess or name our own," but it is rather "the justifying, sanctifying, and saving miracle of the Holy Spirit."[239] From this it also follows that only in light of the Spirit's

235. *GD*, 33–34.
236. Ibid., 224.
237. Ibid., 100.
238. Ibid., 224.
239. Ibid., 308.

priority of the gift of our "mouths and ears and eyes for God's revelation," can theology begin to open up to the soteriological setting of the problem that "there is no human way to a knowledge of God in himself, that God himself and God alone is here the only way and goal";[240] "the only way" in which "indeed *God's* Word, which we may not take on our lips or repeat," crucially, "differs radically from all the words that we speak."[241] Succinctly put, Barth stresses the priority of the ontic over the noetic in Scripture's knowledge of God.

> God is Father, Son, and Spirit, subject, and never as such God objectively in himself. Christian revelation is trinitarian revelation, and this very firmly rules out any possibility of seeing God behind or above in his deity apart from his personality. To try to grasp his nature apart from his personality unavoidably means trying to get away from the knowledge of revelation understood as an act. . . . He is Father, Son, and Spirit from eternity to eternity. Once we abstract away, even for a moment, from the speaking person that addresses us, that address us; once we dissolve the deity in a general truth or idea that is no longer a person, we are no longer thinking about God.[242]

If God's deity cannot be known apart from the regeneratively concrete act of the Spirit's electing illumination in the biblical prophets and apostles, it follows that, moreover, only in the light of its soteriological setting can Barth's emphasis on God's absolute freedom be grasped.[243] As Barth writes,

> the whole amazing doxology of the Christian church and theology in no sense has its point in itself but in him [God] alone by whom it is occasioned and to whom it applies, in the good pleasure with which he accepts it. It is not for us to say that he *must* accept it with good pleasure. He must if he *wills*, if *he* wills. He can say *Yes*, and does say Yes. But it is obvious that he can also say *No*, and does say No. In face of us clever theologians, who always try to do more than is fitting for us, and in face of the human race as a whole insofar as we have only representative significance, he has reserved it for himself to be the one thing in all the fine things that

240. Ibid., 399.

241. Ibid., 62.

242. Ibid., 368.

243. Cf. ibid., 33–34. "God in his omnipotence might himself gather and claim a church without any means, but he has preferred to deal with us through means, that is, through human ministry."

we think and will and feel regarding him, to be the head without which all things are at every moment nothing, absolutely nothing. "When thou hidest thy face, they are frightened; when thou takest away their breath, they die and return to dust" (Ps. 104:29). Christian theology and the Christian church live by the fact that God himself makes himself heard in free grace. They know and confess that we live by the Word that proceeds from God's mouth (Matt. 4:4). They know and confess that God can also take back this life-giving Word of his without being any the less glorious or divine or worthy to be praised. God would not be *God* if he did not have this freedom. . . . But this freedom is the freedom of God's election of grace, of predestination.[244]

Thus Barth on the absolute freedom of God in God's election of Scripture and its reader; on the unidirectional, external and gracious character of God's "life-giving Word" in the biblical canon and theology. Put differently, Barth is uninterested in construing the divine-human relation of being and act in Scripture as any sort of consubstantiality or coinherence. Rather, "eternal predestination must not be confused with determination, with a decision regarding us whereby God has fixed his action for all time," for "predestination is the divine decree in action, the divine decreeing concerning us in which at every moment God is free in relation to us and goes forward with us from decision to decision."[245] That is Barth's way of securing God's saving action as characteristic of the absolute freedom of the Spirit's unidirectional relation to Scripture and the reader. Just as only "from decision to decision" of God can Scripture be recognized as an object of and created by "the divine decree in action," so only through and by God acting from one moment to another in his relation to Scripture and to his reader, is he "himself heard in free grace." On Barth's reading, since "God alone can be a competent witness on his own behalf," the biblical witnesses "claim no credibility for themselves";[246] instead, only as fellow elects do they address their readers, that is, they address them by *and* through the regeneration of the Spirit acting freely in one being with the Father and the Son. It is the Reformed construal of Scripture's respect for the tautology of the Creator-Redeemer Spirit as pure deity and Christ's saints as participants created by the illuminating Spirit's gratuitous but objectively commanding regeneration that Barth characterizes constructively as the "biblical attitude":

244. Ibid., 445–46.
245. Ibid., 450, 180–81.
246. Ibid., 222.

> The biblical attitude, that of the prophets and apostles, is the at-
> titude of witnesses, the attitude that put the scriptures in the canon
> and called their text holy, the attitude not of spectators or report-
> ers or thinkers, but of people who come down from an absolute
> presupposition, the *Deus dixit*, with all the irresistible momentum
> of a boulder rolling down a mountainside.[247]

More closely—and this is the second theme—Scripture's "attitude of witnesses" points *beyond* its created knowledge of God to God's own knowledge of God in himself, to God acting as the one who is "*a se*."[248] On his readings of Aquinas and Gerhard in §16, Barth argues for a distinc-tion between the two just-mentioned kinds of knowledge of God. If "[t]o comprehend is to define," Barth argues "that even to the blessed in heaven, who know God essentially, he is still not comprehensible," just so do "we know God but we do not comprehend him."[249] In this connexion, God's incomprehensibility is a soteriological concept concerning a formal reserve of God's being in his external relations.[250] Contrary to the construal of God "in the sphere of concepts and objects"[251] by Kant, Heidegger, and their theological heirs, the formal reserve is crucial to Barth's understanding of the ontological force of the Reformed emphasis on God's absolute freedom.

> The freedom of God with which, without ceasing to be who he is,
> he can leave his mere incomprehensibility for our comprehensibil-
> ity and even our conceptuality makes room—for what? For a defi-
> nition *ousiôdês*? No. God remains who he is even in his revelation.
> We rather say, For a definition *onomatôdês*, a subjective notion of
> God, a sort of description of God as he is revealed to us.[252]

Thus Barth, once again, on God's action as characteristic of the absolute freedom of God speaking *from his own being*, that is, God speaks as the one is "*a se*."[253] God's aseity, in one sense, is a crucial soteriological theme con-cerning, in short, God's self-existent being, the being of "the total God"[254]

247. Ibid., 288–89.
248. Ibid., 336.
249. Ibid., 352.
250. Ibid., 352–53.
251. Ibid., 353.
252. Ibid., 355–56.
253. Ibid., 336.
254. Ibid., 93. Cf. Hart, *Regarding Karl Barth*, 41. Hart is right that Barth's "episte-mological and ontological assumption" of God's aseity and transcendence "permeates

himself as the uncreated ground to his unbound freedom "in the sphere of concepts and objects."[255]

Crucially, moreover, the *soteriological* theme of divine aseity concerns the ontological force of the uniqueness of God's being "when God names his name" vis-à-vis "when *we* speak about God."[256] God's uniqueness as a soteriological theme in Barth's pneumatological construal concerns *specifically* "[t]he I that addresses us in revelation," "with all marks of individuality, of absolute uniqueness, of specific distinction from every other I."[257] *Beyond* "an inescapable circularity to the church's claims regarding Scripture as God's Word,"[258] and *beyond* the sum of creaturely knowledge of God in the church and in Scripture, Scripture's witness points to God as the self-announced subject of his self-communicative person, the God who "names his name," "only in the first person"[259] "in the most unrestricted sense."[260] In this specific connexion, Barth's trinitarian emphasis on the absolute freedom and aesity of God's subjecthood in Scripture cannot be grasped apart from its soteriological orientation.

More closely, Barth's soteriological primacy concerns the pure deity of God's self-communicative being as the ground of his action: only from his being does God speak and act as God-for-us. Succinctly put, in the light of the ontological force of God's *unbound* action, Barth is able to indicate that no creaturely "participation in the divine substance" and no "confusion of identity between Creator and creature" on the one hand,[261] and that only by God's unbound *action* do we know the deity of the Spirit acting in one *being* with "the total God."[262] As Barth writes, "*God* is always the subject, and God the *subject*, in this concealed and singular address which is not in continuity with other events."[263] "If God *speaks*, then *God* speaks":[264] "indeed *God's*

Barth's theology from the days of his so-called dialectal period through to the very end of *CD* and beyond."

255. *GD*, 353.

256. Ibid., 368–69.

257. Ibid., 368.

258. Bender, "Scripture and Canon in Karl Barth's Early Theology," 183.

259. *GD*, 135.

260. Ibid., 369–70.

261. Ibid., 397.

262. Ibid., 93.

263. Ibid., 61.

264. Ibid., 92.

Word" is "which we may not take on our lips or repeat. It differs radically from all the words that we speak."[265] Just so do God's speech-acts essentially differ from Scripture's human speech-acts:[266]

> The witness of the prophets and apostles . . . is not to the effect that they, the prophets and apostles, *could* talk about God, and for this reason we too, perhaps appropriating their words or at least their thoughts, should also try to do so.[267]

This is so because only from God's being does God act or speak, as Barth continues:

> revelation is God's Word itself, God's own speaking in which he alone is the subject, in which no flesh also speaks, but he and he alone. This is found in scripture, this pregnant *Deus dixit*, God speaking personally as the subject, God as the author, God not only giving authentic information about himself but himself speaking about himself.[268]

Thus Barth on the soteriological theme of divine aseity of the Spirit of God speaking as "no flesh also speaks"; and crucially, on the triune God's own life as the overarching theme of the Reformed scriptural and doctrinal orientation to the externality and unidirectionality of the *Deus dixit* in Scripture.

More closely, Barth's soteriological construal of Scripture's relation to the *Deus dixit*—and this is the third theme—cannot be grasped properly apart from its primacy and priority of the mystery of the relation of God's "being in himself" to "his being for us."[269] In this connexion, one way to construe the pneumatoloical gratuity and dependency of Scripture's new-creaturely elements in the mysterious economy of the divine life concerns the consequence of their divine deployment and human reception and the precedence of the Spirit's "express turning to us."[270] The Spirit's turning, Barth construes, is a trinitarian theme concerning the "*spiratio*, the divine breathing, the *processio spiritus sancti*," "the procession of God from

---

265. Ibid., 62.

266. Ibid., 59.

267. Ibid., 56.

268. Ibid., 57.

269. Ibid., 392; cf. 332: "The indirectness of our knowledge is the correlate of the concealment in which God gives himself to be known. The reality of revelation stands or falls with it."

270. Ibid., 128f.

himself,"[271] "and not from us."[272] Only in virtue of God's turning to us from his being-in-himself (*a se*) to his being-for-us (*pro nobis*)—do the person and work of the biblical witnesses have being. Consequently, their being is external to themselves, created and manifested by the Spirit's life-giving turning to us: their life and work are *derived*. Succinctly put, in his relation to us by the Spirit, the triune God "lives his own life, and in it, and as alone the living one,"[273] "the life of him who is Lord and *a se*."[274] Put negatively, there "can be no confusing of his life with the life of nature or life in nature or in us, even in its highest form." Yet "even in its highest form" creature is only a witness of God's absolute freedom: "if and as we do know God, there breaks upon our vision his concealing incommunicable nature, his eternity, omnipresence, and immutability, forcing us to look not only *far* beyond this life but *totally* beyond it."[275] Barth's view, however, cannot be grasped apart from its soteriological primacy of the Spirit of the triune God as the unbound giver of life in Scripture,[276] God as the self-existent one living, turning, creating, and commanding from and in none other than "his own life." Succinctly put, Barth's pneumatological language of divine life secures the absolute freedom of "the one act of lordship which is grounded in God, which proceeds from God":[277] God's action in and through Scripture's creaturely elements is at once *a se* and *in se*. In this specific connexion, Barth's emphasis on God's "actuosity"[278] as characteristic of the externality of God's self-revelation in Scripture cannot be grasped properly apart from its pneumatologial primacy. As Barth writes, "There *is* a 'beyond' in scripture. This is the Word of God, namely, revelation."[279]

All this suggests that Barth is uninterested in describing the divine-human relation in Scripture as one of coinherence or consubstantiation. On his reading, instead, if "[o]nly the Word of God can bear witness to

---

271. Ibid., 128–29, 134.

272. Ibid., 135: "the triune God, inexhaustibly living, immutably the subject, from himself, and not from us."

273. Ibid., 415, 403.

274. Ibid., 215.

275. Ibid., 402–3. For a more qualified and fuller development of the concept of divine life, see Webster, "God's Perfect Life," 143–52.

276. *GD*, 403: "the creator of life."

277. Ibid., 226.

278. Ibid., 372–73, 401f.

279. Ibid., 215.

the Word of God in scripture," it also follows that "[r]ecognition of the authority of the Bible coincides with recognition of God as its author."[280] Note his crucial language of "coincidence." Constructively, it secures the gratuity of "holy scripture" as "a contingent entity,"[281] in the "unique and totally incalculable"[282] mystery of the economy of God's self-communication. Negatively, it underscores the externality of Scripture. In relation, Hart is right that the relation between the Word and Scripture "is not a union of identity, but one of indwelling, and it is not permanent but temporary."[283] Time in Scripture, for instance, is bound by the Spirit's unbound electing, creating, and commanding illumination, that is, by "the quality of God in virtue of which he contains in himself the meaning of time."[284] Time in Scripture, in a sense, is a soteriological theme of God's merciful turning to creation. Creaturely history in Scripture, like the canonical text and its churchly undertakings, has neither its unity nor "meaning" in itself. Barth's view of history's unity and meaning cannot be grasped apart from its the pneumatological priority and primacy of God's sovereign freedom in and "totally beyond" the creaturely realm. As Barth writes, "God's freedom has to be God's lordship over time and space. It is lordship backwards only if he created time and space, and forwards only if he rules them, and only if he is present every moment in them as Lord" who "is not contained in space, but himself gives space and the things that are in it their being."[285] Thus Barth on Scripture's pneumatological priority and primacy of God's unbound freedom in *and* above time, and on witness as characteristic of Scripture's contingent "being" in the saving economy of God's sovereign and electing creativity. From all this it is clear that the concept of the *Deus dixit* in Scripture refers to Barth's recognition of the sovereign freedom of God's self-communicative being in the Word and Spirit. The Spirit's election of the biblical witnesses is a soteriological theme stressing the unbound and concrete, merciful creativity of God in the unidirectional relation of divine command to human obedience in Scripture, as Barth writes, once again: "predestination is the divine decree in action, the divine decreeing

280. Ibid., 222.

281. Ibid.

282. Ibid., 130.

283. Hart, *Regarding Karl Barth*, 35.

284. *GD*, 436.

285. Ibid., 435.

concerning us in which at every moment God is free in relation to us and goes forward with us from decision to decision."[286]

"Decision" is a key word in Barth's characterization of Scripture as canon *and* divine command in "Das Schriftprinzip der reformierten Kirche" lecture and later in *CD* I. Although Barth's initial construal of the three themes and his corresponding language of the triune economy of the Spirit's regenerative relation to Scripture are at best preliminary, we can easily see that his pneumatological emphasis on the unidirectional and external character of the relation cannot be grasped properly apart from Barth's soteriological concept of the *Deut dixit* in Scripture. One important implication of Barth's trinitarian conviction about the precedence and externality of the Spirit's commanding, regenerative activity in Scripture and in the reader concerns Barth's enduring bibliological emphasis on *prayer* as the mode of the obedience of human witness to revelation. For now, we simply note that Barth's pneumatological primacy is entirely characteristic of his soteriological emphasis on *prayer* as essential to the Reformed *pneumatological* orientation to the Bible and doctrine:

> Those who stand before God in the Spirit can only pray. They do not think they already are or have to do or possess anything. To pray is to not to have. We must all seek. We can pray only like the publican in the temple, from a distance (Luke 18:13). . . . We know that what is born of flesh is flesh. We know that we can stand before God only in God and by God, and that only is born of the Spirit. We know we cannot equate this new, regenerate person, this subject that can truly, indicatively, say of itself, "I believe, I obey," that we cannot equate this person with ourselves. We must stay with petition: *Come*, Creator Spirit. We cannot make it into an indicative or a perfect, as though the Spirit *had* come. Here . . . we have a perpetual operation. This is how we stand before God, how we receive revelation, how we are the Lord's (Rom. 14:8), in this way and no other.[287]

"Das Schriftprinzip der reformierten Kirche"

The soteriological primacy of Barth's Reformed pneumatological orientation to Scripture and church in the foregoing is entirely characteristic of

286. Ibid., 450, 180–81.
287. Ibid., 127.

"Das Schriftprinzip der reformierten Kirche" lecture of 1925.[288] In it, he stresses the pneumatological primacy in the "*Reformed* doctrine of the Bible."[289] Appearing in *Zwischen zum Zeiten* following his lecture tour in Switzerland, it was Barth's landmark theological publication[290] and a significant piece of evidence of his self-described recognition of the Reformed Scripture Principle.[291] If Barth's recognition of the publication is visible, strange, we argue, is its marginal place in recent construal of his view on the Bible.[292] Moreover, if our reading is plausible, it reinforces our view that more than the church history of confession,[293] and more than the authority of the church's valuation of "the divinely appointed vocation" of the biblical prophets and apostles,[294] what Barth finds most attractive in the Reformed (and more generally, Protestant) Scripture Principle concerns, instead, the Reformed pneumatological primacy of the absolute freedom and pure deity of the triune God's self-communicative being. Put differently, it concerns the Reformed *soteriological* emphasis on God's "unfathomable mystery"[295]—"God himself as *Subject*, as acting in history, the eternity as the limit of time, the event without analogy"[296]—on the "sober distance" between the Redeemer and his regenerates.[297] It is this soteriological emphasis on the pneumatological primacy of divine action in the church's relation to Scripture that Barth identifies as "one of the most fundamental

288. First published in *ZZ* 3 (1925), 215–45.

289. "Das Schriftprinzip," 520.

290. For his less direct and substantial reflections on Scripture in other public lectures in 1924–1925, see "Menschenwort und Gotteswort in der christlichen Predigt" in *ZZ* 3 (1925), 119–40; reprinted in *Vorträge und kleinere Arbeiten 1922–1925*, 426–57 (esp. 451f). "Kirche und Theologie" in *ZZ* 4 (1926), 18–40; reprinted in *Vorträge und kleinere Arbeiten 1922–1925*, 644–82 (esp. 656f).

291. Barth, *Revolutionary Theology in the Making*, 167.

292. See, for example, Lauster, *Prinzip und Methode*, 263 n. 38; Thompson, "Witness to the Word," 168–97.

293. Plasger, "Du sollst Vater und Mutter ehren!," 404; Plasger, "Wort vom Wort," 43–58 (esp. 47–49). Plasger is right that the Scripture Principle is central to Barth's Reformed identity. But on Plasger's reading of Barth, God's canon seems to collapse into the church's canon. Similar inattention to their crucial asymmetry is visible also in U. H. J. Körtner's reading of Barth in his treatment of "Die Krise des protestantischen Schriftprinzips," in *Theologie des Wortes Gottes*, 302–7.

294. Bender, "Scripture and Canon in Karl Barth's Early Theology," 187.

295. "Das Schriftprinzip," 503.

296. Ibid., 506.

297. Ibid., 536.

principles of the proclamation of our Reformed church."[298] In this specific connexion, Barth's soteriological emphasis on the Spirit's unidirectional mobilization of Scripture's regenerative humanity is prominent in at least two concepts in the lecture.

The first concept concerns the consequence of witness as characteristic of Scripture's regenerative humanity and the precedence of "the event without analogy,"[299] namely, the "pure, profound and divine" "gospel" of the Spirit's illuminating witness to Christ speaking in person in the Bible.[300] The Bible, Barth construes, is manifested "under a sphere of very strange human words"[301] that crucially serve none other than "the unique role and meaning of the divine."[302] By indicating the "pure" deity, priority and uniqueness of God's use of the biblical text to address the "Christian church,"[303] Barth can stress the ecumenical character of the Reformed characterization of Scripture's "human words" as *witness*. Succinctly put, it is Scripture's "human words" not first or finally as mere text, but it is the "human words" first and finally as a purposively created being bound to the Spirit's unbound witness in the church, that Barth construes the biblical canon *is* first and finally a *witness*. In this connexion, the canonical witness *is* outside of itself, Barth stresses: the witnesses *are* writers from without, and can be "heard" only by the "prism of their"—utterly broken (gebrochen)— "words, God himself"—"[o]therwise God himself is not *heard*."[304] Succinctly put, not only is their unity *external* to their words, the "divine" "meaning" mediated'—spoken by Christ's Spirit—by means of them *is* "without analogy."[305]

Put differently, ingredient in Barth's radical asymmetry between God's command of Scripture's "meaning" and the church's resultant obedience is Barth's *self-delimited* recognition of the priority and precedence of *divine action* in the external, contingent and unidirectional relation of the

298. Ibid., 504.

299. Ibid., 506.

300. Ibid., 503.

301. Ibid., 505.

302. Ibid., 506.

303. Ibid.

304. Ibid., 509. Cf. Mangina, *Karl Barth: Theologian of Christian Witness*, 16. Mangina is perceptive of the inherent "brokenness" in human words in relation to revelation: "The life that is ours in Christ is ours only through the cross—and therefore through the death of the present fallen world. But if so, our language too must be 'broken' if it is to bear its peculiar witness."

305. "Das Schriftprinzip," 512–14.

precedence of the canonical witness to the consequence of proper human recognition of the Spirit's mysterious objectivity in and through Scripture. Scripture's Reformed reception, as Barth construes it, concerns the onto-logical force of two interrelated aspects of the pneumatological primacy in the biblical witness: first, witness *is* characteristic of the canon for "only God himself can witness from God";[306] second, only *from* God through his attesting *action* does the canonical witness come to our attention and become a witnessing object of human recognition because "God can be recognized only through God."[307] Constructively put, Barth's reading of the Reformed scriptural and doctrinal orientation "means to create a space and to let a space be created for God's unique Word."[308] Recognizing the biblical canon as witness *by the Spirit of the Word*, in one crucial way, means: "To speak of God can only mean to let God speak."[309]

> The biblical texts do not wish to be God's Word, but as such speaks and is heard, is discovered and gives itself to be discov-ered. . . . Not human inerrancy (Irrtumslosigkeit)—in isolation (in keiner Beziehung)—makes these witnesses into witness of God himself, but the light of divine truth (das Licht göttlicher Wahrheit), illuminates in them the evidence (Zeugnissen) of fal-lible people like us.[310]

Thus Barth on the Reformed pneumatological construal of the external-ity of witness as characteristic of Scripture's "human words," and on the ecumenical character of the interrelated Reformed soteriological orienta-tion to the utter divine-human dissimilarity of witness, action and being in Scripture. Just as only by and through the Spirit's unbound witness comes Scripture as a witness from revelation to the church, so only in virtue of the Spirit's gratuitous electing illumination in Scripture comes the church's rec-ognition of the canon as a witness *through* the event of the Spirit's unbound self-announced presence of Christ, "the event without analogy."[311]

More closely—and this is the second concept—the biblical canon as the self-presence of the triune God is God's decision *a se*. God's presence in and through Scripture is God's capacity for Scripture's "human words," not

306. Ibid., 508–9.
307. Ibid., 508.
308. Ibid.
309. Ibid.
310. Ibid., 517–18.
311. Ibid., 506.

the capacity of Scripture's "human words" for God. God's use of the "human words" is creative—*ex nihilo*—ever fresh: the unidirectional relation of their new being to their old being *comes* to the church's attention only as a consequence of the Spirit's preceding mortifying and vivifying regeneration. That is, only in virtue of the electing God's unbound deployment *is* Scripture holy. If Scripture's holiness as canon is in Christ by the Spirit, it is not *in se*: just as its canonicity is always an *alien* event as an alien *event*, so is its recognition by the church in the *living* Spirit's self-revelation.

> Revelation stands, no it happens (nein sie geschieht), for us in the Scripture, it happens, there is no escape here (heir kein Ausweichen): in the biblical texts, in the words and sentences, in what the prophets and apostles as his witnesses intended to say and have said. . . . The texts come to us not as "Quellen," but as witness (Zeugnis). And the witness is not sought in some facts behind the sources, but in the texts. To understand this circle therein one must not jump out of it.[312]

Thus Barth on witness as characteristic of "the biblical *texts*" and on the event character of the textual witness as a created, contingent instrument of God's unbound mercy. In this sense, Barth's *soteriological* concept of "canonicity" is a corollary of the concept of the unity of Spirit's free act of election, inspiration, and illumination, *not vice versa*.[313] That is also to say, theology's construal of Scripture's canonicity and unity can no more be read back into the Spirit's unidirectional relation to Scripture, than can divine command be conflated with church obedience.

Succinctly put, as obedience, "canonization" stands for the church's solemnization of the ontological force of "God's unique voice" in the canon, the *vox Dei* that the church in due diligence distinguishes from its own voice, as Barth writes, "The Reformed church values the Bible not at all as 'Quelle,' but as *law* (Gesetz). Scripture stands severely *over against* the church."[314] In this connexion, one way to construe the self-critical theological force of the Reformed Scripture Principle is that in the Bible's relation to the church there is no "sense of continuity, but an establishment (Grundlegung), new high miracle, this momentously spoken imperious Word of God in the same unconditional sense as revelation itself."[315] On

312. Ibid., 516–17.
313. Ibid., 510.
314. Ibid., 525.
315. Ibid., 526.

Barth's reading, "that is the *Reformed* doctrine on Scripture": "The Church lives from revelation, from participating in none other than divine decision in God's self-knowledge."[316] Crucially, that means only by deferring to the Spirit of the Word's incarnate one, does the church dare "to speak of God because it is itself addressed by God"[317] as the God of the same Jesus Christ of the biblical prophets and apostles through *the Spirit's witness*. For

> this participation (Teilnahme) is mediated, not unmediated. Between the Word of God that became flesh [cf. Joh. 1.14] there and then, and the Word of God that is here and now and should be proclaimed and heard, stands (not to separate from the [first] but to distinguish between the two) the Word of God as Holy Scripture, the bridge across the abyss of time, the Word of God that makes us *partake* (teilhaftig) of revelation with the apostles and prophets *coincidentally* (gleichzeitig)—us who are *not* apostles and prophets, *not* witnesses to revelation in this fundamental sense (grundsätzlichen Sinn), who have *not* seen the resurrection, and have *not* heard the unique voice (einmalige Stimme) which Moses and Paul heard.[318]

Thus Barth on the ontological force of the Reformed pneumatological concept of canonicity of the *vox Dei* in Scripture, God's "unique voice" whose churchly recognition is firstly, finally, and entirely *contingent* upon God's *fresh* self-identification *a se* with "the unique voice that Moses and Paul heard."

Only in the light of the external and event character of the *vox Dei* in Scripture—in the light of God speaking in Scripture as a "*divine* decision, which humanly considered, must always be made again"[319]—is Scripture properly heard and proclaimed as canonical witness to the Spirit of the incarnate Word who came and is to come. Just as only by God's act does the church come to recognize the unity of his act, so only by God's act does the church come to recognize the unity of God's uses of Scripture as canon. Canonization "from the standpoint of the (revelation-recognizing) church," *contra* naturalist and historicist views, is "not historical, but dogmatic" (nicht historisch, sondern dogmatisch, vom Standpunkt der (Offenbarung erkennenden) Kirche),"[320] nor is it first, finally, and entirely

---

316. Ibid., 520.
317. Ibid.
318. Ibid.
319. Ibid., 523.
320. Ibid., 511.

the church's decision. Only in virtue of the decision of God who *acts, is* Scripture the canon and does its canonicity *come* to our attention. Barth's Reformed soteriological orientation to the *pneumatological* relation of the canon to canonization cannot be grasped apart from its ontological force.

The ontological force of Barth's pneumatological view of canon crucially concerns the unbound, saving relation of the Spirit of Jesus Christ to the biblical witnesses and their readers. Only by participating in the unidirectional relation of the Spirit *and* Scripture to the church, does the church confess the miraculous, sanctifying recognition of the identity of Jesus *in* the Spirit's regenerative economy. Put differently, only by being made a real participant in the Spirit's regenerative economy between the two advents of Christ, can *and* must the church as a new creature work out its proper witness in the miraculous and unidirectional relation of the new creation to the old one. On Barth's reading, Scripture *comes* to the church *by* Christ's commanding Spirit as God's preceding redemptive self-presence to the pilgrim church in the concrete task of pure witness.[321] By recognizing the positive and purposive character of the Spirit's regenerative use of Scripture, Barth can devise certain "'probabilities (Wahrscheinlichkeiten)'" for "the theological task of a pure historical science of the Bible."[322] This Barth does so crucially in the light of the ontological force of the pneumatological primacy and priority of the Reformed Scripture Principle, as he writes: "the incarnate, crucified Christ, whose life is hidden and is revealed only insofar as he is revealed through his Spirit, in the concrete decision on a razor's edge between unbelief and faith, between offence and grace."[323] By grace *can* "a pure historical science of the Bible" be a "theological task." That is also to say, only "through his Spirit" the "task" can be "theological" and a "historical science of the Bible" can be "pure." Succinctly put, as Barth writes earlier in the *GD*, in the light of the absolute precedence and freedom of the Spirit "we know nothing about a church where there is no scripture."[324] For

---

321. Barth, "The Concept of the Church," 294. "The Church is the Church of forgiven thieves, who wait for their redemption. This fact does not destroy the authority of the Church, but it does mark its limit."

322. "Das Schriftprinzip," 536. Lauster briefly discusses this lecture in a footnote where he notes the concept of witness as a trace of Barth's Reformed orientation, but strangely omits Barth's explicit indication of the constructive interrelation of theological work and historical study of Scripture (Lauster, *Prinzip und Methode*, 263 n. 38).

323. "Das Schriftprinzip," 527.

324. Ibid., 215.

> God is the living God whom we have learned to know in the doc-
> trine of the Trinity, and that his is immutable subjectivity, so that we
> are again leaving it in his hands whether there is revelation across
> the times and in the history of all times, whether there is church.[325]

Thus Barth on the Reformed church as the Spirit's "pure" reader of Scripture, and the overarching soteriological theme of the Reformed utter respect for the absolute freedom and lordship of the triune God speaking as
none other than "the living God" in Scripture.

From all this it is clear that the landmark 1925 publication affords us
a significant entrée for understanding his Reformed identity, a prominently
pneumatological orientation that he wished to be known as entirely characteristic of his project of theological renewal. Moreover, it is clear that
Barth's *pneumatological* view of canonical witness as being characteristic of
Scripture's "human words" cannot be grasped apart from its soteriological
orientation. Only as the Spirit's new-creaturely witness *to Jesus Christ*, does
the canon come to the church's attention as "the Church of forgiven thieves,
who wait for their redemption,"[326] Barth writes in "The Concept of the
Church" lecture in 1927. One way to put Barth's point on "pure" witness as
characteristic of the Reformed Scripture Principle concerns once again the
soteriological theme of the uniqueness of the incarnate one in the Spirit's
unidirectional relation to the biblical witnesses and the church, as we shall
see in the next chapter. For now, we shall simply note that on Barth's reading, the witness of the canon's "human words" are by the Spirit bound to the
Spirit's self-witness to Jesus Christ, but the self-witness of Christ's Spirit is
unbound to the writers or their "words."

Summary

I began this chapter by suggesting the formative significance of Barth's increasing self-identification with the Reformed Scripture Principle in the complex process of his theological renewal. I have sketched his view of Scripture
by reading a series of Barth's correspondence and works from 1916 to 1925: a
representative selection of his sermons, extramural lectures in relation to the
nature of Scripture, a biblical commentary (in two editions), and two lectures
series on historical theology and the prolegomena to his first dogmatics.

325. Ibid., 205.
326. Barth, "The Concept of the Church," 294.

From all this, Barth's emphasis on the external and unidirectional relation of the divine-human witness of Spirit and Scripture to the church is arguably, occasionally visible, while it is fair to say it is not consistent throughout his writings. By understanding the antecedence, uniqueness, and prevenience of divine action in Scripture, Barth is able to describe Scripture as an event of the Spirit bearing witness to the Spirit's past activity and of *this* Spirit's dynamic self-witness as ground to the simultaneity of election, inspiration, and illumination as *one* act of *divine autopistia*.[327] The charge that in Barth, illumination collapses into revelation, or the due weight of Scripture's human elements is overlooked, simply does not stick,[328] for at least two reasons.

The first reason is that Barth stresses the logical priority of the Spirit's illumination of the new person of the biblical witnesses in their old one, so that recognition of their eschatological humanity is a corollary of the recognition of the soteriological primacy of God in Scripture and the reader. In the reader and Scripture—and this is the second reason—illumination is external, contingent, and necessary to human recognition of revelation as God's unbound free act of life-giving mercy, so that only by virtue of the Light of the Spirit does Scripture's humanity as witness to revelation come to our attention. If Barth's critics think he has a pneumatological deficit, it is in part because they overlook the precedence of illumination and the consequence of human recognition of revelation as none other than revelation *in illumination*—without exception.

Further, Barth's bibliological orientation to the unity of the Spirit's electing, creative, and perfecting activities helps illuminate his increasingly attentive and respectful recognition of "the testimonies in which the past solemnly confessed its faith on the basis of scripture and the Spirit" so that in attentiveness and respect for the Spirit's past and present work in the saints, "individuals in their own historical place have to see in such confessions the faith of a very special past, that is, that of the church which has baptised them."[329] One way to put Barth's point concerns the teaching office of the Spirit,[330] the Spirit's office as "the point of reference to which

---

327. *GD*, 249.

328. Thompson, "Witness to the Word," 189f. "Barth himself has been accused (quite reasonably in my view) of having collapsed the Spirit's illumination into the concept of revelation."

329. *GD*, 239–40.

330. Ibid., 192.

all church authorities relate, in which they are grounded, and by which the are superseded."[331] That is also to say, the recognition of the Spirit's use of Scripture presupposes the recognition of the Spirit's use of the ministry of the churches through the ages. Thus, of churches, Barth writes, "We are not simply to think and speak in detachment from them, as though the church began only today with us—not even if we use the Bible."[332]

In next chapter we shall see increasing precision in Barth's constructive construal of the external and unidirectional relation of the canon to the church in the saving economy of the Spirit. For now, we simply note that Barth is aware of the church's service in the economy of Christ's Spirit in Scripture, a service that Barth construes, moreover, under the soteriological theme of the biblical canon as a pure witness in illumination. All this is illustrated in a passage in his concept of "pure"[333] human witness:

> As regards the word "pure," it is better than "right" or "correct" because it better denotes what is meant, that is, it brings out its specific content better. What I say that doctrine must be pure . . . I mean that it should be clear and transparent like polished glass. It is not there for its own sake but so that we may see through the human word to the present, living Word of God. The less it puts a third thing between God's Word and us; the more it removes every third thing and displaces everything that is falsely divine or over-arrogantly human; the more positively it is merely a reference or a pointing of the finger compelling us to look at the other thing with which it is indirectly identical; the more clearly the hidden Word of God can shine through the concealing human word, the more it is *pure* doctrine. It was not for nothing that in the Middle Ages a crystal-clear and polished glass vessel was one of the most familiar symbols for Mary. The Logos seeks vessels such as this . . . This is not to say that even where the doctrine is purest, God will really confess it, speaking when we speak. It is not to say that he cannot speak even through the medium of very impure doctrine. But God's freedom does not alter the fact that we are set a task (to be pure in our talk about God). When we have done everything that we are required to do, we should still say that we are unprofitable servants (Luke 17:10). But those who infer from this that we may be insolent servants show thereby that they do not understand the matter at all.[334]

331. Ibid., 249.
332. Ibid., 239.
333. Ibid., 274.
334. Ibid.

By way of anticipation: Barth's Reformed concepts of God and in and through the pure witness of the canon will gain increasingly greater profile in his lectures on the Gospel of John and *ChD*, as we shall see in next chapter.

3
Dominus Illuminatio Mea
The School of the Biblical Witness

THIS CHAPTER UNPACKS CERTAIN characteristics of Barth's Reformed view of the biblical witness and its reader. It examines especially their anthropological and creaturely orientation as an extension of his concept of the triune God. To this end, we can proceed through a focused reading of his lectures on the Gospel of John and the first volume of *Die christliche Dogmatik im Emtwurf*. If our reading of Barth is plausible, it reinforces our crucial point about the formative significance of Barth's Reformed pneumatological emphasis, and illuminates the material difficulty faced by certain mischaracterizations of his scriptural and doctrinal orientation. On Barth's "dialectical" orientation, for example, Jüngel observes that in the late 20s "the dialectical theologians were . . . beginning to attempt" "a nontheological basis for speech about God," an attempt that "Barth opposed."[1] The theological character of Barth's constructive objection is visible in the material. Barth's objection generally concerns a twofold damaging, prominent view of the person and work of the biblical witnesses: (a) domestication of divine illumination and revelation in the biblical witnesses, and (b) absolutization of their written testimony as a self-determined, self-sufficient, and nearly self-existent entity. By contrast, the Münster material arguably affords a different picture substantially. In it Barth's soteriological, and characteristically Reformed, emphasis on the absolute precedence of the Spirit's illumination is crucial.[2] Put differently, more than a mere respect

---

1. Jüngel, *Karl Barth*, 38f.

2. *Contra* Thompson's claim that Barth has "collapsed the Spirit's illumination into the concept of revelation" (Thompson, "Witness to the Word," 189f).

for the church and its tradition,[3] and more than just a different way of construing Scripture,[4] Barth's self-identification with the Reformed Scripture Principle crucially affords him an "open" characterization of the humanity of the biblical witnesses.[5] By Barth's bibliological theme of "illumination," I mean, in a nutshell, his reference to the Spirit's uncreated Light as unbound, external and necessary to the created light of Jesus and his biblical witnesses: their lights need to be illuminated to illuminate. The theme does not displace human agency from God's saving economy; instead it is a device to underscore certain ontic, noetic, and teleological—and on our part, *hypothetical*—conditions of the human agency of Scripture. Under these hypothetical conditions the human agency is described neither deified nor absolutized; rather, it is characterized as a gratuitous, ever-fresh creation of the Redeemer for the sake of his pure deity in his self-revelation. In a

3. Plasger, "Wort vom Wort," 45–48f. Cf. Barth, "Church and Theology," 303: *"Pure* doctrine is doctrine conforming to the Scripture and to the Spirit. Such doctrine leaves the divine Word free, above the claims of all human speaking of and about God."

4. *B-Bultmann*, 28–29. On 10th December, 1926, Bultmann tells Barth that fundamental is their difference on the externality and necessity of the Word and Spirit in Scripture and the reader. In John's Gospel Bultmann perceives "that the proclaimer Jesus Christ becomes the proclaimed Jesus Christ. I have the impression that you [Barth] do not see this problem, which to me seems to be a true theological problem, indeed, the problem of NT theology in general." He continues, "the Word became flesh, a someone who has said something. The synoptists tell us about this someone and something. It makes no difference here that in Christian proclamation the synoptics are heard as Christian talk about Jesus, or, historically formulated, are seen in a Pauline or Johannine light. They do not simply say, as John does, that Jesus presented himself as the revealer; instead they tell us how he did so, which John does not. This fact seems to be brought out most clearly, and the problem presented most pressingly, when with the help of historical criticism one tries to show what, then Jesus said." Cf. Rumscheidt, "The Barth-Bultmann Correspondence," 65–74. In relation, when addressing a question about the dogmatic foundation between his view of Scripture and Bultmann's, Barth referred to "the aseity of God" as a key concept. Barth, *Gespräche 1964–1968*, 290f.

5. Schmid rightly observes that even though Barth and Gogarten both have an "actualistic" concept of revelation, Gogarten's is *"consistently actualistic*, his actualism is structurally fundamental nature, unlike Barth's orientation which is "hypothetical, open, pointing-beyond-itself—it is structurally restrictive," that is, in the form of a witness to revelation rather than in the form of domestication of revelation himself (Schmid, *Verkündigung und Dogmatik in der Theologie Karl Barths*, 83). See also McCormack, *Karl Barth's Critically Realistic Dialectical Theology*, 392. McCormack cites Barth's realization of Gogarten's "hidden doctrine" in a letter to Thurneysen on 10 June 1926: "This evening, I suddenly comprehended much of Gogarten's hidden doctrine. Above all, it became very clear to me that with Gogarten, it is once again a question of a clear grasping after the *est*, of nothing else!" (*B-Th*, II, 422. McCormack's translation).

way, the concept of illumination therefore prefaces certain ontic and noetic *soteriological* conditions which God supplies and under which he makes himself known to us. Whether or not Barth is successful and consistent throughout his writings, one essential aspect of his characterization is his respect for the soteriological primacy of the sanctifying creativity of Christ's Spirit and the corresponding *asymmetrical* divine-human relation as an asymmetrical divine-human *relation*.

One way to put his point about the relational character of Scripture is his critique of the "absolute man" in Europe's intellectual history since the Renaissance.[6] A significant example of the critique, we shall see, is his construal of John as an "enlightened man."[7] Barth does so by way of an expansive exegetical description of the Spirit's illumination in and through the Evangelist, to underscore, we suggest, "the objectivity of the sacraments" and "the concreteness of the divine command"[8] in the human testimony and reception of Scripture. If Barth's soteriological recognition of the due weight of humanity is entirely characteristic of his pneumatological view of Scripture, we suggest that it is in part because, as P.T. Nimmo perceives, there is "no such thing as a command of God in the abstract, but only a command of God as part of a concrete relationship with an individual in the covenant of grace."[9]

That is also to suggest that the soteriological primacy in his anthropological orientation cannot be grasped properly apart from his pneumatological priority. In this specific connexion, Barth's consistent anthropological

6. Cf. *PT*, 13–14f (ET 13–4f); 19–20 (ET 22–23). Of "the absolute man," Barth writes, is he who "discovers his own power and ability, the latent potentiality of his humanity (that is, in his human being as such), and looks upon it as the final, the real, the absolute, I mean as something 'detached,' self-justifying, with its own authority and power, which he can therefore set in motion in all directions and without any restraint—this man is absolute man." For more qualified accounts on Barth's *Protestant Theology in the Nineteenth Century*, see Webster, *Barth's Earlier Theology*, 91–117; see also Wood, *Barth's Theology of Interpretation*, 51–99.

7. *EJE*, 2–4 (ET 2–4).

8. Wood, *Barth's Theology of Interpretation*, 90–94; 84–85. Wood notes the precedence of the ontic over the noetic in Barth's reading of the history of dogma: "Barth argues that the modern inability to meaningfully enter these debates reflects a modern christological deficiency that can only be described as both error and sin. That is, we suffer from a spiritualistic and arbitrary moralism that cannot accept the realism of the biblical testimony to the incarnation, 'a horror of the being of God in his revelation' and a rejection of the ontological significance of the classical claim that Jesus Christ is true God and true man."

9. Nimmo, *Being in Action*, 39.

interest is emphatic in his maturing view of Scripture on the one hand, and in his significant demarcation between the incarnate one and the biblical prophets and apostles on the other. On Barth's reading, the demarcation concerns the asymmetrical relation of the Word to *his* witnesses as no more than *witnesses* by virtue of the Spirit's illuminating regeneration. As H. Hartwell puts it: "They exist and are real and genuine only if and when and as long as they owe their existence to an act of God."[10] Succinctly put, his account of the Reformed emphasis on illumination is visible in Barth's bibliological concept of the divine action. In this chapter, we shall attempt to show just how this is so. If the marginalization of his lectures on John's Gospel in recent readings of his bibliology is strange, we suggest that the lectures afford compelling exegetical evidences of Barth's Reformed orientation. One such evidence is his construal of John the Evangelist.

Erklärung des Johannes-Evangeliums

At Münster his "Hauptvorlesung" was the exegetical lectures on the Gospel of John when he became Professor of Dogmatics and New Testament Exegesis in 1926.[11] A prominent theme in his construal of the Fourth Gospel is the Spirit's unbound illumination of the Evangelist and the readers. The Spirit's relational primacy in Scripture, Barth observes, concerns an ontological problem[12] to John and his readers, namely, the mysterious hypostatic relation of the Word to Jesus of Nazareth.[13] More closely, if the Evangelist stresses the incarnate Word's hypostasis as one of subject, *not*

10. Hartwell, *The Theology of Karl Barth*, 33.

11. The stylistic and textual features and historical backgrounds of the lectures, which he repeated in Bonn, with slight variations, are well documented. See Webster's careful and detailed description (Webster, "Barth's Lectures on the Gospel of John," 211–31). Cf. Martin, "The Gospel of John," 31–42. Fürst, *EJE*, vii–xii (ET ix–xii). Plasger, "Wort vom Wort," 43–58. Wengst, "Der Zeichenbegriff in Barths Kommentar zum Johannesevangelium," 30–42. Boer, "'Bedrängnis muß groß sein . . .,'" 8–29. J.P. Martin notes the continuity from the Romans commentary regarding Barth's references to the precedence, transcendence and immanence of God (Martin, "The Gospel of John," 38–39). Cf. Already by the fall of 1925, he had begun to indicate the significance of the lectures, in part for clarifying his fundamental differences with Bultmann. *B-Th II*, 397; *B-Bultmann*, 33; 56.

12. Cf. Barth construes it as the ontological force of the incarnate Word's "essential offensiveness" (Infragestellung alles Seins und alles Seinenden) (*EJE*, 30 (ET 25), 45 (ET 37), 67–68 (ET 54–55)).

13. *B-Bultmann*, 28–29.

nature, it also follows that, Barth argues, an prominent theme in John is the apostolic emphasis on the absolute freedom, sovereignty, and necessity of the action of the triune God as characteristic of Jesus Christ's contingent self-presence to and through the new creation in the old one. In this connexion, being neither absolute nor occasional,[14] the Apostle's self-described relation to the miracle of the saving and sanctifying Light of the incarnate Word is best described as coincidental.[15] By acknowledging the miracle of illumination as key to construing the concrete relation of John's new person to his old one, Barth can indicate gratefully and confidently—but without positing ontically—Scripture's eschatological humanity *and* historicity as "creatura verbi divini" *and* "simul justus et peccator," in two ways.

The first way concerns the primacy of the illuminating Spirit in the person and work of a biblical apostle. Put negatively, "[t]here is need to appeal for the assistance of grace," Barth introduces the point, for if "the natural man does not understand the things of the Spirit of God,"[16] our recognition of John as an "enlightened man" (erleuchtet Mensch) "presupposes that he is first known and acknowledged precisely in his humanity."[17] Being human, the apostle is only a *witness* to and through the divine Light of his salvation and vocation, and *not* as the Light himself. "[B]ecause," quoting Augustine Barth writes, "those who wrote the scriptures were also men, they do not shine of themselves"—"it is precisely in this sense that the other John, the Baptist, says of himself: I am not the Christ."[18] Just as

14. For one of Barth's strongest critics on the point, see Hamer, *L'Occasionalisme Théologique de Karl Barth*, 167. Wood suggests that Runia makes "an implicit criticism of perceived occasionalism in Barth" (*Barth's Theology of Interpretation*, 38 n. 127). Although just short of committing to a divine-human consubstantiation in Scripture, Runia argues that the biblical witnesses "are not only witnesses to revelation, in a limiting and distinct way, but they themselves *belong to the revelation*. Their speaking and writing *is* revelation" (*Karl Barth's Doctrine of Holy Scripture*, 35). For other excellent analyses of Barth's critics concerning human agency, see Webster, *Barth's Moral Theology*, 1; Asprey, *Eschatological Presence in Karl Barth's Göttingen Theology*, 241–43; Clough, *Ethics in Crisis*, xii; 6ff; ecclesiology, see Flett, *The Witness of God*, 188–89 n. 50.

15. *EJE*, 107 (ET 87). The notion of coincidence is important to Barth's understanding of ἐγένετο (v. 14) as the Word's "mode of coming" to the biblical witnesses and through them to the reader. For a more qualified and comprehensive treatment of the notion, see Webster, "Barth's Lectures on the Gospel of John," 211–31.

16. *EJE*, 1 (ET 1).

17. Ibid., 2–4 (ET 2–4).

18. Ibid., 3 (ET 2). "the deity, ontological distinction, essential offensiveness" (Infragestellung alles Seins und alles Seinenden) and sovereign self-determination of the Word in relation to "the concealed truth, Jesus Christ, in the proclamation of the Evangelist."

Christ's demarcation from his biblical witnesses is ingredient in his self-presence to and through them,[19] so is the Spirit's enduring distinction from them ingredient in his regeneration of the new person in the old one in their humanity as a sanctified field of his self-determined illumination: "They cannot impart illumination of the understanding. They themselves need illumination." (Die Erleuchtung zum Verständnis aber können sie nicht vermitteln, sind sie doch selber der Erleuchtung bedürtig gewesen.)[20]

The apostolic need of the Spirit to act—and this is the second way—is indicative of his externality and necessity as characteristic of their ministry.[21] Constructively, Barth sees that John comes to us from "a concrete, specific situation whose form (Gestalt) does not depend at all on us," but that the form rather "lies in the matter (Sache) itself."[22] The objectivity of John's humanity is indicative of "our help" that

> comes from the Lord who has made heaven and earth (Ps. 121:2). . . . [Scripture] as witness which itself needs witness and expects witness—the witness that its subject (Gegenstand) must give. This giving is an event, an action, the action of God in the strictest sense of the term.[23]

Thus Barth on John's contingent, but by no means occasional, ministry. Succinctly put, John comes and testifies to us, only in and through the Spirit. For if the "Gospel comes to us with the promise that God himself will confess it,"[24] the Apostle is obliged to "[the Logos and the incarnate one] as the definitions of one and the same subject (Subjektes), to think of them in *concert* (zugleich)," just so is the witness of John obliged to the prior action of the Spirit and the Word.[25]

> To see him as an apostle we need the same illumination that he needed and received in order to be an apostle. He does not proclaim God without God, nor may he be known as one who proclaims God without God. His word is qualified as address in

19. Ibid., 30 (ET 25); 67–68 (ET 54–55).

20. Ibid., 3 (ET 3).

21. Cf. In his reading of 6.39–40 Barth construes the ministry of the biblical witness as an "Indicative!" to Christ in virtue of "the work of Jesus" in the hope of the coming of the "the eternal life," not their ministry as "a pile of ancient documents" (*EJE*, 294–95).

22. Ibid., 4 (ET 3).

23. Ibid., 9 (ET 7).

24. Ibid., 9 (ET 7).

25. Ibid., 107 (ET 86–87).

the sense described, as holy scripture, in virtue of (kraft) God's address to us by means of the words of this man. We have to speak, not of quality, nor of the qualified nature (Qualifiziertheit), but of the qualifying of his word (Qualifikation seines Wortes), not of a being (Sein) but of an action (Tun), the divine action in virtue of which his word is qualified as an address.[26]

Thus Barth on the consequence of the externality of the instrumentality of "the words of this man" and the precedence and prevenience of "the divine action in virtue of which his word is qualified as an address."[27] Barth's concept of John's person and work stresses God's self-communicative action as a necessary *and* unbound condition of the Evangelist's apostolic qualification.[28] In this sense, a complimentary aspect of the unidirectional relation of John's new creatureliness to his old one[29] is his instrumentality in virtue

26. Ibid., 8 (ET 6).

27. Put differently, Scripture is "only apparently nearer" to us "than God" whose scriptural self-presence is his action, not mere human valuation (ibid., 3 (ET 3)). See also Barth's emphasis in vv. 1.3–4 on the Word's "absolute distinctiveness" (absoluten Andersartigkeit) to "*all* things that came into being" foundational to his sovereign immediacy to them who, the creatures, "in no sense stand *beside* him . . . or *without* him" (ibid., 41 (ET 34)).

28. Ibid., 32 (ET 27). "wo die in die Verkündigung des Evangeliums verhüllte Wirklichkeit, Jesus Christus, gewaltig seinen Platz einnimmt, wo die Gleichung zur Auflösung kommt: καὶ αὕτη ἐστὶν ἡ μαρτυρία τοῦ Ἰωάννου: v 19ff." See in the original: Barth's accent on the event (denoted by the verb "kommt"), the radically explosive character of the divine unveiling of the concealment of revelation of Jesus Christ as the Word overshadowing and upholding John's witness.

29. Cf. *UCR III*, 352–53. Barth thinks that the fellowship (Gemeinschaft) of the saints is the fellowship of the living, but makes a crucial distinction between the "ecclesia *triumphans*" and the "ecclesia *militans*" to secure, in a sense, divine freedom in the anticipatory, eschatological and fluid orientation of the witness of Scripture in the hearing of the saints on pilgrimage towards the resurrection. "Wir leben oder sterben, so sind wir des Herrn. Die *eine* Kirche—nicht um eine zwiefache handelt es sich bei diesen Begriffen, sondern um die um die *eine* Kirche in zwiefacher Hinsicht—ist 'ecclesia *triumphans*', Gemeinschaft der der Auferstehung wartenden Toten in Abrahams Schoß, *und* 'ecclesia *militans*', Gemeinschaft der im Glauben und Gehorsam hier und jetzt Wandernden, der dem Tode entgegeneilenden Lebenden, und zwar auch Gemeinschaft dieser mit jenen, jener mit diesen. In der Kirche sind Abraham, Isaak und Jakob heute mit uns und wir mit ihnen." ["In life as in death, we belong to the Lord. The *one* church – not a twofold church in these concepts, but *one* church in two aspects—is 'ecclesia *triumphans*', a community of the resurrection-awaiting-dead in Abraham's blossom, *and* 'ecclesia *militans*', a community in the faith and obedience of the pilgrims here and now, of the living in the shadow of death, and indeed a community of the former with the latter as well as [a community] of the latter with the former. In the church Abraham, Isaac and Jacob are with us today and we with them."]

of the Spirit's self-determined gift[30] of his apostolic mission to the church. The church's resultant reception of Scripture has a noetic force that is *derived* from the biblical witnesses. But the words of their testimony crucially "do not illuminate unless they are illuminated"[31] by the Light of their "Sache within the domain of its own logic and ethic" (Sache im Rahmen ihrer eigenen Logik und Ethik):[32] "the apostles do not speak to us as such unless it is ever and again given to them to do so by God."[33]

Put slightly differently, an ingredient aspect in Barth's concept of Scripture as the self-communicative action of the Word is recognition of the Spirit's regenerative relation to the apostle's humanity.[34] Recognition of the apostle's sanctified humanity requires the Spirit's sanctifying illumination, for, Barth stresses, "without which we cannot perceive the light of scripture" and "for which we can only pray."[35] By understanding prayer and Scripture as interrelated complementary themes of the idiom of illumination, Barth can secure the soteriological character of the themes as well as the instrumentality and necessary gift of the sanctified person. He can stress the logical priority of the new person in the task of attending to the ontological problem of the *simul justus et peccator* in the Apostle and the proper reader, so that, Barth emphasizes, we come to Scripture, "not as teachers (Lehrer) but as students (Schüler), not as those who know (Wissende) but as those who do not know, as those who let ourselves be told what the Gospel, and through it the divine wisdom (Weisheit), is seeking to tell us."[36]

If, moreover, by the Spirit we become grateful students of the illuminated light of "his existence and function as the human witness who

---

30. A gift "in a way that does not bind him from whom every good gift comes" (*EJE*, 10 (ET 8)).

31. Ibid., 9 (ET 7).

32. Ibid., 11 (ET 8–9).

33. Ibid., 9 (ET 7).

34. Ibid., 41 (ET 34). "It is related (bezieht) to God, it is not *nothing*, but *something*, it *is* something insofar as it is related to the Word." *Contra* K. Nürnberger who suggests Barth's scriptural orientation as a mere antithesis of God and humanity in *Theology of the Biblical Witness*, 23.

35. Ibid., 10–11 (ET 8–9). Barth construes the prayer for illumination as one in an "openness," "readiness," and "willingness" of a pure "heart" and "continence" to *adapt* (fügen) to our enduring need of the grace by which John *is*.

36. Ibid., 11 (ET 9).

stands between revelation and humanity,"[37] our description of the divine action in and through John's humanity must take heed of an apostolic warning. On Barth's reading, John warns about "the danger of confusion that can arise, and therefore about the required criticism with which such a man [that is, "someone other than Christ himself . . . speaks about Christ"] must be differentiated from the one about whom he speaks."[38] Our construal of the speech-acts of the apostolic testimony, in this sense, demands *theological* "criticism." Such "criticism" for Barth is not one that imposes a concept of speech-act on John or domesticates illumination in the apostle's humanity or ours. Instead, Barth construes it as one that draws out the ontological force of the externality of John's new humanity in the old by indicating the externality of the divine action by virtue of which John *comes* to us in the light of the *whole* being of the Word. If "[f] or the Evangelist the Word is not just the words that Christ *speaks* but the Word that he *is* in his whole manifestation (Erscheinung),"[39] Barth perceives that "[c]anonical Scripture . . . means scripture to which we stand in that relation from the very first, a Word that is spoken to us from the very first in the name of God,"[40] so that in illumination the Apostle "cannot think of regarding himself as the bearer of the final Word even relatively or on earth."[41] Succinctly put, the Word's hypostatic union has only *one* human subject, namely, Jesus Christ, to whom and in relation to whom biblical writers are only witnesses. As Torrance puts it:

> The mighty living Word of God is not encapsulated in the written words of Bible, far less is that Word personally incarnated in the Bible as it is in the Lord Jesus Christ, for there is no hypostatic union between the Word of God and the word of man in the Bible.[42]

37. Ibid., 19 (ET 16).

38. Ibid., 19 (ET 17). Cf. "Wherever this *confusion* (Verwechslung) kicks in, the witness, instead of remaining a witness, begins to behave (gebärden) as the Revealer, instead of Christ and the Sache of God, points to his own heart and makes *his* [pointing] hand the Sache" (ibid., 68–69 (ET 55–56)).

39. Ibid., 31 (ET 26). The important emphases in the original are omitted in Bromiley's translation. "Denn Evangelisten ist der Logos nicht nur das Wort, das Christus *spricht*, sondern das Wort, das er in seiner ganzen Erscheinung *ist*." Barth has in mind Bultmann for whom Jesus was "strictly only the Revealer" and A. Schlatter who "has it that the Evangelist is referring to the words from the lips of Jesus."

40. Ibid., 5–6 (ET 4–5).

41. Ibid., 133–34 (ET 108–9).

42. Torrance, *Karl Barth, Biblical and Evangelical Theologian*, 91.

If our reading is plausible, the common construal of Barth domesticating of divine action in the human action of Scripture or the reader is problematic. More closely, the problem concerns the primacy and mystery of God in the essential dissimilarity of *subjecthood* between Jesus and his biblical witnesses as well as in their common *nature* as creature. Barth overlooks neither their utterly dissimilar subjecthood or agency nor their common sanctified nature, for an essential insight of his John is the recognition of the drama of the Spirit's utterly concrete work in and through Christ's flesh that was *there*.

> The so-called "historical Jesus," abstracted from the action of the Word, is *not* revelation! . . . Revelation is nowhere and never the work of the σάρξ as such, not even the σάρξ of Christ; it is completely (ganze und gar) the work of the *Logos* that has become σάρξ. *He* is the Jesus Christ who will authoritatively take up the word in the Gospel. If Jesus Christ does *not* do this work of his, the σάρξ can and must conceal, hide, and shut, even though it is the σάρξ of Christ. So just as certainly it can and must reveal when Jesus Christ *does* this work of his through it! No one has emphasized as much as the Fourth Evangelist that Christ can both reveal himself and not reveal himself. . . . As σάρξ, if he *will* not reveal himself, he is *not* revealed but is concealed and offensive (ärgerlich)! His revelation cannot be known except through this danger of offense (Gefahr des Ärgernisses), since it can be known only in the flesh. Flesh would not be flesh without the full possibility of offence. For the Logos would not be the Logos if he did not have and exercise in the flesh the full freedom to give *and* to withhold.[43]

Thus Barth on John's recognition of the ontological problem of the incarnate Word who "shares the same nature with the person of the Father in the same dignity and perfection."[44]

---

43. Ibid., 114–15 (ET 92–93).

44. Ibid., 26 (ET 22). The Reformed concept of the hypostatic union of subject (as opposite to nature) in the incarnation enables Barth to speak of Jesus Christ's sinlessness as a corollary and affirmation of the incarnate Word's deity without compromising the integrity of the createdness of the flesh. And that is also to say, the concept of the sinlessness of Christ is related to the Reformed teachings on the hypostatic union and human depravity. In a sense, this is one reason why fundamental is Barth's conviction about the humanity's inherent inability to indicate, let alone reveal, the Word. Cf. *UCR III*, 103–4f. Barth's bibliology of the incarnation will be treated momentarily in our reading of the *ChD*.

More closely, on Barth's reading, the Johannine view on the two natures refers to a hypostasis of the *subject* in the Word and the Nazarene,
not to a hypostasis of two entirely dissimilar natures.[45] If the dissimilarity
between Jesus and John has to do less with their human nature,[46] but more
with their subjecthood or person, and recognition of the hypostasis of the
incarnate one is a necessary condition of recognizing John's humanity as
a witness to the Word,[47] it follows that Barth's demarcation between revelation and witness once again comes under the theme of divine action.
Succinctly put, "revelation is an event (Ereignis), an *action* (Handeln) of
the Word," just so is John's new humanity.[48] It is rather by the action of the
divine Word, *not* by the flesh, that the apostles testifies to the *who* in the
incarnation: "he [the Word] *has done* that. The apostolic witness is that
he did that."[49] Once again: "Can one fail to recognize that here revelation
is presented as a closed circle (Kreis) into which no-one can leap (here-
inspringen) from outside? . . . *He* [the Word] convinces, *he* convicts, *he*
compels, *he* decides. He is subject and not object in this action."[50] Crucially,
only from within this "closed circle" of the economy of God's action of covenantal promise and fulfilment[51] comes our proper recognition of John's
provisional (old) and eschatological (new) humanity being caught up in
between the first and second advents of the incarnate Word whose "*other*
form (Gestalt), which coincides (zusammenfällt) with the *resurrection* of
the flesh, still awaits us."[52] In the light of Christ's *parousia* Barth argues that
the relation of John's old humanity to the incarnate Christ is not to be read
back into the relation of John's new humanity to the ascended Christ: just

45. For a more qualified account of Barth's christology, see Webster, "Barth's Lectures
on the Gospel of John," 211–31.

46. Cf. Hart, "Calvin and Barth on the Lord's Supper," 47ff: "this relationship of 'hypostatic union' is unique, and does not pertain to any other God-given sign."

47. If "revelation does not become a state or quality or property of the flesh," nor does
the new humanity of his witnesses, we suggest, become domesticated in the old humanity; for Barth, knowledge of the unidirectional relation of the new to the old is a corollary
of the Spirit's gift of the knowledge of Christ (*EJE*, 113f (ET 92f)).

48. Ibid., 113f (ET 92f). Cf. Ibid., 120 (ET 97), 294. In relation to the apostolic reference to the Word as subject and agent of the incarnation, Barth takes the view that the
divine Word is in complete freedom with respect to Christ's earthly σάρξ on which the
"Apostolic indication (Schauden) does not depend."

49. Ibid., 118 (ET 95–96).

50. Ibid., 92 (ET 75).

51. Ibid., 115–16 (ET 95).

52. Ibid., 117 (ET 95).

as John's testimony is best described as eschatologically provisional, just so is our construal of his humanity and ours in Christ.[53]

From all this it is clear that John's Gospel affords Barth exegetical clarity for the primacy of illumination[54] in the Reformed scriptural and doctrinal orientation to the Word and Spirit on the one hand and to Scripture's humanity and ours on the other. Moreover, Barth's recognition of John's eschatological humanity is visible, especially in terms of the Spirit's work in the Apostle's relation to the Light of the Word's hypostatic union of subject in Jesus. An essential theme in Barth's construal of the relation of the Word to John is his concept of the utter dissimilarity between the incarnate one and his human witnesses as well as their common human delimitations as *creatura verbi divini* and their eschatological provisionality in the face of the *parousia*. Although these lectures are Barth's exposition of the Fourth Gospel with his students in mind, not a treatise on theological metaphysic, we can easily see the significance of his breathtaking sketch of the Johannine ontic and noetic relation of the Light of the Word to the incarnation, especially in terms of his increasingly resourceful idiom of witness. The idiom will appear, sometimes almost *verbatim*, in the *ChD*.

In the *ChD*, a picture of continuity of what we already highlighted here and in Chapter 2 is visible, for instance: in §4.2 "The Word of God as canon" where he underscores God's Word as the gratuitous ground to the humanity of Scripture;[55] in §20.1–4 "God in the witness of the prophets and apostles" where he underscores the pure deity and freedom of the divine

---

53. Cf. Ibid., 116–17 (ET 94): "that is, [if] in Christ [the incarnation] has brought the true (wahre) and eternal tabernacle, the real (eigentliche), universal, and ultimate (endgültige) σκηνοῦν of God μετ' αὐτῶν (Rev. 21.3) has still to come eschatologically." Barth's eschatology and doctrine of the resurrection cannot be treated here. The eschatological accent of Barth's emphasis on the incarnation as the Word's concealed—*indirect*—self-presence is, however, clear. One way to put Barth's seminal point is the contingency or non-permanence of the Word's self-presence to all human witnesses *before* the eschaton. Hence Scripture, as it were, is construed as a contingently illuminated path *en passant* to the resurrection. "Ist sie doch nach Hebr. 9, 9 eine παραβολὴ εἰς τὸν καιρὸν τὸν καιρὸν τὸν ἐνεστηκόα, und wenn nun auch die messianische Gegenwart die Erfüllung dieser παραβολη/, d.h. in Christus die wahre, die ewige Stiftshütte nahe herbeigebracht hat, so steht das eigentliche, universale, endgültige σκηνοῦν Gottes μετ'αὐτῶν (Apk. 21, 3) als endgeschichtlich doch noch aus." [Is there a παραβολὴ εἰς τὸν καιρὸν τὸν ἐνεστηκόα after Heb 9, 9, and whether the messianic presence has now also brought about in Christ the fulfilment of this παραβολη/, i.e., the true and eternal tabernacle in which the real, universal, and final σκηνοῦν of God is μετ'αὐτῶν (Rev 21, 3) endures until the eschaton.]

54. *Contra* Thompson, "Witness to the Word," 189f.

55. *ChD*, 60–64.

Word of the incarnate one, namely, Jesus Christ, who speaks and is heard as inalienably *subject* of absolute, unbound precedence and prevenience in and through the biblical witness.[56] To draw out the ontological force of the Reformed concept of divine-human dissimilarity in the unidirectional relation of the Spirit and Jesus to the biblical witnesses, we shall sidestep these sections to reserve space for a close reading of some crucial aspects of Barth's pneumatological understanding of Scripture's anthropological orientation in *Die Christliche Dogmatik im Entwurf.*

Die Christliche Dogmatik im Entwurf

"I was and I am an ordinary theologian, who does not have the Word of God at his disposal, but, at best, a 'Doctrine of the Word of God.'"[57] Thus Barth on his anthropological orientation in his first monograph in dogmatics. If common construal of his view of Scripture tends to perceive his scriptural and doctrinal orientation as domestication of divine action in the human,[58] we suggest that it is in part because it tends to overlook his Reformed concept of divine-human dissimilarity and the resultant emphasis on the externality of illumination, revelation, and Scripture.[59]

56. Ibid., 435–50; 461–74.

57. Ibid., 8.

58. Cf. J.W. Hart observes that even though "he is moving to the place where he can finally ground revelation in itself rather than on human possibilities," "Barth still makes an essential connection between revelation and humanity's existential situation" (Hart, *Karl Barth vs. Emil Brunner*, 86). Gogarten makes a similar point that Barth's episte-mological foundations might not be as different from that of Bultmann as Barth might think. Gogarten argues that there is a certain account of a phenomenologically posited divine-human relation as Barth's "fundamental, not only occasional" source for dogmat-ics (66–67) which orients Barth's "*pre*-understanding about the sense and possibility of dogmatics" (62), and indicates therefore Barth's hypocrisy against him and Bultmann for their ordering biblical exegesis to philosophy or the "Weltanschauung" (66–67). Gog-arten, "Karl Barths Dogmatik," 60–80. In a letter to Gogarten in 1922, Barth asked his friend, "*What* will be the authority through the authority of God's Word?" and shared his clear scepticism towards depicting a proper theological response to the question in the terms of the "I-Thou" community ("die 'Ich-Du'-Gemeinde"), for example, the social order of state, law, family, and so on. For Barth, that sort of concept of God is dangerous and self-defeating in combating against German idealism (Barth, 23 Dec 1922 in *Rudolf Bultmann-Friedrich Gogarten Briefwechsel 1921–1967*, 267–73).

59. Chung argues that here Barth's Reformed orientation is "more prominent" than it is in the Göttingen dogmatics. My contention is quite simply that Barth's self-described orientation to the Reformed needs to be kept in view in reading the *ChD* (Chung,

In this connexion, a key issue is whether or not Barth envisions any possibility of creaturely transference in, or domestication of, divine self-revelation in Scripture.[60] In response to this question, our answer is *negative*.[61] Our reading of §15.1–3 will show just how all this is so, by way of two interrelated points.

The first point concerns Barth's crucial distinction between the internal and external relations in the life of the triune God. In the light of the distinction, Barth stresses that Scripture's relation to Jesus is not to be read back into the Spirit's relation to the Word.[62] "The Word is there, where God himself is, namely, ἐν ἀρχῇ, in initio, in principio of everything that is."[63] The Word remains transcendent in his immanence in the created world: "That the Word is here, spoken and heard, takes no more and no less than God himself. *He* must speak it."[64] In short, "there is . . . no symbol of God— there are symbols for gods, but not for God" "because he lives and is utterly only in the first grammatical person" as "the inalienable subject," so that

---

Admiration and Challenge, 88–89). See also: M. Menke-Peitzmeyer's brief but perceptive observation of the Reformed character of Barth's doctrine of the Trinity in the ChD (Menke-Peitzmeyer, *Subjekitivität und Selbstinterpretation des dreifaltigen Gottes*, 276). Freudenberg is right that the Reformed Scripture Principle is key in the GD, ChD, and CD (Freudenberg, *Karl Barth und die reformierte Theologie*, 238–39).

60. See Frei, "An Afterword," 95–116 (esp. 101–8). Even though Frei makes a very perceptive observation on Barth's position on the relation between Word and human existence and on Bultmann's clear disagreement on the issue, here, ironically, he seems to downplay Barth's divine-human distinction between revelation and the biblical witnesses, between the Spirit and the reader, and between human speech-acts and God's speech-acts, and between God and the created world, by inflating the capacity or significance of human capacity for the incarnate one's ineffable presence and by reducing Scripture's divine content into creaturely categories.

61. Cf. Barth's christological primacy in his concept of divine-human dissimilarity in construing the priority and externality of illumination in Scripture's relation to the reader (*ChD*, 257f, 232–39, 245–56, 268–80, 289ff). See also Torrance's reading that Barth's appearance of having "the hearing man" "'co-posited' in the address of the Word of God" needs to keep in view of that for Barth "man" is understood *not* in generality but in the utter particularity of Jesus Christ as the Word (Torrance, *Karl Barth: An Introduction to His Early Theology*, 141–43).

62. Cf. *ChD*, 245f. Before turning fully to the theme of the incarnation, Barth speaks at great length on the Son's relation to the Father and the Spirit as fundamentally different from the Son's relation to the created world and secures, by way of an exegetical excursion to the prologue of John's Gospel, an important recognition of the absolute priority, pure deity, and sovereignty of God's inalienable immediacy in the doctrine of the Word.

63. Ibid., 245.

64. Ibid.

Barth finds any sort of ontological construal of a creaturely possibility of a *deus ex machina* problematic—a heresy characteristic of naturalist and historicist concepts of Scripture and the reader.[65]

Constructively, moreover, Barth's recognition of the Bible's human reality and creaturely elements as ingredient in theology's construal of the triune God's *opus ad extra* is crucial to his bibliological convictions about the priority and primacy of divine agency. He is convinced that only by virtue of the Spirit's work *a se* does the Word's contingent scriptural address come to our attention as the Spirit *pro nobis*.[66] The logical priority of the *gift* of the new humanity of Scripture and the reader is Barth's seminal point. God's mercy is wholly *contingent* upon the unity of his internal and external life, not *vice versa*: God's being is *his* freedom and decision absolutely. By contrast, his mercy is absolutely necessary to our life in relation to his and to who we are in relation to who he is.[67] Put differently, the doctrines of the Word's prevenience and precedence are two complementary aspects of the same idiom of the distinction between the ontological and economic Trinity:[68] "It is not revelation and reconciliation that create the Son, but the Son creates revelation and reconciliation."[69] By recognizing the biblical witness as God's external work, Barth can confidently indicate the externality of Holy Scripture as the Word, "He, the Word, is not nearly the naturally available and known relation of God to the world, the divine world-principle, of which Philo and his equals saw likewise, or the world

---

65. Ibid., 291. Cf. Williams rightly observes that Barth's concept of *extra calvinisticum* is ingredient in Barth's resistance to any form of *communicatio idiomatum* in the relation of revelation and Scripture, that the Word "must not need creation as a means of self-realization or self-interpretation," that Barth "wishes at all costs to avoid" a certain "anthropological determination" that has "a concept of revelation defined in advance of his exegesis" ("Barth on the Triune God," 147–93).

66. *ChD*, 257–63.

67. As McCormack puts it, "the Word does not have to be addressed to human beings to be what it is. The Word is what it is essentially as a result of the free communication which exists between the members of the godhead. That the Word is *also* directed to human beings is a fact but not a necessity" (McCormack, *Karl Barth's Critically Realistic Dialectical Theology*, 441).

68. Cf. Barth's extensional concept of "Fleischwerdung" (*ChD*, 290–99). Barth stresses that indicates the whole Godhead acts as subject in the "Menschwerdung": "the Father as 'fons actions,' the Son as his 'medium,' the Holy Spirit . . . as his 'terminus,'" arguing that the flesh which the Word assumed must be wholly human, that is, "he might then not be the revealer" but is rather of the sinful nature (Natur) of Adam (300–301).

69. Ibid., 257.

itself, if one still prefers rash speculation."[70] As Torrance puts it, revelation "cannot be perceived through the inspection of history, even of New Testament history, far less the history of the Church throughout the centuries."[71] Constructively, in the created world, Barth construes, "revelation-time is not any time, but revelation can be revealed any time."[72]

More closely—and this is the second point—the same creaturely delimitation to the Word's flesh in Barth's trinitarian concept of "Fleischwerdung" is crucial.[73] Barth stresses that the whole Godhead acts as subject in the "Menschwerdung": "the Father as 'fons actions,' the Son as his 'medium,' the Holy Spirit, . . . as his 'terminus,'" arguing that the flesh, which the Word assumed is the nature (Natur) of Adam,[74] "might . . . not be the revealer."[75] Christ's deity (Gottsein) and his humanity (Menschein) are neither to mix (vereinerleien) nor to separate: in Barth's view, theology is to construe the relation instead "as unity (Einheit) in the *dissimilarity* and as dissimilarity in the *unity*"[76] "as unity in the full unity of the act and recognition of revelation (Offenbarungserkenntnis)."[77] If Scripture's Jesus speaks and is heard only by virtue of the *whole* Godhead in action,[78] it also follows that

70. Ibid. Cf. In his objection to historical-critical method that trivializes the Word's claim of the text, Schmid perceptively observes, "The scientific character, the propriety of the ontological [question] like the hermeneutical question itself must be configured to the peculiarity of the object, not vice versa." (Die Wissenschaftlichkeit, die Sachgemäßheit der ontologischen wie der hermeneutischen Frage muß sich nach der Eigenart des Gegenstandes richten, nicht umgekehrt.) (Schmid, *Verkündigung und Dogmatik in der Theologie Karl Barths*, 117). *Contra* Kirchstein's reading which tends to overlook Barth's emphasis on the externality and contingency of revelation in relation to the biblical text (Kirchstein, *Der souveräne Gott und die heilige Schrift*, 167).

71. Torrance, *Karl Barth: An Introduction to His Early Theology*, 110.

72. *ChD*, 319.

73. Ibid., 290–99. Cf. Barth's corresponding self-delimitation in all human teachings and dogmas including the Chalcedonian formula (ibid., 364).

74. Ibid., 300–301.

75. Ibid., 299.

76. Ibid., 301.

77. Ibid.

78. Cf. Ibid., 311–13. "Offenbarung ist ein Mehr gegenüber jener ewigen Geschichte Gottes." As he identifies revelation *ad intra* as an "extension" (Mehr) to the "eternal event (Geschehen) between God Father, Son and Holy Spirit," Barth is construing the human person of the Nazarene as the Word's *special* provision to create (erschaffen) "a distinct I" as his "representative, his Platzhalter, his symbol to be in Geschichte," so that the human reception of Christ is contingent upon the Word's free use of this "distinct I," upon a *special* action of the whole Godhead.

Scripture is, as Barth construes it, a corollary of the ontological problem of Jesus Christ as God's absolute freedom as God-for-us,[79] the "doctrine of *anhypostasis* and *enhypostasis* of the human nature (Natur) of Christ."[80] In this sense, by the Spirit Scripture's "terminus a quo is the λόγος ἄσαρκος," Barth stresses, the Word *is* "wholly not object, not human, not flesh, but perfect subject, unrestricted (uneingeschränkt) God,"[81] so that to recognize the human reality of the biblical witnesses is to be moved and taught by divine address, in order to turn and stand "under a prayer: that in the revelation the true God becomes true human."[82]

From all this it is clear that, on Barth's reading, it is "not its character as 'Quelle' for the knowledge about the historical Jesus," "but its character as witness of [the Word made flesh] as that out of the conception of the Holy Spirit" that the church characterizes Scripture as *Holy* Scripture.[83] A prominent theme, moreover, is Barth's critique of the damaging eschatological[84] and hamartiological[85] deficits in historicist and naturalist bibliologies that are unable or unwilling to grasp the "pure mercy of God" in the "witness-character" of the "historical kernel of those statements" in the light of the historical revelation's essential dissimilarity to, and inaccessibility from, general history.[86] In Barth's words, "revelation . . . *as* Geschichte [is] decisively *more* than Geschichte."[87] Even though Barth's employment of the terms of "Urgeschichte" and "Übergeschichte" ap-

---

79. Ibid., 304–8, 362–64.

80. Ibid., 352.

81. Ibid., 364.

82. Ibid., 306. Barth will expound at length the concept of prayer as a soteriological orientation of a believer to God whose creative action is an ontic necessity that precedes and determines any noetic relation to revelation, Scripture and doctrine in his reading of Anselm in 1930. Cf. *Anselm*, 35ff.

83. *ChD*, 334.

84. Ibid., 276–77, 334, 341–46.

85. Ibid., 310–11, 326–33, 347–64.

86. In his reading of Barth's scriptural orientation, even though Frei is aware of the irreducibility of the history of revelation, he downplays (i) the dissimilarity between that special history and general history, and (ii) God's contingent action as gracious (external!) ground to the integrity not only of the text or its witness, but of readerly undertakings also. That sort of trivialization of the spiritual specificity of text-reader relation is a damaging distortion of Barth's soteriological view of Scripture. After indicating the literary and linguistic integrity of the Bible, Frei adds immediately, "but . . . that unlike any other depicted world it is the one common world in which we all live and move and have our being" (Frei, "An Afterword," 114).

87. Ibid., 311–12.

pears rather awkward and clumsy at times, we can easily see that he does not rely on it to sketch the doctrine of history because he has acquired greater resources from Reformed theology for his concept of God in the *Romans*. We can see, moreover, that he secures divine freedom and transcendence more basically and crucially by prefacing, qualifying, and enclosing the doctrine of history by a sophisticated doctrine of the Trinity and an increasingly precise, though no less self-critical, sketch of the nature of revelation in the economy of the Word. He accomplishes all this by way of regular excursions to the school of the Bible and his Reformed tutors as fellow readers of the scriptural text.

It is true that Barth did not always succeed in making his Reformed scriptural orientation sufficiently explicit. And a result is that the significance of his self-identification with the Reformed Scripture Principle is often downplayed in favour of a distorted picture of his concept of Jesus Christ that is disconnected from his pneumatological emphasis on illumination. In the *CD* I, Barth will reinforce his Reformed commitments in the *ChD* through a more precise construal of the human reality in Scripture, especially the soteriological character of the pneumatological relation of Jesus Christ to the biblical witnesses. For now, we shall simply note that with respect to his ontology of Scripture there is a picture of strong continuity between the *ChD* and *CD* I.

Summary

We began this chapter by suggesting the prominence of Barth's Reformed orientation to revelation as an ontological problem of the being of the *whole* Godhead in *action*. More than mere "dialectical opposition" between God and humanity,[88] we have seen Barth's *soteriological* emphasis on the concrete provisionality of Scripture's human reality as *simul justus et peccator* and creaturely elements as *creatura verbi divini*. His soteriological emphasis is visible in his expansive sketch of the Reformed primacy of illumination in the unidirectional relation of the Word's "Fleischwerdung" to Scripture's witness as externally characteristic of the eschatological, new existence of the biblical prophets and apostles in their old existence. In this connexion, we have seen that it was crucial to recognize Barth's distinction between the ontological and economic Trinity in the Word's relation to the Nazarene

---

88. Cullberg, *Das Problem der Ethik in der dialektischen Theologie I*, 38.

on the one hand and between the relation of the pure deity of the triune God to the humanity of Jesus and the relation of Jesus to creation on the other. With this sophisticated trinitarian characterization of revelation as divine action in time, Barth can identify a crucial distinction between the history of revelation and general history and between divine speech-acts and human speech-acts in Scripture, and can stress that Scripture's witness to revelation comes to us from, by and in none other than the Spirit's sanctifying illumination. As Torrance reflecting on Barth's observation of the externality of the Spirit and Scripture sums it up,

> It is through its unique relation to this speaking and acting God as the sovereign Lord of all that is, that the Bible is and becomes and is recognized to be what it *is* as "the Word of God." That is why the Bible is the Word of God before we know it to be so, for its truth as God's Word is not lodged in the Bible itself but in God from whom it comes and to whom it directs us.[89]

By understanding the external character of the objectivity of the relation of Jesus to Scripture, Barth can confidently indicate the Spirit's self-witness as characteristic of the truth of the biblical witness on the one hand, and the scriptural testimony as indicative of the Word's absolute freedom and prevenience on the other. In Schmid's words, "Through God's Word humanity is locked up in this dialogue, but humanity does not constitute the same independent presupposition which would somehow be ontologically or hermeneutically applied and methodologically analyzed."[90] If common construal mischaracterizes Barth's confidence as domestication of illumination in the Bible or the reader, it is in part because it often strangely overlooks his prominent Reformed scriptural and doctrinal orientation to (a) the biblical witnesses as the Spirit's "children of God" and (b) to their witness as canon, namely, the sign of Christ's commanding self-presence to the church. As Barth construes this twofold view of Scripture in the *CD* I/1, "God is Lord in the wording of his Word."[91] We shall see how this is so by turning now to the *CD* I.

---

89. Torrance, *Karl Barth: Biblical and Evangelical Theologian*, 90.
90. Schmid, *Verkündigung und Dogmatik in der Theologie Karl Barths*, 118.
91. *CD* I/1, 139.

4

Dominum et Vivificantem
Biblical Witnesses as Children of God

TO RECAPITULATE: OUR SKETCH of Barth's account of the Protestant Scripture Principle has been a partial treatment designed to orient our focused reading of his relevant lines of argument in the first volume of the *Church Dogmatics*. In examining the material our exposition shall be limited to, with a few exceptions, his characterization of the relation of divine agency to the human agency of the biblical witness. In general we shall avoid developmental questions concerning the relation of the *CD* I to relevant sections in the *GD* and *ChD* or a comprehensive sketch of the architecture and corresponding theological or hermeneutical significance of the first volume. Essential as these tasks are, excellent studies can be found elsewhere.[1] If our reading is plausible, certain common mischaracterizations of his relation to the Bible[2] as well as his anthropological

1. See, for example, Wood, *Barth's Theology of Interpretation*, 100–174; Webster, *Barth*, 49–74; Webster, *Holy Scripture*, 5–67. For thematic treatments of Barth's ontology: in relation to biblical interpretation as characteristic of *CD*, see Watson, "The Bible," 57–71; with respect to Barth's pneumatological characterization of Scripture, see Paddison, *Scripture*, 111; in relation to method and preaching in *CD* I, see Schmid, *Verkündigung und Dogmatik in der Theologie Karl Barths*, 145–80; in relation to Scripture, exegesis and ethics in *CD* I, see Nimmo, "Exegesis, Ontology and Ethics" 171–87; Nimmo, *Being in Action*, 17–40; in relation to relevant considerations regarding scriptural authority, inspiration and interpretation in conversation with evangelicalism, see McCormack, "The Being of Holy Scripture is in Becoming," 55–75; Vanhoozer, "A Person of the Book?," 26–59.

2. See, for example, Gibson's characterization of Barth's concept of biblical witness as "positing . . . the relationship between revelation and the Bible" (*Reading the Decree*, 185–88); Bentley's construal of Barth's concept of Scripture tends towards a direct identity between God's use of Scripture and the church's, *The Notion of Mission in Karl Barth's*

and pneumatological orientations,[3] we suggest, are problematic.[4] Just as problematic is a tendency to trivialize the polemics and "rhetorical directedness"[5] of his presentation of the Protestant Scripture Principle in relation to the church principle in the form of sixteenth-century Roman Catholicism and the "Christian principle" of Protestant modernism.[6] By contrast, one way to read his Protestant Scripture Principle, I argue, is to attend to Barth's account of God's soteriological primacy. On Barth's account, the primacy can be understood in terms of the Spirit's unidirectional, unbound relation to Scripture and the reader, a concrete relation that is "in virtue of the fact that Jesus Christ intercedes for us, taking our place before the Father, and in virtue of the illuminating and purifying work of the Holy Spirit upon us."[7] Put differently, as Barth writes, "Whatever God may say to us, it will at all events be said in this relationship of renewal," "this final, consummating, eschatological relation."[8] We stress that on Barth's reading, revelation is reconciliation:[9] "His presence by the Word is His presence of the coming One, coming for the fulfil-

---

Ecclesiology, 25–30; Bender strangely overlooks Barth's emphasis on the externality of Spirit and Scripture, "Scripture and Canon in Karl Barth's Early Theology," 183–84; likewise, McGlasson asserts that intrinsically "the text of the Bible, the language of its witness, is not distant from its divine Object," (*Jesus and Judas*, 41–43); like problems can be seen in Thompson's reading of revelation as intrinsic to the scriptural text in Barth, "Witness to the Word," 168–97; Vanhoozer's more sophisticated reading, "A Person of the Book?," 26–59, and Runia's, *Karl Barth's Doctrine of Holy Scripture*, 3; Wolterstorff's distortion of Barth's concept of Scripture's humanity, *Divine Discourse*, 63–74; Lauster's portrayal of Barth professing "a kind of hermeneutical immediacy," (*Prinzip und Methode*, 261); Kirchstein's talk of a concept of a creaturely analogy to divine aseity in Barth, *Der souveräne Gott und die Heilige Schrift*, 179–92; Runia, *Karl Barth's Doctrine of Holy Scripture*, 35.

3. Jenson, "You Wonder Where the Spirit Went," 296–304; Williams, "Barth on the Triune God," 147–93.

4. Barth's resistance to construing or practising dogmatics as the church's monologue or self-reflection is explicit (*CD* I/1, 105). "The Church is not alone in relation to God's Word. It is not referred to itself or consequently to self-reflection. It has not the confidence to appeal to itself as the source of the divine Word in support of the venture of proclamation" (100).

5. Wood, *Barth's Theology of Interpretation*, 101–4.

6. *CD* I/1, 258–59.

7. *CD* I/2, 700.

8. *CD* I/1, 142.

9. Cf. Wood, *Barth's Theology of Interpretation*, 108; Hunsinger, *Disruptive Grace*, chapter 7 (149).

ment and consummation of the relation established between Him and us in creation and renewed and confirmed in reconciliation."[10] We suggest that only in the light of its soteriological character can Barth's view of Scripture in *CD* I be properly grasped. With this in mind, we can begin by sketching Barth's account of the relation of divine agency to Scripture's human agency, in two ways.

The first way concerns Barth's construal of the new humanity of a *peccator justus* awaiting the parousia.[11] On his reading, in "the time between" and in Scripture and its readers, "[h]uman words are never final words."[12] Scripture's human witnesses in the "variety of their languages about the reality of revelation," Barth argues,

> are uttering only their penultimate word, not their ultimate. When they are uttering their ultimate word, they say the same thing. This ultimate word, however, is not a further thesis, not a synthesis, but just the name Jesus Christ. By naming Him, they want to let Him who is so named have the final word.[13]

Putting Barth's idea slightly differently, Scripture's relation to Jesus is contingent upon God's absolute freedom in his internal and external relations: If the Godhead is irreducible to human subjectivity,[14] it is in part because "God is no way bound to man": "His revelation is thus an act of His freedom."[15] The absolute freedom of the triune God in the self-revelation of Jesus Christ entails, on the part of all objects of his mercy,[16] his unqualified freedom to accept or to reject the biblical witnesses:[17] "Even as He gives

---

10. *CD* I/1, 142.

11. Ibid., 4–11.

12. Ibid., 142. Cf. The Spirit's economy in and through their eschatological humanity, Barth argues, "is to be understood only in terms of itself and not therefore in terms of a prior anthropology" or "an existential ontological possibility" (ibid., 42).

13. *CD* I/2, 24.

14. Williams, "Barth on the Triune God," 147–93

15. *CD* I/2, 7.

16. Cf. *CD* I/1, 131. Barth stresses that our relation to God is not to be read back into the God's relation to us: "we do not even know we are created merely from being created but only from the Word of God, from which we cannot deduce any independent, generally true insights that are different from God's Word and hence lead up to it."

17. Vanhoozer, "A Person of the Book?," 52 n. 122. Vanhoozer is correct insofar as that Scripture is bound to the Spirit's action and is therefore eschatological in nature (51–52) and purposiveness (52–53). But if Vanhoozer is correct, his assertion that "God in his freedom has tied himself to the biblical texts" (57–58) is questionable. *Contra*

Himself He remains free to give Himself afresh or to refuse Himself. This His new self-giving remains man's only hope."[18] This hope in Barth's view denotes a self-involving openness to God's saving relation to the biblical witnesses: "The New Testament speaks eschatologically when it speaks of man's being called, reconciled, justified, sanctified and redeemed."[19] Succinctly put, Scripture's humanity, on Barth's reading, points away from itself to Christ and refers the "whence" of Jesus first to the work of his Spirit "in such a way that all we think and say about it has its substance not in itself but outside itself in the Word of God, so that what we think and say about this how can never become the secret system of a what."[20] Constructively, Barth's construal of Scripture's eschatological humanity refers to its being sent as a sort of God's creaturely provision contingent upon "the divine creatio continua,"[21] a contingent means of God's "availing Himself of His freedom to come to us Himself in His Word and in His reserving to Himself the freedom to do this again and again."[22] It is Scripture "as an event, and in and with this event the Word

---

Vanhoozer, Barth stresses God's deity and sovereignty as his unqualified freedom with Scripture, as he writes, God "is Lord of the wording of His Word. He is not bound to it but it to Him. He has free control over the wording of Holy Scripture. He can use it or not use it. He can use it in this way or in that way . . . He can choose a new wording beyond that of Holy Scripture" (*CD* I/1, 139). Cf. *CD* I/2, 530–31, 695. For a fuller analysis of Vanhoozer's reading, see Wood, *Barth's Theology of Interpretation*, 142–43.

18. *CD* I/1, 324. Here Barth orients his notion of divine action to his reading of John 17: "God the Father is God who always, even in taking form in the Son, does not take form, God as the free ground and the free power of His being God in the Son. It would not be revelation within the bounds of the biblical witness if God did not also reveal Himself thus, as the Father. . . . God's fatherhood, too, is God's lordship in His revelation."

19. Ibid., 464. Cf. If in Scripture "[w]hat God and His Word are" "is something God himself must constantly tell us afresh," Barth stresses that "there is no human knowing that corresponds to this divine telling"—no "assuming of God's nature into man's knowing," but instead, "only a fresh divine telling" (ibid., 132).

20. Ibid., 164. In his reading of Barth, H. Hübner questions if the concept of the being of human as "outside" God's being is compatible with Act 17.28. He proposes rather: "Denn in aller Eindeutigkeit ist hier das *Sein des Menschen* als im *Sein Gottes* befindlich ausgesagt" (*Evangelische Fundamentaltheologie*, 82–83, emphasis and italics original). He goes on to argue for a dynamic anthropology for scriptural reading on the basis of this concept. To be fair, Hübner is right that in *CD* I Barth unequivocally rejects this deeply disturbing concept of God.

21. *CD* I/2, 688–89.

22. *CD* I/1, 139. Cf. Barth's concept of divine action is "not an ultimate 'assuring' but always a penultimate 'de-assuring' of theology, or . . . a theological warning against theology" whose ideas "are certain in themselves like the supposed axioms" of physical sciences, and therefore "are not related to their theme and content, which alone are

of God exercises its freedom," not Scripture as "a depositum" in the church, that Barth construes Scripture as a "witness to the coming God."[23]

Crucially, Scripture as a miraculous event of divine turning denotes "a free action and not a constantly available connexion, grace being the event of personal address and not a transmitted material condition."[24] If in his being and act God is wholly unbound to the human speech-acts in Scripture, Barth recognizes a formal reserve of the ontological Trinity from the economic Trinity who "can be seen and heard only as the active God."[25] From this it also follows that if God's absolutely free being is characteristic of his action, "[t]his God is not only a God of action," Barth argues, "as the founding of the Sabbath tells us with special beauty. He can not only work; He can also rest from all his works."[26] For Barth, Scripture's divine employment, as with its reception, is contingent upon "a fresh divine telling."[27] Another way to underscore the point about God's absolute freedom with the whole creation is the concept of divine aseity, as Barth writes, "God Himself is in the act": "There is no one and nothing above Him and no one and nothing beside Him, either on the right hand or the left, to condition Him or to be in a nexus with Him. God is a se. This is unreservedly true of His Word."[28] As *creatura verbi divini*, in short: "Even the biblical witnesses themselves cannot and do not try to introduce revelation of themselves."[29]

If and when God deploys the biblical witnesses—and this is the second way—Barth characterizes their person as "a specific subject and being" that "does not subsist of itself, but only in a specific doing."[30] Only in their work

---

certain, which they cannot master, by which they must be mastered" (ibid., 164–65).

23. *CD* I/2, 113.

24. *CD* I/1, 41.

25. Ibid., 332–34, 384–98. Barth is suggesting not that God can be known outside of his works, but rather that even in his actions God's deity is utterly pure.

26. Ibid., 322.

27. Ibid., 132. Hence for Barth there is also no going behind or beyond divine revelation in the concept of divine freedom. Cf. ibid., 305. "God's revelation has its reality and truth wholly and in every respect—both ontically and noetically—within itself. Only if one denies it can one ascribe to it another higher or deeper ground or try to understand and accept or reject it from the standpoint of this higher or deeper ground." Cf. Nimmo, "Exegesis, Ontology and Ethics," 177, 186–87. See also, McCormack, "The Being of Holy Scripture is in Becoming," 55–75 (esp. 66).

28. *CD* I/1, 157.

29. *CD* I/2, 483.

30. Ibid., 369. Notably in the moving §18, "The Life of the Children of God." Moreover, the specificity of their "intention and bearing" (their person) and of their "action

the biblical witnesses are what they are in Christ. We will return to the notion of their ministry or work momentarily. To put Barth's notion of their person slightly differently, he stresses that the peccator justus has his person and vocation, not from himself, but "'from outside,' that is from God":[31] from the Father through the Word in the outpouring of the Holy Spirit.[32] A net effect of all this is a pneumatological construal of the hidden, sanctified person of the biblical witnesses in Christ. Constructively, by recognizing the soteriological relation of their human light to the divine Light of the Holy Spirit of the triune God, Barth can confidently indicate the due weight of their humanity in virtue of revelation in the Spirit's light that I here call "illumination":

> The Christian in *abstracto* we must avoid—the Christian in *concreto* we cannot avoid. It is to him that the Word of God is directed and the gift of the Holy Spirit is made, and upon him that the light of revelation falls. We cannot see this light, which is, of course, always and exclusively the light of God, without seeing the man as well.[33]

In illumination, moreover, "seeker" is characteristic of a biblical witness who is borne to us in a relation in which, Barth argues, "God creates men who do not exist unless they seek Him, and who cannot cease to testify that He has found them."[34] Their testimony and work are a seeking-after-God—a confessing act of their new person in the old, as Barth writes: "What is essentially 'Christian' in this life and doing and not doing can only be the declaration: He and not I! He and not we! He, the Lord! He for us! He in our stead!"[35] The "declaration" of God's primacy and priority is a human work being underwritten by Christ's life-giving Spirit and being carried out by the writer's new person in the old who is "still a sinful creature" "afterwards as well as before."[36] "In face of the sin and death, from which he has come, as a real justus peccator," Barth stresses, "he can only live out and reveal and attest his salvation" by God who "compels him to do this work of revealing

---

and its effect" (their work) refers to the specificity of a *peccator justus* for whom, Barth stresses, neither her person nor her work "can exist without the other any more than being without doing, or doing without being."

31. Ibid., 368.

32. Ibid., 362–71.

33. Ibid., 364; cf. 465.

34. Ibid., 368.

35. Ibid., 368.

36. Ibid., 375.

and attesting and confessing."[37] The precedence and prevenience of God's work is Barth's seminal point.

> When we say man himself, the whole man, we come to what is in fact both in James and also in Paul, not the strict, mathematical centre (which can only be the name of Jesus Christ and faith in Him), but the central area which necessarily circumscribes and indicates that centre: the man who comes necessarily and totally under a new determination is the ἐν Χριστῷ, the man who is the object of that divine act, the man who believes in Jesus Christ. His existence under this determination, his existence therefore under the determination of Jesus Christ and faith in Him, is what Paul so strikingly describes as his work or works.[38]

Thus Barth on the person and work of the biblical witnesses as objects of "the unique love of God for us"[39] in Jesus Christ:[40] Their person, that is, who they are, precedes their decision and action. Their action and decision cannot be grasped apart from their whole person in Christ.

Succinctly put, the objectivity of "the whole man" of the biblical witness comes to our attention, only in Christ and radically outside of the witness himself. If the apostolic faith is "faith in Him," Barth argues: "It is not the case that the time between the ascension and the second coming is to some extent the kingdom of the believing man autonomous in and by virtue of his faith."[41] From this it also follows that it is false that the biblical witness has no referent.[42] On the contrary, as "a sign of what God as the one Lord has done and is for us" the witness of the Bible is "a work . . . in the

---

37. Ibid., 371.

38. Ibid., 367.

39. Ibid., 375.

40. Ibid., 366–67.

41. Ibid., 692–93. Cf. A. Burgess is right that in the "time between" the Spirit's sanctifying work and corresponding created means—among which the biblical canon is unique—is "the determinative context for the nature of the church" (*The Ascension in Karl Barth*, 56). If by the Spirit the significance of church ministry is derived from the significance of the ministry of Scripture, the proper reader can attend to both ecclesial tradition and the biblical canon without trivializing the Spirit's primacy in them. If our reading is plausible, certain recent variations of the reader-principle appear problematic. See for example, K.A. Richardson's thoughtful argument for a reader principle in the relation between Scripture and ecclesial tradition (*Reading Karl Barth*, 99–106).

42. *Contra* Smith, *What is Scripture*, 237.

fact that it is the witness of God's work, and therefore a renunciation of all self-glorifying and all claims."[43]

> Indeed, what God in His love wills from us to His glory is that our existence in the determination which we ourselves give to it should be a sign of the fact that we stand under His predetermination. The fulness of His love is not only that He rescues us from the sin and death to which we should fall victim if left in the determination which we would have given ourselves, but that He claims us for the proclamation of His glory.[44]

Thus Barth on this claim as God's reconciling recreation and redeeming renewal of the "whole man" of the biblical prophets and apostles.

On Barth's reading, God claims the witnesses "for the proclamation of His glory" as God-for-us in the "fulness of His love." This love, Barth argues, is not a necessity by which God is bound, but free mercy of which God is and has shown himself capable through Christ by his Spirit.[45] His Light in their light is his pure mercy. "If God uses man, it is only in the service of His kindness to man."[46] That also to say that "we cannot perceive and understand love in those 'acts' in which it is offered or not offered to God, but only in the being of man as determined in faith by the Word and the Holy Spirit,"[47] "only as man's answer to what God has said to him" in the light of "the meaning and the content of the revealing, manifesting, attesting, confessing, living out and showing forth of the lordship and redemption which has come to the children of God."[48] "In Holy Scripture the love of God to us speaks the language of this fact—the

---

43. Ibid., 401.

44. Ibid.

45. *Contra* Wolterstorff whose reading of the *CD* I tends to overlook the soteriological orientation in Barth's construal of the biblical witnesses (*Divine Discourse*, 63–74). Cf. *CD* I/2, 433. "The crucified Jesus Christ," writes Barth, "does not contract out of the mediatorial position which He adopted in His resurrection and ascension. He does not, therefore, contract out of that solidarity and identity with sinful and afflicted fellow-man, in which as neighbour He crosses the path of His own." For Barth, Scripture's inability to effect "the fulfilment of revelation, the imparting of the Word and Spirit of God" is characteristic of the biblical witness, a divine-human ontic-noetic demarcation that "we cannot try to transcend . . . without destroying its nature as witness" (444).

46. *CD* I/2, 380.

47. Ibid., 400. *Contra* Cullberg, *Das Problem der Ethik in der dialektischen Theologie I*, 38.

48. *CD* I/2, 401.

fact of His election, guidance, help and salvation."[49] The new humanity of the biblical witnesses, Barth argues, "is denied any other being than that which consists in the specific act of seeking": a witness to Christ is first and finally an object of God's action a se—a seeker and follower of Christ in, by and through the Spirit *pro nobis*. A seeker "is forced out of every other being and forced into that of being a seeker after God, and after God in Christ,"[50] "the bearer of their shame and curse."[51]

A net effect of the construal of the seeker is the prominence of Barth's account of the soteriological primacy of the unqualified freedom, externality, and sovereign mercy of the whole Godhead. Barth understands the prophetic and apostolic seekers as no more than witnesses and their seeking as no less than their appeal to illumination by confessing that they are neither the Spirit nor the Christ.[52] More specifically, by "seeking" Barth means:

> from the standpoint of the reconciliation and justification effected in Him [Christ], it means that, bearing our punishment, achieving the obedience we did not achieve and keeping the faith we did not keep, He acted once and for all in our place. We cannot, therefore, seek our own being and activity, so far as they still remain to us, in ourselves but only in Him. Strictly speaking, our being and activity as such can only be this seeking. . . . Our own being and activity stands wholly and utterly under this judgement. . . . Yet this being and activity acquires a direction at the point where everything is done for us, the direction Godward in Jesus Christ. And this is no special work. It is far more. It is the work of all works. It is no special miracle. It is far more. It is the miracle of all miracles. And as such it is the simplest necessity of nature: even more necessary than breath to our body. . . . What matters is emphatically not the

---

49. Ibid., 378.

50. Ibid., 370.

51. Ibid., 382.

52. If our reading is plausible, any talk of divine-human correspondence or domestication of the divine monarchy in Scripture is, in Barth's view, profoundly problematic. *Contra* Moltmann, *Experience in Theology*, 139–40. Moltmann's reading of the "monarchical trinitarian order" tends to relativize the unidirectional character of the order of revelation-scripture-proclamation, characterizing the order as a "biblical-hermeneutical circle" permanently identified with the text and the reader. Cf. *CD* I/2, 400. Barth's refutation of the problematic domestication of a "supernatural quality, a 'habitus'" by way of a direct identity between the human spirit and the Holy Spirit, between the person of the incarnate Word and the person of the biblical witnesses.

> fact that we are seeking. What matters is that if we accept and adopt this direction, we are always seekers.[53]

Thus Barth on seeker as characteristic of the biblical witnesses. Succinctly put, they can be what "they are as the children of God if . . . they are surrounded and borne along by the mercy of God"—to be his "counterpart in the world which now is and passes," his "bearer and representative of this temporal as well as eternal mercy of God" in the work of "proclaiming and showing forth Jesus Christ"[54] in their anticipation of the parousia. On Barth's reading, the work of their new person in their old one comes under the theme of the soteriological primacy of Spirit's eschatological work in and through their humanity. "What they do is the purest form of that work of divine mercy which is assumed by the children of God. They bear witness to Jesus Christ. In that way they order the praise of the children of God; they make it possible as a real praise of the real God."[55] In short: "They will praise God, according to the will of God."[56]

Our sketch of the soteriological emphasis of his concept of the unbound free act of the triune God in and through the eschatological humanity of the biblical witnesses is a way of orienting our reading of Barth's more expansive concept of Scripture in *CD* I/2. If our sketch is plausible, his famous concepts of canon and witness, we suggest, cannot be grasped properly apart from "the evangelical attitude" of the biblical writers as children of God. On Barth's reading, this is an "attitude" characteristic of those who "have actually been helped in Jesus Christ" "as the Helper" and the "help from without,"[57] "the only attitude which we can regard as consistent with witness."[58] Put differently, his concepts of canon

53. *CD* I/2, 391–92.

54. Ibid., 421–22.

55. Ibid., 422. They come to us "for the proper praise of God within this world," crucially not "by self-will, but only by mercy."

56. Ibid., 433.

57. Ibid., 444–45. *Contra* Abraham's construal of a domestication of revelation in "canonical materials, persons, and practices" (29, 467). *Canon and Criterion in Christian Theology*, 363–90 (esp. 367); similarly, *contra* Vickers, "Canonical Theism and the Primacy of Ontology," 159–60, 173. For an example of a trivialization of Barth's soteriological externality of the biblical canon, see Bender, "Scripture and Canon in Karl Barth's Early Theology," 165–80.

58. *CD* I/2, 447. Witness is also characteristic of their commanded work as sanctified love to the neighbour. "Love to the neighbour is weighed, not measured. We are nowhere dispensed either from the great thing, if it is a matter of the great, or from the small, if a

and witness can be described as corollaries of his concept of "divine present" as the Spirit's help to Christ's saints, a soteriological concept around
which, he argues, "the whole doctrine of Holy Scripture circles."[59] We can
sketch his argument in §19.2 and his focused reading of 2 Timothy and 2
Peter, in two interrelated ways.

The first way concerns Barth's construal of the Pauline[60] characterization of the unidirectional relation of the "outbreathing" of the Spirit of God
to Scripture and its readers.[61] As he identifies πᾶσα γραφὴ θεόπνευστος
(2 Tim. 3.16) as Paul's indication of the Spirit himself as the agent of "the
power of the truth of the fact that the Spirit of God is before and above and
in Scripture,"[62] Barth is stressing that the objectivity of the Spirit's relation
to Scripture "cannot be expanded" but is that "to which," for Paul, "only
a—necessarily brief—reference can be made."[63]

Barth does not say the Spirit is mere "power." Rather, the Spirit is the
Spirit's own agent; his relation to Scripture is the mystery of his agency, the
power of his mystery. But his mystery is not mere power, for the Spirit's
agency is irreducible to human agency, or his action to its effect. Neither

---

matter of being faithful in that which is the least. Everything must be done by us at the
right time and in the right place: everything with the clear knowledge that we are unable
even to give the sign, let alone to make it effective, to bring the help which it attests; but
everything with the even clearer knowledge that we are required to give the sign, and to
give it in deed as well as in word, that from the one motive of real obedience we will be
content with the promise; and that therefore as far as we understand and are able there
must be this helping, lightening, comforting, and bringing of joy, and it is our task. If
it does take place, and, quite apart from any claim, if we are in a position to cause it to
happen, why should we not be confident to bear witness to Jesus Christ to our neighbour
in this second form, the form of our little assistance, and therefore be obedient to the
commandment to love him?" In this sense, Barth construes the biblical witnesses by way
of their indication of a total "subjection to the lordship of Jesus Christ, of the comfort
of forgiveness, by which I myself live, of the liberty of the children of God in which I
myself move." Moved by the Spirit they proclaim Christ as he from whom their (and our)
help, in God's mercy, has come and is to come, and to whose advents they devote their
attention, direct their indication, and command their neighbours to do likewise—to love
and praise the Helper with God's help unreservedly as our derived love to "the neighbour" properly understood. *Contra* Wolterstorff's soteriologically deficit in his reading
of Barth's concept of the biblical witnesses in *Divine Discourse*, 63–74.

59. *CD* I/2, 503.

60. Ibid., 503–6. Barth is aware of the complex issue of the epistle's authorship.

61. Ibid., 504.

62. Ibid., 504–5, 515–17.

63. Ibid., 504.

is the criticism of Barth's alleged "Spirit-avoidance"[64] plausible in the face of the text. What Barth avoids is rather a direct identity between the Spirit and the Spirit's work—in significant part because Barth wishes to speak of the Spirit's agency in terms of none other than God's pure deity. To be clear, Barth does not wish to speak of the Spirit's agency in terms of human agency including the human agency of Scripture, still less the human agency of the church. Barth's avoidance of any confusion between divine agency and human agency is not "Spirit-avoidance," a criticism that apparently says more of the critic's pneumatology than of Barth's. Rather, a net effect of all this is Barth's understanding of the relation of the Spirit to Scripture as unidirectional or, in his word— "inaccessible."[65] To paraphrase Barth's datum from his landmark lecture, "Das Schriftprinzip der reformieten Kirche": To speak of the Spirit of God can only mean to let the Spirit of God speak.[66]

If Barth does not isolate the power and economy of the Spirit from the mystery of the whole Godhead, it is in part because Barth is uninterested in subordinating one divine person to another in the presence and work of God, and in part because Barth does not reduce the objectivity of the Spirit to mere human subjectivity.[67]

Negatively put, if God's deity sets the delimitations to all human thinking and speaking of the Spirit and the Spirit's relation to Scripture, Barth thinks that "all that we have to say about [the relation] can consist only in an underlining and delimiting of the inaccessible mystery of the free grace in which the Spirit of God is present and active before and above and in the Bible."[68] To put the delimitation slightly differently, no human construal of the Spirit is to be read back into the Spirit's relation to creatures, for God's absolute freedom is characteristic of the Spirit's contemporaneous presence "before and above and in Scripture,"[69] as Barth writes,

> we cannot attain to it of ourselves any more than we can . . . to the unity of Scripture. If it desires and wills to come, taking place

64. Jenson, "You Wonder Where the Spirit Went," 296–304 (esp. 302, 304).

65. *CD* I/2, 504.

66. "Das Schriftprinzip," 508. "To speak of God can only mean to let God speak."

67. Williams, "Barth on the Triune God," 147–93.

68. *CD* I/2, 504.

69. Cf. *CD* I/1, 139. "God is Lord of the wording of His Word. He is not bound to it but it to Him. He has free control over the wording of Holy Scripture. He can use it or not use it. He can use it in this way or in that way."

within our own encircling exposition—well, it will simply do so, and it will do so the more strongly and gloriously the less we interfere with our clumsy and insolent attempts to attain to it. It is when we are clear that in all our exposition we can only think and explain this event, that we are equally clear that for our part we can never do more than think and explain it. All the possible denials and dissolutions of this present into all kinds of pasts and futures have their source in the fact that this present is not respected as the divine present. It is thought that we can and should turn everything upside down and treat this present as a created human present which we can seize and control.[70]

Thus Barth on Scripture's divine-human demarcation; and on the unbound mystery of the Godhead in the Spirit's relation to the Bible and the reader.[71]

Put differently, moreover, "to look on [the prophets and apostles] . . . always means, to look on Him who has sent them."[72] If our recognition of the God of the prophets and apostles is always his grace, it also follows that the 'divine present' is best described as a pure negation: "the present," Barth indicates, is that "for which we have no word, over which we have no power, of which as such we cannot say anything except this extravagant 'has' and 'is.'"[73] Constructively, what Scripture is concerns "something which has already been formed and given."[74] Once again, for Barth human words and decisions are penultimate and never final: "It is only rhetorically that we call it 'holy' Scripture."[75]

---

70. *CD* I/2, 503; cf. 502: the soteriological emphasis on the externality of "the divine present" is characteristic of Barth's constructive vision of the church's orientation to Scripture as θεόπνευστος. He advises that in our theological characterization of Scripture, "we must first replace the 'has' by a 'had' and 'will have,' and the 'is' by a 'was' and 'will be.' It is only as expounded in this way that the two words correspond to what we can actually know and say: we who are not in a position to carry through that divine disposing, action and decision or to handle them as thought they were ours."

71. Cf. *CD* I/1, 259. If "the Bible whose supremacy we could establish would obviously not be the free Bible," Barth stresses the Bible in Spirit's commanding use as "the Bible that is not yet interpreted, the free Bible, the Bible that remains free in face of all interpretation." *Contra* Ward, less is to be expected from construing Scripture in terms of "what kind of a thing a text in general *is*" (*Word and Supplements*, 137).

72. *CD* I/2, 492.

73. Ibid., 503. That is not to say that we overlook Barth's emphasis on Scripture's humanity, but that instead we stress his characterization of the sort of human persons that the biblical witnesses are in the economy of revelation and salvation.

74. Ibid., 473.

75. Ibid., 497.

If we ascribe to it the character of Holy Scripture, we can do so only because we remember at least its witness to revelation and the event of its prophetic-apostolic function. We can do so only because we reconcile ourselves to its effective power of command, as we ourselves recognise and acknowledge it to be effective. We can do so only as we reconcile ourselves to it, not as one of the living powers and forces of Christian history, but as the one power and force which has created and bears and rules the Church and with it all Christian history, which therefore confronts as the critical norm the Church and all the forces active in the sphere of the Church . . . . It is only in virtue of this separation of itself that the Bible can be set apart. But in virtue of it, it is actually and truly and radically set apart. The objection is to hand: To what extent after all can and should an historical quantity like the Bible be given this basic priority over against all other historical quantities? When the Christian Church makes the act of remembrance and the corresponding self-reconciliation, in which it gives to the Bible the authority of Holy Scripture, and expects to hear in the Bible and only in the Bible the Word of God, does there not take place something which cannot be squared with the majesty of God: the absolutising of a relative, that is, of a word which is always human, and which cannot stand side by side with the One who Himself is and wills to be God alone? And if it cannot do that, as a relative does it not belong to the other relatives of our human cosmos? Does it not belong, in fact, as something which can be compared although it has not yet perhaps been excelled, to that series in which Neo-Protestantism and in another way [sixteenth-century] Roman Catholicism can see it? Does not the Protestant principle attribute too much to the Bible, and too little to God Himself on the one hand, and to all other witnesses of His revelation on the other? The answer is that there is indeed only one single absolute fundamental and indestructible priority, and that is the priority of God as Creator over the totality of His creatures and each of them without exception.[76]

Thus Barth on a key, ecumenical conviction in "the Evangelical Scripture principle" in that, negatively, "nothing was absolutised and no one divinised."[77] Constructively, "the absolute, no, God was present in His Word as the Lord, as the One who commands and the One who shows mercy, as

76. Ibid., 497–98.
77. Ibid., 499.

in the human word of the Bible."[78] The "human words of the Bible" are human by divine mercy and borne to us by God's commanding presence.[79] Succinctly put, "the presence the Word of God itself, the real and present speaking and hearing of it, is not identical with the existence of the book as such,"[80] for it is "the event of what God Himself decides and wills and does in divine freedom and superiority and power."[81] The mystery of God as God-for-us is the mystery of God's agency as Creator and Redeemer. That is Barth's seminal point. In short:

> According to the Bible, the in itself unthinkable coexistence of absolute and relative is made possible by the fact that it does not speak of the absolute but of the goodness and patience of the Creator of all things revealed to us in Jesus Christ, nor does it speak of the relative, but of the creatures of this Creator.[82]

On Barth's reading—and this is the second way—two key characteristics of the biblical witnesses as creatures of the self-announced presence of God are visible. The first characteristic concerns their new person as a free human subject by the virtue of the mystery of the pure deity of the agency of God. For Barth, only in the light of God's pure deity can their pure humanity and their unidirectional relation to the Spirit be grasped. God is unbound to them but they are bound to God. They exist as free, genuine human persons only by virtue of divine turning. They owe their office and ministry to the Spirit's active rule in and over themselves as well as their readers, but not to human valuation including their own,[83] so that the Holy Spirit "indeed in such a way that He is described as the real author of what is stated or written in Scripture."[84] Barth does not suggest that the Spirit's authorship is identical with the authorship of the biblical witnesses. Rather, the theme of authorship denotes a distinction between agents and between offices, a twofold distinction that is essential to their relation. The

---

78. Ibid.

79. Ibid., 473. "If what we hear in Holy Scripture is witness, a human expression of God's revelation," Barth suggests that "what we hear in the witness itself is more than witness, what we hear in the human expression is more than a human expression. What we hear is revelation, and therefore the very Word of God."

80. Ibid., 530.

81. Ibid., 503.

82. Ibid., 498.

83. *Contra* Smith, *What is Scripture*, 237.

84. *CD* I/2, 505.

themes of their authorship and office are derived from the themes of the authorship and office of the Spirit as their maker and their light. The point is visible in Barth's reading of 2 Pet 1.19–21: by the Spirit the light of their sanctified humanity

> is our light in a dark place, when it is not made the object of an ἰδία ἐπίλυσις: i.e., when we allow it to expound itself, or when we allow it to control and determine our exposition. This is because, as the text goes on, it is not given "by the will of men", but in it men spoken as they were "moved by the Holy Ghost", ὑπὸ πνεύματος ἁγίου φερόμενοι, they spoke "from God" (ἀπὸ Θεοῦ).[85]

Thus Barth on Scripture's "inspiration" as originating from, and coming to our attention by, "the miracle of the grace of God to sinners, and not the idle miracle of human words which were not really human words at all," "the miracle" that "is the foundation of the dignity and authority of the Bible."[86] Once again, the theme of the mystery of the Godhead in the agency and work of the Spirit is Barth's seminal point.

More closely, writing and speaking ἀπὸ Θεοῦ, the Spirit's "moved" or inspired writers crucially "lived then and there and not here and now," so that their writing "like every human action, an act conditioned by and itself conditioning its temporal and spatial environment." From this it also follows that, Barth argues, "the prophets and apostles do . . . exist for us only in what they have written."[87] What was "written" by their new person is borne

85. Ibid., 504–5.

86. Ibid., 530. Cf. Demson, *Hans Frei and Karl Barth*. He argues that in contrast to Frei, "Barth gives a wider sense and a content to *inspiration*. The New Testament texts describe the gathering, upholding, and sending of the apostles. Belief in inspiration is the belief that the New Testament texts arise out of and ever cohere in this gathering, upholding, and sending of the apostles by Jesus—they are exponents of it. Belief in inspiration is belief that Jesus actually gathered, upheld, and sent these men and continues to gather, uphold, and send many by making these many participants in the threefold chosenness of the apostles. There is a distinction, but no gap, between the text and what it describes in this regard. There is a distinction in that Jesus, not the text, executes this threefold choosing of many, but there is no gap in that what Jesus does and what the text describes him as doing are one, for Jesus ever utters his own Word as the Word of the appointment, calling, and commissioning of many. Even as in the text he appointed, called, and commissioned the apostles, he appoints calls, and commissions many (or all) by way of the apostles' testimony to his threefold choosing of them. That is Barth's account of inspiration" (109). While Demson draws his evidence largely from the later volumes of the *CD*, his masterful argument holds true for our account of Barth's doctrine of inspiration as well.

87. *CD* I/2, 505.

to us penultimately and contingently, so that their uniqueness corresponds as such to the uniqueness of "the act of revelation in which the prophets and apostles in their humanity became what they were, and in which alone in their humanity they can become to us what they are."[88] For Barth, the eschatological notion of their "becoming" comes under the pneumatological theme of Christ's "Fleischwerdung."[89]

> As to when, where and how the Bible shows itself to us in this event as the Word of God, we do not decide, but the Word of God decides, at different times in the Church and with different men confirming and renewing the event of instituting and inspiring the prophets and apostles to be His witnesses and servants, so that in their written word they again live before us, not only as men who once spoke in Jerusalem and Samaria, to the Romans and Corinthians, but as men who in all the concreteness of their own situation and action speak to us here and now. We can know that in the life of the Church, and indeed in its life with the Bible, it is a matter of this decision and act of God or rather the actualisation of the act of God which took place once and for all in Jesus Christ. In the whole Bible it is always a matter of this act.[90]

Succinctly put, only in light of their whole humanity "of what they had to say and write as eye-witnesses and ear-witnesses"[91] to the Spirit life-giving "actualisation of the act of God which took place once and for all in Jesus Christ" can we begin to grasp the Spirit's gift of their distinction from and relation to the readers.[92]

> The Bible as witness of divine revelation comes to every man, all men, and in a measure includes them in itself. Rightly understood, all humanity, whether it is aware of it or not, does actually stand in the Bible, and is therefore itself posited as a witness of divine revelation. But that this is the case is made possible and conditioned by the fact that in the first instance not all men but certain specific

88. Ibid., 508.

89. Cf. *ChD*, 290–99.

90. *CD* I/2, 531.

91. Ibid., 505.

92. The point about the indivisibility of Scripture's sanctified instrumentality and uniqueness with respect to all other human literature is well stated by Berkouwer. *Holy Scripture*, 139–94. The concept of "*theopneustos* points to an essential relationship between the breath of the Spirit and the graphê. This is the mystery of Scripture which the church desired to express in its confession. This mystery is the uniqueness through which Holy Scripture in all its humanity was distinguished from all other human writing" (140).

men stand in the Bible: that is, the men who in face of the unique and contingent revelation had the no less unique and contingent function of being the first witnesses. Because there were and still are those first witnesses, there could and can be second and third witnesses. We cannot speak about Yahweh's covenant with Israel without at once speaking of Moses and prophets. Similarly in the New Testament, indissolubly bound up with Jesus Christ, there are the figures of His disciples, His followers, His apostles, those who are called by Him, the witnesses of His resurrection, those to whom He Himself has directly promised and given His Holy Spirit. The Church can say anything at all about the event of God and man only because something unique has taken place between God and these specific men, and because in what they wrote, or what was written by them, they confront us as living documents of that unique event. To try to ignore them is to ignore that unique event. The existence of these specific men is the existence of Jesus Christ for us and for all men. It is in this function that they are distinguished from us and from all other men, whom they resemble in everything else.[93]

Thus Barth on their uniqueness and common eschatological humanity with the saints,[94] and on the Spirit's life-giving animation as formative of the instrumentality of their written witness as canon in virtue of God's use of it.

A free divine decision is made. It then comes about that the Bible, the Bible in *concreto*, this or that biblical context, i.e., the Bible as it comes to us in this or that specific measure, is taken and used as an instrument in the hand of God, i.e., it speaks to and is heard by us as the authentic witness to divine revelation and is therefore present as the Word of God. It is present in a way we cannot conceive.[95]

Notice Barth stressing a theological subordination of epistemic issues concerning Scripture to the ontological force of the eschatological humanity of the biblical prophets and apostles.[96] Succinctly put, the ontological question of Scripture—for instance, a proper theological characterization of what it is by regeneration—has logical priority over epistemological questions. In discerning what Scripture is in God's use of it, the church, Barth argues,

93. *CD* I/2, 486.

94. Cf. Berkouwer. *Holy Scripture*, 139–94.

95. *CD* I/2, 530.

96. *Contra* Abraham's reading of Barth's scriptural orientation as a sort of project to secure a "criterion of truth which is internal to theology itself" (*Canon and Criterion in Christian Theology*, 367).

"can do so only to the best of its knowledge and judgement, in the venture and obedience of faith, but also in all the relativity of a human knowledge of the truth which God has opened up to them."[97] Scripture-reading is a creaturely act of discipleship directed by the life-giving Spirit as Lord of the reader and the text. Likewise, Scripture's self-described relation to God in Jesus Christ "are," Barth stresses, "not guarantees," but, as genuinely human, "can only be an assurance,"[98] "[f]or," in short: "the Bible is a sign which, it cannot be contested, does at least point to a superior authority confronting the proclamation of the Church."[99]

Borne to the saints by the self-announced presence of Christ's commanding Spirit—and this is the second key characteristic—the canon is "a sign of the promised help of God" in "Jesus Christ as the Helper,"[100] a sign of "the lordship of the triune God in the incarnate Word by the Holy Spirit."[101] By stressing the concrete character of the Spirit's help and the logical priority of regeneration, Barth can recognize the due weight of human factors in the complex process of the canon's composition and reception as episodes in the history of salvation and sanctification. A net result of Barth's view is a self-critical caution against imposing any human criterion of the divine or the human over Scripture,[102] for bound inescapably to regeneration, proper recognition of God's relation to us in Scripture is neither unaided nor spiritually neutral.[103] It is not the canon as a sign of a sort of "coinherence of Bible and church"[104] or a sort of consubstantiation between the biblical

97. *CD* I/2, 473. In this sense, "knowledge of priority of God" is best described as "the knowledge of the divine benefit" (499).

98. Ibid., 453.

99. Ibid., 457.

100. Ibid., 447.

101. Ibid., 457.

102. Berkouwer, *Holy Scripture*, 70. "He who approaches the canon from a perspective which sharply differentiates between the divine and the human, will not even recognize the validity of speaking about a canonical 'problem'; for in such a view the divine definitely rules out the possibility of a problem. The result is the apparent failure to appreciate the fact that human considerations did play a large role in the formation of the canon."

103. Ward, *Word and Supplements*, 137. *Contra* Ward, less is to be expected from construing Scripture in terms of "what kind of a thing a text in general *is*."

104. Lindbeck, "Scripture, Consensus, and Community," 78. Neither is Barth's canon a sign of self-described, "authorized" readers or "authorized interpretation of the sacred text," a sign of human self-entitlement to revelation, *contra* Wolterstorff, *Divine Discourse*, 224–25. Likewise, *contra* Abraham's construal of a domestication of revelation in

writers, the scriptural text and the Spirit,[105] but it is the canon as "a single and simultaneous act of lordship by the triune God" that Barth construes the Word's self-communicative action by the Spirit as the "truth and force of Holy Scripture."[106]

> To say "the Word of God" is to say the Word of God. It is therefore to speak about a being and event which are not under human control and foresight. Our knowledge of this being and event does not justify us in thinking and speaking of them as though they were under our control or foresee when we know this Word, when we know, then, what we are saying when we say that the Bible is the Word of God. That we have the Bible as the Word of God does not justify us in transforming the statement that the Bible is the Word of God from a statement about the being and rule of God in and through the Bible into a statement about the Bible as such. When we have the Bible as the Word of God, and accept its witness, we are summoned to remember the Lord of the Bible and to give Him the glory. It would not strictly be loyalty to the Bible, and certainly not thankfulness for the Word of God given and continually given again in it, if we did not let our ears be opened by it, not to what it says, but to what He, God Himself, has to say to us as His Word in it and through it. With this recognition and adoration of the sovereignty of Him whose Word the Bible is, the knowledge of its inspiration, its character as the Word of God, will always have to begin.[107]

Thus Barth on God's help as the "whence" of the church's recognition of the instrumentality and humanity of the canonical witness in the mysterious economy of the Spirit's sanctifying self-manifestations. As Berkouwer puts it, "in sacred Scripture we never confronted God speaking outside of human media, outside of the horizontal perspective and history. We meet the Word of God as canon precisely in the witness of the prophets and the

---

"canonical materials, persons, and practices" (29, 467) (*Canon and Criterion in Christian Theology*, 363–90, esp. 367). For a different but no less problematic trivialization of the externality of the Spirit and Scripture in Barth's concept of canon, see Bender's sophisticated reading, "Scripture and Canon in Karl Barth's Early Theology," 165–80.

105. McGlasson asserts that "the text of the Bible, the language of its witness, is not distant from its divine Object" (*Jesus and Judas*, 41–43); similarly, Thompson, "Witness to the Word," 168–97.

106. *CD* I/2, 539.

107. Ibid., 527.

apostles."[108] By stressing the priority of God in the biblical prophets and apostles as *peccatores iusti*, Barth can avoid "a competition syndrome"[109] that is characteristic of the "absolute man" of modernism, and can stress instead the Reformed soteriological primacy that the loving help of the *viva vox Dei* "confronts man in his own creaturely existence."[110] By recognizing the precedence of regeneration, Barth can, moreover, profess that Scripture "does not lie—and this is why prayer must have the last word—not in our power but only in God's, that this event should take place and therefore this witness of Scripture be made to us."[111]

> The Bible must be known as the Word of God if it is to be known as the Word of God. The doctrine of Holy Scripture in the Evangelical Church is that this logical circle is the circle of self-assuring, self-attesting truth into which it is equally impossible to enter as it is to emerge from it: the circle of our freedom which as such is also the circle of our captivity.[112]

Thus Barth on the "door of the Bible texts can be opened only from within," on the "door of the Bible" on which the reading church is summoned to keep "knocking."[113] For Barth, the church's scriptural orientation properly belongs to the idiom of prayer. Finally, if the church confesses the Scripture as God's Word, Barth thinks that the church then acknowledges that "faith

---

108. Berkouwer, *Holy Scripture*, 73.

109. Ibid., 198. For an example of this "syndrome," see Cullberg, *Das Problem der Ethik in der dialektischen Theologie I*, 38.

110. Berkouwer, *Holy Scripture*, 73. "When the Word of the Lord comes to a man, it comes into his own life on his own level. It doe not come in a strange extraterrestrial or supratemporal manner, consequently making it unnecessary to distinguish it from other voices because it is incomparably and therefore irresistibly unique."

111. *CD* I/2, 531. For a thoughtful reflection on the concept of inerrancy of Scripture in Barth and in North American evangelicalism, see McCormack, "The Being of Holy Scripture is in Becoming," 55–75 (esp. 65–70). McCormack rightly points out that "Barth's denial that the Bible has either an intrinsic or a permanently bestowed capacity to be an adequate bearer of the Word of God is, in large measure, simply a function of the Reformed character of his Christology" (70).

112. Ibid., 535.

113. Ibid., 533–35. Cf. *CD* I/1, 136. For Barth that means the primacy of the Spirit's unbound freedom before, above and under the human reality and creaturely elements in Scripture and the reader. "Only in God's Word do we find the normal order of the natural and the spiritual. But in God's Word we do find it, and we should not allow the aberrations of human spiritual in its flight from nature to lead us into an attempt to level up or even reverse the order. In theological and ministerial utterance we have to be clear, then, what it means to employ naturalistic terms."

in the inspiration of the Bible stands or falls by whether the concrete life of the Church and of the members of the Church is a life really dominated by the exegesis of the Bible."[114] Biblical exegesis in Barth's soteriological construal is the church's open, self-involving acknowledgement of the priority and primacy of the Spirit in the life of the biblical witnesses as well as the life of all the saints; an acknowledgement also of the ontological force of God's sanctifying use of the canonical text as his unique witness and authority on earth before the parousia, a miraculous sign of his promised help and present love to his waiting saints. That is also to say, for Barth, a proper doctrine of inspiration is, in short, to give way to God's sovereign and merciful use of Scripture by summoning the church's due diligence and expectancy in the school of the prophets and apostles: "[t]he existence of the biblical texts summons us to persistence in waiting and knocking."[115]

Summary

What does Barth mean by "Holy Scripture"? We suggested that his characterization of the scriptural texts could not be grasped properly apart from its soteriological primacy and priority of the activity of the triune God. Succinctly put, on Barth's reading, revelation is reconciliation. Another way to put it is the priority of the ontic over the noetic in Barth's anthropology of the biblical witnesses. In this sense we stressed Barth's understanding of the biblical witnesses as *peccatores iusti*. Their new person in the old, we indicated, is borne to us contingently by the outpouring of the Holy Spirit whose relation to the regenerates is and remains unbound absolutely: their "whole man" is claimed by God for his glory, love, and praise.[116]

To identify an exegetical basis of Barth's construal of the person and work of the biblical writers, we read his expositions of 2 Pet and 2 Tim. In them we observed an apostolic self-delimitation to and by the Spirit's relation to the scriptural text, so that "all that we have to say about [the relation] can consist only in an underlining and delimiting of the inaccessible mystery of the free grace in which the Spirit of God is present and active before and above and in the Bible."[117] That is, we said, on Barth's account, the Spirit's relation to Scripture is unidirectional.

114. *CD* I/2, 533; cf. 537.
115. Ibid., 533; cf. 534–35.
116. Ibid., 401.
117. Ibid., 504.

In the light of Barth's account of the primacy and priority of the Spirit in and through Scripture, we sketched two creaturely characteristics of the biblical witnesses in illumination: first, they spoke and wrote ἀπὸ Θεοῦ: their witness is only in virtue of God's use of it; second, recognition of God's deity and their sanctified humanity is bound inescapably to the Spirit's regeneration; finally, we saw, Barth stresses prayer as characteristic of church's scriptural orientation in the light of his soteriological conviction that the "door of the Bible texts can be opened only from within."[118]

We discussed several implications of Barth's view of the biblical witnesses for a theological characterization of Scripture and the reader. For Barth, theology's construal of Scripture does neither legislate God's use nor engage in "a kind of hermeneutical immediacy."[119] Neither does it allow the reader's theorization[120] to become conflated with the Bible or to claim any necessary correspondence between the text and its reception.[121] Nor does Barth perceive the Spirit's objectivity merely as power or human subjectivity.[122] Instead for him a proper theological construal of Scripture can only open up to the divine economy in whose reality and on whose terms the text has its being.[123] As this reality is its own primary agent and subject in relation to which Scripture's creaturely element is derivatively genuine and correspondingly secondary, this means that, in the very least, our theological descriptions of Scripture are delimited by the reality of the regeneration of the biblical witnesses and their proper readers, and therefore will not be confined to, or specified by, theologically unconstrained characterizations of text, language, history, humanity, and so on.[124] For Barth, a proper theo-

118. Ibid., 533–35. Cf. *CD* I/1, 136. For Barth that means the primacy of the Spirit's unbound freedom before, above and under the human reality and creaturely elements in Scripture and the reader. "Only in God's Word do we find the normal order of the natural and the spiritual. But in God's Word we do find it, and we should not allow the aberrations of human spiritual in its flight from nature to lead us into an attempt to level up or even reverse the order. In theological and ministerial utterance we have to be clear, then, what it means to employ naturalistic terms."

119. Lauster, *Prinzip und Methode*, 261.

120. Ward, *Word and Supplements*, 137.

121. Lindbeck, "Scripture, Consensus, and Community," 78; Abraham, *Canon and Criterion in Christian Theology*, 363–90.

122. Jenson, "You Wonder Where the Spirit Went," 147–93.

123. Cf. Wood, *Barth's Theology of Interpretation*, 173–74.

124. That is also to say, for Barth, exegetical method needs be neither disorderly nor absolutistic if the antecedently determined being of the biblical text (and the corresponding responsibility of the reading church) in the divine economy is to be respected. Cf. Barth, *Erklärung des Phillipperbriefes*, preface).

logical description of Scripture must therefore resist generalizing, trivializing, or simulating God's use of it, but we must instead reckon with the biblical witnesses and their text with what they are by the sovereign mercy that God has for us in Jesus Christ.

Conclusion

WE BEGAN THIS STUDY by stating its modest intention and self-conscious limitations as no more than a preliminary sketch of certain aspects of Barth's Reformed scriptural orientation to the biblical prophets and apostles as *peccatores iusti*. Moreover, we considered Barth's occasional, bibliological reference to the unbound, saving, and sanctifying activity of the Spirit *of the triune God*. We noted Barth's conviction about the pure deity and one being of the agency of the Godhead as theology's delimiting, ontic and noetic context for confessing, thinking, and speaking of, the pure deity of the agency of the Spirit of Scripture. One implication of Barth's conviction about the distinction between divine and human agencies is the priority of divine action in his anthropology of the biblical witnesses: They *are* by virtue of none other than their use by God who acts in absolute freedom as God-for-us. In response to certain recent, problematic readings of Barth's concept of Scripture,[1] this formal sounding language of divine action is a way of drawing out the theological force of Barth's twofold emphasis on the externality and precedence of the Spirit's unidirectional use of the canon on the one hand and the due weight of the humanity of the biblical witnesses in the saving economy of revelation on the other. In this sense, we argued that if Barth's soteriological construal of their historicity is a constructive theme of the Spirit's election, sanctification, and deployment of their *whole* humanity, the new *and* old, the well-known criticism of Barth as a "pneumatic" tells us less about Barth but more about his critics and

---

1. See, for example, Thompson, "Witness to the Word," 168–97; Bender, "Scripture and Canon in Karl Barth's Early Theology," 165–80; Kirchstein, *Der souveräne Gott und die Heilige Schrift*, 179–92; McGlasson, *Jesus and Judas*, 41–43; Gibson, *Reading the Decree*, 185–88; Plasger, "'Du sollst Vater und Mutter ehren!,'" 404; Lauster, *Prinzip und Methode*, 261.

their problematic concept of the Spirit's self-objectivity in Christian biblical studies.[2] When we look into Christian biblical studies we see a range of issues raised in the church's characterizations of the reality in which Scripture is borne to us.[3] It is, however, not my intention to cover all these topics. In place of a conclusion we shall simply address several problems in certain prevalent readings of Barth in the light of his soteriological construal of Scripture.

One succinct way to put his soteriological construal is by grasping his constructive, but no less polemical, notion of the externality of Scripture: just as Scripture is *outside* of itself, so as canon it is *extra ecclesiam*.[4] The notion is in a sense his theological critique of historicist and naturalist anthropological orientations that are unwilling or unable to respect the unbound mystery of the ontological Trinity. If our reading of Barth's notion of externality is plausible, its marginal profile in such construal of his scriptural orientation as "post-critical" (R. Smend) or "meta-critical" (E. Jüngel) is problematic.[5] Moreover, we can arguably see problems in the absent discussion of his constructive, ecumenical vision of "the theological task of a pure historical science of the Bible"[6] in the prevalent, but deeply problematic, characterization of his scriptural orientation as an "antihistorische Revolution."[7] We can see at least two issues with these readings.

The first issue with the marginalization of his concept of externality is a soteriological deficit that tends to overstretch his theological optimism by, for instance, mistaking his confidence in the Spirit and Scripture as confidence in creatures, be they the church or the readers.[8] In these readings of Barth as in the sophisticated but problematic project of "canonical

---

2. Jülicher, "A Modern Interpreter of Paul," 72–73.

3. For a more in-depth sustained discussion on Scripture's humanity and historicity, see, for example, Berkouwer, *Holy Scripture*, chapters 5–8.

4. *CD* I/1, 164, 259. Cf. Berkouwer, *Holy Scripture*, 88.

5. E. Jüngel's very perceptive reading comes short of indicating Barth's concept of contingent illumination ("Theologie als Metakritik," 91–98); Smend, "Nachkritische Schriftauslegung," 215–37. See also, Wallace, *The Second Naiveté*, 12.

6. "Das Schriftprinzip," 536. Cf. Barth, *Harnack*, 96; Barth, *Gespräche 1963*, 238–53 (esp. 243). We can see similar problems in the widespread inattentiveness to his soteriological orientation of Scripture's humanity and historicity to illumination. Cf. Pannenberg, "The Crisis of the Scripture Principle," in *Basic Question in Theology*, 1:1–14.

7. Lauster, *Prinzip und Methode*, 259–64. Graf, "Die 'antihistorische Revolution,'" 377–405.

8. Bender, "Scripture and Canon in Karl Barth's Early Theology," 165–80.

heritage,"[9] the soteriological deficit is especially visible in its complacency towards the essential and unique, *confrontational* character of the biblical canon as divine command. The complacency can be further described as a conflation between divine command and human obedience, a form of domestication of divine giving in human receiving.[10] Crucially in Barth's construal of Scripture's externality human participation receives its due significance as a consequence of renewal by Christ's Spirit.[11] As Wood perceives, for Barth "Scripture is not in the first instance a 'text' of one sort or another, so that general considerations of texts to generate or to constrain meaning straightforwardly apply," but "[w]hat scripture is is determined not by its evident resemblance to other cultural productions, but by its relationship to God's Word."[12] By understanding the precedence of God, Barth can underscore the *spiritual* character and ends of the *whole* humanity of the biblical witnesses, and can stress their gratuitous instrumentality in Christ's commanding self-presence to the saints on pilgrimage towards the parousia. The point on the gratuity of their divine employment is neither a direct identification of the human speech-acts of the biblical witnesses with the speech-acts of God, nor a sharp material divine-human distinction. Instead, Barth stresses the logical priority and necessity of the Spirit's fresh gift of human openness to the biblical witness as Christ's self-announced presence that purifies our attention and fills our hearts with genuine humility and gratitude before Scripture as the Word of God.

Conversely, the second key issue is an inattentiveness to Barth's logical priority and necessity of the Spirit's concrete gift of person in the biblical witnesses *and* their readers. Put slightly differently, the issue is inattentiveness to the logical priority of the ontological problem of Scripture over epistemological or methodological concerns. By respecting God's absolute freedom, priority, and primacy, Barth can confidently refuse to approach the Bible as some sort of *deus ex machina*, or, as it were, through the 'backdoor' by positing revelation in reason or experience[13] including

9. Abraham, *The Divine Inspiration of Holy Scripture*, 58–67, 74, 89; *Canon and Criterion in Christian Theology*, 363–90, 467; *Crossing the Threshold of Divine Revelation*, 3–5; *Canonical Theism: A Proposal for Theology and the Church*, 2–5.

10. Lindbeck, "Scripture, Consensus, and Community," 78; Lindbeck, "The Church's Mission to a Postmodern Culture," 183; Hofmann, *Die Bibel ist die Erste Theologie*, 287–91.

11. *CD* I/2, 531.

12. Wood, *Barth's Theology of Interpretation*, 176.

13. Cf. Heidegger, "The Onto-theo-logical Constitution of Metaphysics," 70–71 (esp. 125); "Kant's Thesis about Being," 339–43; 362. See also Moltmann, *Experience in Theology*, 139–40, 171–79.

their expressions in the scriptural text.[14] Although human factors have due weight in the formation and reception of the canon, Barth believes that if "God is *a se*" "[t]here is no one and nothing . . . to condition Him or to be in a nexus with Him,"[15] so that the inattention to God's unbound, pure deity in and through the biblical witness amounts to be a sort of *spiritual* epidemic. The epidemic is more than a mere intellectual crisis in the church, more than a doctrinal and exegetical deficit in biblical and theological studies; it demands more than mere readerly discipline[16] or a merely different way of reading Scripture—for, Barth argues, it is the life-giving Spirit of Christ who does the giving, renewing, and absolving of the proper person in the reader, preacher, or teacher for conversion, repentance, and obedience. Instead of human valuation, decision, or re-flexivity including their own,[17] they owe the gift[18] of their sanctified life and work rather to the miracle of "the *divine creatio continua*":[19] only by

14. McGlasson, *Jesus and Judas*, 15, 41–43. Cf. J. Barr's discussion on Barth's concept of the referential character of the language or "thought-categories" of the biblical writers, *The Bible in the modern world*, 91–92. For a more qualified treatment of the point, see, Hunsinger, *Disruptive Grace*, chapter 9: "Barth consistently rejected the kind of scriptural interpretation which saw no discrepancy between text and referent" (210). See Molt-mann's argument of a "biblical-hermeneutical circle" for a permanent, direct identity between the reader and the text, *Experience in Theology*, 139–40.

15. *CD* I/1, 157; 36. Cf. In a speech in Bièvres, 20 Oct 1963, Barth's response to a question about canonicity reaffirmed his enduring view of God's being-in-the-Word as free ground of the relation of Scripture to the church (*Gespräche 1963*, 195–99).

16. Briggs, *Words in Action*, 148–53; Briggs, *The Virtuous Reader*, 66–67.

17. The point is overlooked by J. Schickler. In his thoughtful study, he construes the theme of the risen Christ as the theme of "the capacity of a self-conscious subject to find . . . its subjectivity in its objectivity all the way down to the material level," the ca-pacity that is an "organ of absolute self-cognition, the unifier of all other faculties" that "might hence be called the Christ or resurrection-faculty"; posits this capacity generally in human cognitivity (*Metaphysics as Christology*, 7, 145).

18. In his profound discussion about the concept of gift, and especially ironically in light of his critique of M. Heidegger and J.-L. Marion, J. Milbank apparently does not see a problem in domesticating divine giving in the human receiving of faith and theology. If he seems to suggest the Spirit as "the gift of relation" that can be posited in "a Christian ontology" or creatures themselves in general, it is perhaps in part because Milbank ap-parently does not distinguish the ontological Trinity from the immanent Trinity, and in particular, between God's person and work in his internal and external relations ("Can a Gift be Given?," 119–61). Similarly, R.T. Shorthouse problematically regards the biblical Abraham and Moses as intrinsically capable of inhabiting the "ontological viewpoint" of God as "the Other" (*Textual Narratives and a New Metaphysics*, 91–98, 139).

19. *CD* I/2, 688–89.

virtue of the unbound freedom of the Spirit *a se* as the Spirit *pro nobis* does his scriptural address come to our attention.

If my sketch is plausible, I suggest that less is to be expected from readings that isolate Barth's immediate undertakings with the scriptural text from his soteriological orientation to God's action as unbound, external, and necessary to the biblical writers and their readers alike,[20] just so are readings of Barth that tend to trivialize the significance of biblical exegesis in his theological renewal unpromising.[21] Instead we suggest that a reading of Barth's renewed relation to the Bible can be more accurate and fruitful when it attends to his Reformed Scripture Principle. By recognizing Scripture's anthropological objectivity as a consequence of the self-objectivity of the life-giving Spirit, Barth can stress that if by Spirit we are in Christ we can understand the Bible and its history objectively. Yet for Barth, the objectivity of the outpouring Spirit of God is not mere human subjectivity in the light of the pure deity and one being of God's agency. By recognizing God's agency as irreducible and necessary to the human agency in Scripture and theology, Barth can speak of a sort of self-involving sensibility in biblical and theological studies. The sort of self-involving sensibility that he brought to his theological task emerged, we saw, from a clash between his modern Protestant heritage and his Reformed conviction about the eschatological comprehensiveness of the Spirit's economy of revelation and salvation. Once again: "the point is not to keep the historical-critical method of biblical and historical research developed in the last centuries away from the work of theology, but rather to fit that method, and its refinement of the way questions are asked, into that work in a meaningful way."[22]

Contrary to his critics who characterize his scriptural orientation as "anti-historical" or, in the word of Harnack, "scandalous,"[23] the material affords, we said, an arguably different picture. In it, more than his obvious

---

20. See, for example, Kirchstein, *Der souveräne Gott und die Heilige Schrift*, 30–31; the eschatological perfection of the Spirit's inspiration of the writers includes their authorial intention and hidden person that can come to our attention by none other than the Spirit's illumination of Christ's self-announced presence. In his careful reading of Barth's doctrine of inspiration, C. Carter seems hesitant about this crucial point concerning their hiddenness in Christ and apparently conflates the new and old persons of the biblical witnesses ("Karl Barth on the Imago Dei," 123).

21. Fisher, *Revelatory Positivism*, 194–211. In his thoughtful analysis of "Barth's Critique of Metaphysics in Theology," he tends to overlook the formative significance of Barth's identity as a reader and preacher of Scripture.

22. Barth, *Harnack*, 96.

23. Zahn-Harnack, *Adolf von Harnack*, 415 (ET 30–31).

polemics against historicism and naturalism in liberal Protestantism,[24] and related personal and institutional forms of elitism and corruption,[25] Barth recognizes the primacy and priority of God's saving economy in Scripture's divine deployment and the resultant priority of the history of revelation, salvation and reconciliation in Christian biblical and theological studies.

More closely, by stressing Barth's account of the primacy of divine mercy, we did not at any rate suggest a hamartiological deficit in his recognition of human factors, for instance, in the complex process of canonization. On the contrary, we argued that as he stresses the gravity of human depravity in the church and its intellectual life, Barth is able to acknowledge God's sovereign freedom as the light in which sinful humanity and all our transgressions are to be reckoned; hence his insistence on the externality of the Word and Spirit, and on prayer as essential to theology's recognition of the *whole* humanity of the biblical witnesses as *peccatores iusti*. Succinctly put, his confidence in the Spirit of Scripture is not identical with his confidence in Scripture and the church, but his confidence in the church and Scripture is a corollary of his confidence in God as Lord in complete victory over sin. As Barth writes,

> If we believe that the Lord is mightier than the sin which indisputably reigns in the Church, if we believe that He is the victor in the struggle against grace which is indisputably widespread even in the Church, then we can count on it that a genuine knowledge and confession in respect of the Canon, and therefore a knowledge and confession of the genuine Canon, is not at least impossible in the Church, not because we have to believe in men, but

---

24. Dorrien, *The Barthian Revolt in Modern Theology*, 10–11; Wall, "Ways of Polemicizing," 401–14; Stegeman, "Ethics or Dogmatics," 415–32.

25. Cf. *CD* I/2, 510–11. See Barth's objection to anti-Semitism, a warning that applies broadly to "hostility simply to foreign blood and the like" (and, in Canadian context, I think, at least equally, for instance, to First Nations, all visible minorities and genders) in churches and their institutions. "By being hostile to Jewish blood, the world simply proves that it is the world: blind and deaf and stupid to the ways of God, as they are visibly before it in the existence of this people. And if the Church tries to co-operate in this hostility to Jewish blood, it simply proves that it too has become blind and deaf and stupid . . . Once we have raised even our little finger in Anti-Semitism, we can produce such vital and profound reasons in favour of it, and they all apply equally well to the Bible, not only to the Old but also to the New Testament, not only to the Rabbi Paul but also to the Rabbi Jesus of Nazareth of the first three Gospels." *Contra* G. Lüdemann's reading of Barth's concept of Scripture as anti-Semitic, *The Unholy in the Holy Scripture*, 126–27.

because if we are not to give up our faith we have to believe in the miracle of grace.[26]

His confidence in Scripture as canon is substantially different from the sort of confidence that reduces divine authority to human authorities, the mystery of the Godhead to doctrine, or divine command to human obedience. Conversely, a reading of Barth's construal of the Spirit and Word that overlooks his recognition of the due significance of Scripture's humanity and the human factors in canonization—a sort of docetic reading of his theology—we said, is just as problematic. Doctrinally put, Pelagianist, semi-Pelagnianist, docetic, or similar conceptual distortion of God's relation to Scripture is entirely uncharacteristic of Barth. Instead, Barth is, we stressed, mindful of the disease of *confusio hominem* in the church's characterization of history, the biblical canon, and the saints, by seeking for a "better" description of the divine-human relation in Scripture *and* scripture-reading, and once again, "better in the sense that in it, God, in his unique position over against man, and especially religious man, might be clearly given the honour we found him to have in the Bible."[27] By recognizing Scripture's divine employment as God's free acts of grace, Barth can speak confidently *and* self-critically of a contingent, purposive communion of the biblical prophets and apostles and the saints, by characterizing the communion in the terms of the unbound freedom of God as God-for-us.

If our account of Barth is plausible, we suggest that it can at least provide a constructive, theological account of the career of Barth's scriptural orientation as well as a serviceable position for readers in their approach to the *Church Dogmatics*.

Much work remains, especially a further study of his sermons, biblical exegesis, both published and unpublished, and *CD* II-IV. The preparatory task has been pursued through mapping his soteriological characterization of the eschatological humanity of the biblical witnesses, the uniqueness of their written testimony as canon, and the priority and necessity of God's unbound use of Scripture in the subsequent, gracious gift of the person of a proper reader. If our reading is plausible, this study, moreover, reinforces the suggestion that Barth's decision to inhabit the Reformed tradition was as consistent with his biblical exegesis in his sermons and commentaries as it was formative of his identity as a biblical theologian. From our point about his Reformed identity it also follows

26. *CD* I/1, 598.

27. Barth, "A Thank-You and a Bow—Kiekegaard's Reveille," 97.

that his concepts of canon and witness cannot be grasped properly apart from his visibly polemical, but essentially constructive, view that perfect dogmatic clarity and consensus in Christian bibliology is contingent upon the mercy of God's sanctifying self-presence. If Barth speaks of Scripture in such astonishingly confident ways, it is, in crucial part, because for him God has relieved the proper reader from having to secure the unity, authority, clarity and reliability of the biblical canon.[28] Once again: "To speak of God can only mean to let God speak."[29]

The point about the absolute freedom of God in and through Scripture brings us to the final point: What may be said of Barth's place in Christian bibliology? Did Barth succeed in his theological programme of reordering the dogmatic foundations in modern bibliological discussions concerning, for example: the primacy and priority of the work of the Spirit of Christ in the church's characterization of the biblical prophets and apostles, their written testimony and the proper reader; prayer as the church's scriptural and doctrinal orientation to God's unbound relation to the text and witness of Holy Scripture? And along these lines, did Barth's occasional, bibliological references to the Spirit of God open up further theological characterization of human work in Christian biblical and theological studies? Did Barth's soteriological orientation to the Spirit and Scripture help remind readers of the freedom, patience and faithfulness that God has for us in Jesus Christ who is our common future and present helper, of whom the prophets and apostles spoke and wrote as his Spirit's witnesses?

Whatever decision readers might make about the brief list of Barth's contribution as sampled above, this study suggests that one thing is clear: his view of Scripture helps open up lines of inquiry about the Spirit in the person and work of the biblical witnesses and the church's orientation to the biblical canon as God's Word. And not least in that regard, Barth helps illuminate a profoundly constructive alternative to the post-Renaissance Protestant thoughts of cultural progression, historicism, naturalism, and religious experience, admonishing Christian theology to keep seeking in prayer a more attentive, more expectant, more open, more patient, humbler, and purer desire, diligence, understanding and skill to be open to God's relation to Scripture. For Barth, in the light of that relation, no "finished works" can be and needs be spoken of in Christian theology.[30]

28. Cf. *CD* I/2, 503.

29. "Das Schriftprinzip," 508.

30. *Römerbrief 1922*, vi (ET 2–3).

Much research into his sermons, biblical exegesis and *CD* II-IV remains to be pursued beyond this study as it joins others in the constructive work for a deeper understanding of Barth's theological ontology of Holy Scripture.

Bibliography

Ables, T. "The Grammar of Pneumatology in Barth and Rahner: A Reconsideration." *International Journal of Systematic Theology* 11 (2009): 208–24.

Achelis, E. C. "Noch einmal: Moderne Theologie und Reichsgottesarbeit." In *Vorträge und kleinere Arbeiten 1905–1909*. Zürich: TVZ, 1992.

Asprey, C. *Eschatological Presence in Karl Barth's Göttingen Theology.* Oxford: Oxford University Press, 2010.

Abraham, W. J. *Canon and Criterion in Christian Theology: From the Fathers to Feminism.* Oxford: Clarendon, 1988.

———. *Crossing the Threshold of Divine Revelation.* Grand Rapids: Eerdmans, 2006.

———. *The Divine Inspiration of Holy Scripture.* Oxford: Oxford University Press, 1981.

Abraham, W. J., J. E. Vickers, and Natalie B. Van Kirk, eds. *Canonical Theism: A Proposal for Theology and the Church.* Grand Rapids: Eerdmans, 2008.

Balthasar, Hans Urs von. *Karl Barth: Darstellung und Deutung seiner Theologie.* Köln: Jakob Hegner, 1951; ET: *The Theology of Karl Barth, Exposition and Interpretation.* Translated by E. T. Oakes. San Francisco: Ignatius, 1992.

Barr, J. *The Bible in the Modern World.* London: SCM, 1973.

Barth, K. "Antwort an D. Achelis und D. Drews." In *Vorträge und kleinere Arbeiten, 1905–1909*, edited by H. A Drewes and H. Stoevesand. Zürich: TVZ, 1992.

———. *Barth-Brunner Briefwechsel 1916–1966.* Zürich: TVZ, 2000.

———. *Come Holy Spirit: Sermons by Karl Barth and Eduard Thurneysen.* Translated by G. W. Richards, E. G. Homrighausen, and K. J. Ernst. Edinburgh: T. & T. Clark, 1934.

———. "Das Evangelium in der Gegenwart." *Theologische Existenz heute* 25. Munich, 1935.

———. *Die christliche Dogmatik im Entwurf: 1 Band: Die Lehre vom Worte Gottes: Prolegomena zur christlichen Dogmatik 1927.* Edited by H. Stoevesandt. Zürich: TVZ, 1982.

———. *Die kirchliche Dogmatik.* Munich: Chr. Kaiser, 1932, and Zürich: TVZ, 1938–1965; ET: *Church Dogmatics.* Translated by G. T. Thomson et al. Edinburgh: T. & T. Clark, 1956–1975.

———. "Der Christliche Glaube und die Geschichte." In *Vorträge und kleinere Arbeiten, 1909–1914*, edited by H. A. Drewes and H. Stoevesandt, 149–212. Zürich: TVZ, 1993.

———. *Der Römerbrief (Erste Fassung), 1919.* Edited by H. Schmidt. Zürich: TVZ, 1985.

———. *Der Römerbrief, 1922.* Zürich: TVZ, 1984; ET: *The Epistle to the Romans.* Translated by E. C. Hoskyns. London: Oxford University Press, 1968.

Bibliography

————. *Die Protestantische Theologie im 19. Jahrhundert.* Zürich: TVZ, 1985; ET: *Protestant Theology in the Nineteenth Century.* Translated by B. Cozens and J. Bowden. Grand Rapids: Eerdmans, 2002.

————. *Die Theologie Zwinglis 1922/1923.* Vorlesungen Göttingen Wintersemeser 1922/1923. Zürich: TVZ, 2004.

————. *The Early Preaching of Karl Barth: Fourteen Sermons with Commentary by W. H. Willimon.* Translated by J. E. Wilson. Louisville: Westminster John Knox, 2009.

————. *Erklärung des Johannes-evangeliums (kapitel 1–8) Vorlesung Münster, Wintersemester 1925/1926, wiederholt in Bonn, Sommersemester 1933.* Edited by W. Fürst. Zürich: TVZ, 1976; ET: *Witness to the Word: A Commentary on John 1 by Karl Barth, Lectures at Münster in 1925 and at Bonn in 1933.* Translated by G. W. Bromiley. Grand Rapids: Eerdmans, 1986.

————. *Erklärung des Philipperbriefes.* Zürich: Evangelischer, 1947; ET: *The Epistle to the Philippians.* Translated by J. W. Leitch. Louisville: Westminster John Knox, 2002.

————. *Fides quaerens intellectum: Anselms Beweis der Existenz Gottes im Zusammenhang seines theologischen Programms.* Edited by E. Jüngel and I. U. Dalferth. Zürich: TVZ, 2002; ET: *Anselm: Fides Quaerens Intellectum.* Translated by I. W. Robertson. Pittsburgh: Pickwick, 1975.

————. *Fragments Grave and Gay.* Edited by M. Rumscheidt. Translated by E. Mosbacher. London: HarperCollins, 1971.

————. *Gespräche 1959–1962.* Edited by E. Busch. Zürich: TVZ, 1995.

————. *Gespräche 1963.* Edited by E. Busch. Zürich: TVZ, 2005.

————. *Gespräche 1964–1968.* Edited by E. Busch. Zürich: TVZ, 1997.

————. *God In Action.* Translated by E. G. Homrighausen and K. J. Ernst. Edinburgh: T. & T. Clark, 1936.

————. *Karl Barth–Eduard Thurneysen Briefwechsel, 1913–1921.* Edited by E. Thurneysen. Zürich: TVZ, 1973; ET: *Revolutionary Theology in the Making: Barth–Thurneysen Correspondence, 1914–1925.* Translated by J. D. Smart. Richmond, VA: John Knox, 1964.

————. *Karl Barth–Eduard Thurneysen Briefwechsel, 1921–1930.* Edited by E. Thurneysen. Zürich: TVZ, 1987; ET: *Revolutionary Theology in the Making: Barth–Thurneysen Correspondence, 1914–1925.* Translated by J. D. Smart. Richmond, VA: John Knox, 1964.

————. *Karl Barth–Martin Rade: Ein Briefwechsel.* Gütersloh: Gütersloher Velagshaus, 1981.

————. *Karl Barth–Rudolf Bultmann Briefwechsel, 1911–1966.* Edited by B. Jaspert. Zürich: TVZ, 1994; ET: *Letters 1922–1966.* Edited by B. Jaspert. Translated by G. W. Bromiley. Grand Rapids: Eerdmans, 1981.

————. "Moderne Theologie und Reichsgottesarbeit." In *Vorträge und kleinere Arbeiten, 1905–1909,* edited by H. A Drewes and H. Stoevesand, 341–47. Zürich: TVZ, 1992.

————. *Konfirmandenunterricht 1909–1921.* Edited by J. Fangmeier. Zürich: TVZ, 1987.

————. *Offene Briefe 1909–1935.* Edited by H. von Dietcher Koch. Zürich, TVZ: 2001.

————. *Predigten 1913.* Edited by N. Barth and G. Sauter. Zürich: TVZ, 1976.

————. *Predigten 1914.* Edited by U. J. Fähler. Zürich: TVZ, 1987.

————. *Predigten 1915.* Edited by H. Schmidt. Zürich: TVZ, 1996.

————. *Predigten 1916.* Edited by H. Schmidt. Zürich: TVZ, 1998.

————. *Predigten 1917.* Edited by H. Schmidt. Zürich: TVZ, 1999.

————. *Predigten 1918.* Edited by H. Schmidt. Zürich: TVZ, 2002.

———. *Predigten 1919*. Edited by H. Schmidt. Zürich: TVZ, 2003.

———. *Predigten 1920*. Edited by H. Schmidt. Zürich: TVZ, 2005.

———. *Predigten 1921*. Edited by H. Schmidt. Zürich: TVZ, 2007.

———. *Predigten 1921–1935*. Edited by H. Finze. Zürich: TVZ, 1998.

———. "A Thank-You and a Bow—Kiekegaard's Reveille: Speech on Being Awarded the Sonning Prize." In *Fragments Grave and Gay*, edited by M. Rumscheidt, 95–101. Translated by E. Mosbacher. London: HarperCollins, 1971.

———. *Theology and Church: Shorter Writings 1920–1928*. Translated by T. F. Torrance. London: SCM, 1962.

———. *The Theology of John Calvin*. Translated by G. W. Bromiley. Grand Rapids: Eerdmans, 1995.

———. *The Theology of the Reformed Confessions*. Translated by D. L. Guder and J. J. Guder. Louisville: John Knox, 2002.

———. "23 Dec 1922." In *Rudolf Bultmann–Friedrich Gogarten Briefwechsel, 1921–1967*, edited by H. G. Göckeritz, 267–73. Tübingen: Mohr Siebeck, 2002.

———. *Unterricht in der christlichen Religion, I. Prolegomena, 1924*. Edited by H. Reiffen. Zürich, TVZ, 1985; ET: *The Göttingen Dogmatics: Instruction in the Christian Religion*. Vol. 1. Translated by G. W. Bromiley, and edited by H. Reiffen. Grand Rapids: Eerdmans, 1991.

———. *Unterricht in der christlichen Religion. 2: Die Lehre von Gott/Die Lehre vom Menschen, 1924/1925*. Edited by H. Stoevesandt. Zürich: TVZ, 1990.

———. *Unterricht in der christlichen Religion. 3: Prolegomena, 1924*. Edited by H. Reiffen. Zürich, TVZ, 1985.

———. *Vorträge und kleinere Arbeiten, 1905–1909*. Edited by H. A Drewes and H. Stoevesand. Zürich: TVZ, 1992.

———. *Vorträge und kleinere Arbeiten, 1909–1914*. Edited by H. A. Drewes and H. Stoevesandt. Zürich: TVZ, 1993.

———. *Vorträge und kleinere Arbeiten, 1922–1925*. Edited by H. A Drewes. Zürich: TVZ, 1990.

———. *The Word of God and the Word of Man*. Translated by D. Horton. London: Hodder & Stoughton, 1928.

———. "Zwinglis '67 Schlussreden' aus das erste Religionsgespräch zu Zürich 1523." In *Vorträge und kleinere Arbeiten, 1905–1909*, edited by H. A Drewes and H. Stoevesand, 104–19. Zürich: TVZ, 1992.

Bender, K. J. "Christ and Canon, Theology and History: The Barth–Harnack Dialogue Revisited." In *Theology As Conversation: The Significance of Dialogue in Historical and Contemporary Theology: A Festschrift for Daniel L. Migliore*, edited by B. L. McCormack and K. J. Bender, 3–29. Grand Rapids: Eerdmans, 2009.

———. *Karl Barth's Christological Ecclesiology*. Aldershot: Ashgate: 2005.

———. "Scripture and Canon in Karl Barth's Early Theology." In *From Biblical Criticism to Biblical Faith: Essays in Honor of Lee Martin McDonald*, edited by W. H. Brackney and C. A. Evans, 164–98. Macon, GA: Mercer University Press, 2007.

Bentley, W. *The Notion of Mission in Karl Barth's Ecclesiology*. Newcastle upon Tyne: Cambridge Scholars Publishing, 2010.

Bergant, D. *Scripture: History and Interpretation*. Collegeville, MN: Liturgical, 2008.

Berkouwer, G. C. *Holy Scripture*. Translated and edited by J. B. Rogers. Grand Rapids: Eerdmans, 1975.

————. *The Triumph of Grace in the Theology of Karl Barth*. Translated by H. R. Boer. Grand Rapids: Eerdmans, 1965.

Boer, D. "'Bedrängnis muß groß sein . . . ' Einführung in Karl Barths 'Erklärung des Johannesevangeliums.'" *Zeitschrift für dialektische Theologie* 16 (2000): 8–29.

Bourgine, B. *L'Herméneutique Théologique de Karl Barth. Exégèse et dogmatique dans le quatrième volume de la Kirchliche Dogamtik*. Leuven: Leuven University Press, 2003.

Bradshaw, T. *Trinity and Ontology: A Comparative Study of the Theologies of Karl Barth and Wolfhart Pannenberg*. Edinburgh: Rutherford, 1988.

Briggs, R. S. "Speech-Act Theory." In *Words and the Word: Explorations in Biblical Interpretation and Literary Theory*, edited by D. G. Firth and J. A. Grant, 75–110. Downers Grove, IL: InterVarsity, 2009.

————. *The Virtuous Reader: Old Testament Narrative and Interpretive Virtue*. Grand Rapids: Baker Academic, 2010.

————. *Words in Action: Speech Act Theory and Biblical Interpretation: Toward a Hermeneutic of Self-Involvement*. Edinburgh: T. & T. Clark, 2001.

Burgess, A. *The Ascension in Karl Barth*. Aldershot: Ashgate, 2004.

Burnett, R. E. *Karl Barth's Theological Exegesis: The Hermeneutical Principles of the Römerbrief Period*. Tübingen: Mohr Siebeck, 2001.

Busch, E. *Karl Barth and the Pietists: The Young Karl Barth's Critique of Pietism and Its Response*. Translated by D. W. Bloesch. Downers Grove, IL: InterVarsity, 2004.

————. *Karl Barth: His Life from Letters and Autobiographical Texts*. Translated by J. Bowden. London: SCM, 1976.

Carter, C. "Karl Barth on the Imago Dei: Typology and the *Sensus literalis* of Holy Scripture." In *Go Figure! Figuration in Biblical Interpretation*, edited by S. D. Walters. Eugene, OR: Pickwick, 2008.

Chung, S. W. *Admiration and Challenge: Karl Barth's Theological Relationship with John Calvin*. New York: Peter Lang, 2002.

Clough, D. *Ethics in Crisis: Interpreting Barth's Ethics*. Farnham, UK: Ashgate, 2005.

Colwell, J. *Actuality and Provisionality: Eternity and Election in the Theology of Karl Barth*. Edinburgh: Rutherford, 1989.

Cullberg, J. *Das Problem der Ethik in der dialektischen Theologie I. Karl Barth*. Uppsala: A.-B. Lundequistska, 1938.

Cullmann, O. "Les problèmes posés par la méthode exégétique de l'école de Karl Barth." *Revue d'histoire et de philosophie religieuses* 8/1 (January–February 1928): 70–83.

Cunningham, M. K. "Karl Barth." In *Christian Theologies of Scripture: A Comparative Introduction*, edited by J. S. Holcomb, 183–201. New York: New York University Press, 2006.

Dawson, R. D. *The Resurrection in Karl Barth*. London: Ashgate, 2007.

Demson, D. E. *Hans Frei and Karl Barth: Different Ways of Reading Scripture*. Grand Rapids: Eerdmans, 1997.

Donfried, K. P. *Who Owns the Bible? Toward the Recovery of a Christian Hermeneutic*. New York: Crossroad, 2006.

Dorrien, G. *The Barthian Revolt in Modern Theology: Theology Without Weapons*. Louisville: Westminster John Knox, 2000.

Drews, P. "Zum dritten Mal: Moderne Theologie und Reichgottesarbeit." In *Vorträge und kleinere Arbeiten 1905–1909*. Zürich: TVZ, 1992.

Fähler, J. *Der Ausbruch des 1. Weltkrieges in Karl Barths Predigten 1913–1915*. Las Vegas: Peter Lang, 1979.

Fisher, S. *Revelatory Positivism? Barth's Earliest Theology and the Marburg School.* Oxford: Oxford University Press, 1988.

Flett, J. G. *The Witness of God: The Trinity, Missio Dei, Karl Barth, and the Nature of Christian Community.* Grand Rapids: Eerdmans, 2010.

Frei, H. W. "An Afterword: Eberhard Busch's Biography of Karl Barth." In *Karl Barth in Re-View: Posthumous Works Reviewed and Assessed,* edited by H. M. Rumscheidt, 95–116. Pittsburgh: Pickwick, 1981.

———. "The Doctrine of Revelation in the Thought of Karl Barth, 1909–1922: The Nature of Barth's Break with Liberalism." PhD diss., Yale University, 1956.

Freudenberg, M. *Karl Barth und die reformierte Theologie.* Neukirchen-Vluyn: Neukirchener, 1997.

Ford, D. *Barth and God's Story.* Frankurt: Peter Lang, 1981.

———. "Barth's Interpretation of the Bible." In *Karl Barth: Studies of His Theological Method,* 55–87. Oxford: Clarendon, 1979.

Genest, H. *Karl Barth und die Predigt: Darstellung und Deutung von Predigtwerk und Predigtlehre Karl Barths.* Neukirchen-Vluyn: Neukirchener, 1995.

Gerhard, J. *On the Nature of Theology and Scripture.* Translated by R. J. Dinda. St Louis: Concordia, 2006.

Gibson, D. "The Day of God's Mercy: Romans 9–11 in Barth's Doctrine of Election." In *Engaging with Barth: Contemporary Evangelical Critiques,* edited by D. Gibson and D. Strange, 136–67. Nottingham, UK: InterVarsity, 2008.

———. *Reading the Decree: Exegesis, Election and Christology in Calvin and Barth.* London: T. & T. Clark, 2010.

Gogarten, F. "Karl Barths Dogmatik." *Theologische Rundschau,* Neue Folge 1 (1929): 60–80.

Gorringe, T. *Karl Barth: Against Hegemony.* Oxford: Oxford University Press, 1999.

Graf, F. W. "Die 'antihistorische Revolution' in der protestantischen Theologie der zwanziger Jahre." In *Vernunft des Glaubens. Wissenschaftliche Theologie und kirchliche Lehre. Festschrift zum 60. Geburtstag von W. Pannenberg,* edited by J. Rohls and G. Wenz, 377–405. Göttingen: Vandenhoeck & Ruprecht, 1988.

Greggs, T. *Barth, Origen, and Universal Salvation: Restoring Particularity.* Oxford: Oxford University Press, 2009.

Gunton, C. *The Barth Lectures.* Transcribed and edited by P. H. Brazier. London: T. & T. Clark, 2007.

Hamer, J. *L'Occasionalisme Théologique de Karl Barth: étude sur sa méthode dogmatique.* Paris: Desclée de Brouwer, 1949.

Hart, J. W. *Karl Barth vs. Emil Brunner: The Formation and Dissolution of a Theological Alliance, 1916–1936.* New York: Peter Lang, 2001.

Hart, T. "Calvin and Barth on the Lord's Supper." In *Calvin, Barth, and Reformed Theology,* edited by N. B. MacDonald and C. Trueman, 29–56. Milton Keynes: Paternoster, 2008.

———. *Regarding Karl Barth: Toward a Reading of His Theology.* Downers Grove, IL: InterVarsity, 1999.

Hartwell, H. *The Theology of Karl Barth.* London: Gerald Duckworth, 1964.

Heidegger, M. "Kant's Thesis about Being." In *Pathmarks,* edited by W. McNeill. Cambridge: Cambridge University Press, 1988.

———. "The Onto-theo-logical Constitution of Metaphysics." In *Identity and Difference,* translated by J. Stambaugh. New York: Harper & Row, 1969.

Bibliography

Hofmann, P. *Die Bibel ist die Erste Theologie: ein fundamentaltheologischer Ansatz.* Paderborn: Ferdinand Schöningh, 2006.

Hübner, H. *Evangelische Fundamentaltheologie: Theologie der Bibel.* Göttingen: Vandenhoeck & Ruprecht, 2005.

Hunsinger, G. *Disruptive Grace: Studies in the Theology of Karl Barth.* Grand Rapids: Eerdmans, 2000.

———. *How to Read Karl Barth: The Shape of His Theology.* New York: Oxford University Press, 1991.

Jenson, R. W. *Alpha and Omega: A Study in Theology of Karl Barth.* New York: T. Nelson, 1963.

———. "You Wonder Where the Spirit Went." *Pro Ecclesia* 2/3 (1993): 296–304.

Jülicher, A. "A Modern Interpreter of Paul." In *The Beginnings of Dialectical Theology,* edited by J. M. Robinson, 72-73. Translated by K. R. Crim. Richmond, VA: John Knox, 1968.

Jüngel, E. *God's Being Is In Becoming: The Trinitarian Being of God in the Theology of Karl Barth: A Paraphrase.* Translated by J. Webster. Grand Rapids: Eerdmans, 2001.

———. *Karl Barth: A Theological Legacy.* Translated by G. E. Paul. Philadelphia: Westminster John Knox, 1986.

———. "Theologie als Metakritik: Zur Hermeneutik theologischer Exegese." In *Barth-Studien,* 91-98. Cologne: Benziger, 1982.

Kelsey, D. H. "The Bible and Christian Theology." *Journal of the American Academy of Religion* 48 (1980): 400–401.

Kirchstein, H. *Der souveräne Gott und die Heilige Schrift: Einführung in die Biblische Hermeneutik Karl Barths.* Aachen: Shaker, 1998.

Knight, J. A. "The Barthian Heritage of Hans W. Frei." *Scottish Journal of Theology* 61/3 (2008): 307–26.

Kooi, C. van der. *As In a Mirror: John Calvin and Karl Barth on Knowing God: A Diptych.* Translated by D. Mader. Leiden: Brill, 2005.

Körtner, U. H. J. *Theologie des Wortes Gottes: Positionen—Probleme—Perspektiven.* Göttingen: Vandenhoeck & Ruprecht, 2001.

Lauster, J. *Prinzip und Methode. Die Transformation des protestantischen Schriftprinzip durch die historische Kritik von Schleiermacher bis zur Gegenwart.* Tübingen: Mohr Siebeck, 2004.

Lindbeck, G. "The Church's Mission to a Postmodern Culture." In *Postmodern Theology: Christian Faith in a Pluralist World,* edited by F. B. Burnham. San Francisco: HarperCollins, 1989.

———. "Scripture, Consensus, and Community." In *Biblical Interpretation in Crisis,* edited by R. J. Neuhaus, 74–101. Grand Rapids: Eerdmans, 1989.

Lüdemann, G. *The Unholy in the Holy Scripture: The Dark Side of the Bible.* Translated by J. Bowden. Louisville: Westminster John Knox, 1997.

MacDonald, N. B. *Karl Barth and the Strange New World within the Bible: Barth, Wittgenstein, and the Metadilemmas of the Enlightenment.* Carlisle, UK: Paternoster, 2000.

Mangina, J. L. *Karl Barth on the Christian Life: The Practical Knowledge of God.* New York: Peter Lang, 2001.

———. *Karl Barth: Theologian of Christian Witness.* Louisville: Westminster John Knox, 2004.

Marga, A. *Karl Barth's Dialogue with Catholicism in Göttingen and Münster*. Tübingen: Mohr Siebeck, 2010.

Martin, J. "The Gospel of John." In *Karl Barth in Re-View: Posthumous Works Reviewed and Assessed*, edited by H. M. Rumscheidt, 31–42. Pittsburgh: Pickwick, 1981.

McCormack, B. L. "The Being of Holy Scripture is in Becoming." In *Evangelicals and Scripture: Tradition, Authority and Hermeneutics*, edited by V. Bacote, L. C. Miguélez, and D. L. Okholm, 55–75. Downers Grove, IL: InterVarsity, 2004.

———. "Historical Criticism and Dogmatic Interest in Karl Barth's Theological Exegesis of the New Testament." In *Biblical Hermeneutics in Historical Perspective*, edited by M. S. Burrows and P. Rorem, 322–31. Grand Rapids: Eerdmans, 1991.

———. *Karl Barth's Critically Realistic Dialectical Theology*. Oxford: Clarendon, 1995.

———. *Orthodox and Modern: Studies in the Theology of Karl Barth*. Grand Rapids: Baker Academic, 2008.

———. "Participation in God, Yes, Deification, No: Two Modern Answers to an Ancient Question." In *Denkwuerdiges Geheminis: Festschrift fuer Eberhard Juengel zum 70 Geburtstag*, edited by I. U. Dalferth, J. Fischer, and H .-P. Grosshans, 347-74. Tübingen: Mohr Siebeck, 2004.

———, and K. J. Bender, eds. *Theology As Conversation: The Significance of Dialogue in Historical and Contemporary Theology: A Festschrift for Daniel L. Migliore*. Grand Rapids: Eerdmans, 2009.

———, and G. Neven, eds. *The Reality of Faith in Theology: Studies on Karl Barth Princeton-Kampen Consultation, 2005*. New York: Peter Lang, 2007.

McDowell, I. M. "Principle and Practice: Karl Barth's Scripture Principle and His Exegetical Practice." ThM diss., Trinity Divinity School, Illinois, 2006.

McGlasson, P. *Jesus and Judas: Biblical Exegesis in Barth*. Atlanta: Scholars, 1991.

McKim, D. K., ed. *How Karl Barth Changed My Mind*. Grand Rapids: Eerdmans, 1986.

Menke-Peitzmeyer, M. *Subjekitivität und Selbstinterpretation des dreifaltigen Gottes. Eine Studies zur Genese und Explikation des Paradigmas 'Selbstoffenbarung Gottes' in der Theologie Karl Barths*. Münster: Aschendorff, 2002.

Milbank, J. "Can a Gift be Given? Prolegomena to a Future Trinitarian Metaphysic." In *Rethinking Metaphysics*, edited by L. G. Jones and S. E. Fowl, 119-61. Oxford: Blackwell, 1995.

Neuser, W. H. *Karl Barth in Münster 1925–1930*. Zürich: TVZ, 1985.

Nimmo, P. T. *Being in Action: The Theological Shape of Barth's Ethical Vision*. London: T. & T. Clark, 2007.

———. "Exegesis, Ontology and Ethics: Karl Barth on the Sermon on the Mount." In *Christology and Scripture*, edited by A. T. Lincoln and A. Paddison, 171–87. New York: T. & T. Clark, 2007.

Nürnberger, K. *Theology of the Biblical Witness: An Evolutionary Approach*. Münster: Lit, 2002.

Oh, P. S. *Karl Barth's Trinitarian Theology: A Study in Karl Barth's Analogical Use of the Trinitarian Relation*. London: T. & T. Clark, 2006.

Paddison, A. *Scripture: A Very Theological Proposal*. London: T. & T. Clark, 2009.

Pannenberg, W. *Basic Questions in Theology*. 2 vols. Translated by G. H. Kelm. Philadelphia: Fortress, 1970–71.

Plasger, G. *Die relative Autorität des Bekenntnisses bei Karl Barth*. Neukirchen-Vluyn: Neukirchener, 2000.

Bibliography

———. "'Du sollst Vater und Mutter ehren!' Karl Barth und die reformierte Tradition." In *Karl Barth in Deutschland (1921–1935). Aufbruch-Klärung-Widerstand*, edited by M. Beintker, C. Link, and M. Trowitzsch, 393–405. Zürich: TVZ, 2005.

———. "Wort vom Wort. Systematisch-theologische Überlegungen zur Bedeutung des Verhältnißes von Dogmatik und Schriftauslegung anhand von Karl Barths Erklärung des Johannesevangeliums." *Zeitschrift für dialektische Theologie* 16 (2000): 43–58.

Richardson, K. A. *Reading Karl Barth: New Directions for North American Theology.* Grand Rapids: Baker Academic, 2004.

Robertson, G. A. "'Vivit! Regnat! Triumphat!': The Prophetic Office of Jesus Christ, the Christian Life, and the Mission of the Church in Karl Barth's *Church Dogmatics* IV/3." ThD diss., University of Toronto, 2003.

Rumscheidt, H. M., ed. *Adolf von Harnack: Liberal Theology at Its Height.* London: Collins, 1988.

———. "The Barth-Bultmann Correspondence." In *Karl Barth in Re-View: Posthumous Works Reviewed and Assessed*, 65-74. Pittsburgh: Pickwick, 1981.

Runia, K. *Karl Barth's Doctrine of Holy Scripture.* Grand Rapids: Eerdmans, 1962.

Schickler, J. *Metaphysics as Christology: An Odyssey of the Self from Kant and Hegel to Steiner.* Aldershot: Ashgate, 2005.

Schlegel, T. *Theologie als unmögliche Notwendigkeit. Der Theologiebegriff Karl Barths in seiner Genese (1914–1932).* Neukirchen-Vluyn: Neukirchener, 2007.

Schmid, F. *Verkündigung und Dogmatik in der Theologie Karl Barths. Hermeneutik und Ontologie in einer Theologie des Wortes Gottes.* Munich: Chr. Kaiser Verlag, 1964.

Scholl, H. *Karl Barth und Johannes Calvin: Karl Barths Göttinger Calvin-Vorlesung von 1922.* Neukirchen-Vluyn: Neukirchener, 1995.

Shorthouse, R. T. *Textual Narratives and a New Metaphysics.* Aldershot: Ashgate, 2002.

Smend, R. "Nachkritische Schriftauslegung." In *Parrhesia: fröhliche Zuversicht: Karl Barth zum 80. Geburstag am 10. Mai 1966*, edited by E. Busch, J. Fangmeier, and M. Geiger, 215-37. Zürich: EVZ, 1966.

So, D. W. K. *Jesus' Revelation of His Father: A Narrative-Conceptual Study of the Trinity with Special Reference to Karl Barth.* Milton Keynes: Paternoster, 2006.

Spencer, A. J. *Clearing a Space for Human Action: Towards an Ethical Ontology in the Early Theology of Karl Barth.* New York: Peter Lang, 2003.

Stegeman, D. N. "Ethics or Dogmatics? The Case of 'Rendtorff vs Barth.'" In *Religious Polemics in Context Papers Presented to the Second International Conference of the Leiden Institute for the Study of Religions Held at Leiden April 2000*, edited by T. L. Hettema and A. van der Kooij, 27–28. Assen: Royal van Gorcumeds, 2004.

Stroble, P. E., Jr. *The Social Ontology of Karl Barth.* San Francisco: Christian Universities, 1994.

Thomson, I. *Heidegger on Ontotheology: Technology and the Politics of Education.* Cambridge: Cambridge University Press, 2005.

Thompson, M. D. "Witness to the Word: On Barth's Doctrine of Scripture." In *Engaging with Barth: Contemporary Evangelical Critiques*, edited by D. Gibson and D. Strange, 168–97. Nottingham, UK: InterVarsity, 2008.

Torrance, A. J. *Persons in Communion: An Essay on Trinitarian Description and Human Participation: With Special Reference to Volume One of Karl Barth's* Church Dogmatics. Edinburgh: T. & T. Clark, 1996.

Torrance, T. F. *Karl Barth: An Introduction to His Early Theology, 1910–1931.* London: SCM, 1962.

———. *Karl Barth: Biblical and Evangelical Theologian*. Edinburgh: T. & T. Clark, 1990.

Trowitzsch, M. *Karl Barth heute*. Göttingen: Vandenhoeck & Ruprecht, 2007.

Trueman, C. "Calvin, Barth, and Reformed Theology: Historical Prolegomena." In *Calvin, Barth, and Reformed Theology*, edited by N. B. MacDonald and C. Trueman, 3–26. Milton Keynes: Paternoster, 2008.

Vanhoozer, K. J. "A Person of the Book? Barth on Biblical Authority and Interpretation." In *Karl Barth and Evangelical Theology: Convergences and Divergences*, edited by S. W. Chung, 26–59. Grand Rapids: Baker Academic, 2006.

Vickers, J. E. "Canonical Theism and the Primacy of Ontology: An Essay Concerning Human Understanding in Trinitarian Perspective." In *Canonical Theism: A Proposal for Theology and the Church*, edited by W. J. Abraham, 156–74. Grand Rapids: Eerdmans, 2008.

Wall, E .G. E. van der. "Ways of Polemicizing: The Power of Tradition in Christian Polemics." In *Religious Polemics in Context: Papers Presented to the Second International Conference of the Leiden Institute for the Study of Religions Held at Leiden, 27–28 April 2000*, edited by T. L. Hettema and A. van der Kooij, 401–14. Assen: Royal van Gorcumeds, 2004.

Wallace, M. I. *The Second Naiveté: Barth, Ricoeur, and the New Yale Theology*. Macon, GA: Mercer University Press, 1995.

Ward, T. *Word and Supplements: Speech Acts, Biblical Texts, and the Sufficiency of Scripture*. Oxford: Oxford University Press, 2002.

Watson, F. "Barth's Philippians as Theological Exegesis." In *The Epistle to the Philippians*, xxvi–xxx. Translated by J. W. Leitch. Louisville: Westminster John Knox, 2002.

———. "The Bible." In *The Cambridge Companion of Karl Barth*, edited by J. Webster, 57–71. Cambridge: Cambridge University Press, 2000.

———, ed. *Text, Church, and World*. Grand Rapids: Eerdmans, 1994.

Webster, J. *Barth*. New York: Continuum, 2000.

———. *Barth's Earlier Theology: Four Studies*. New York: T. & T. Clark, 2005.

———. "Barth's Lectures on the Gospel of John." In *What Is It that the Scripture Says? Essays in Biblical Interpretation, Translation, and Reception*, edited by P. McCosker, 211–30. London: Continuum, 2006.

———. *Barth's Moral Theology: Human Action in Barth's Thought*. Grand Rapids: Eerdmans, 1998.

———. *Confessing God: Essays in Christian Dogmatics II*. London: T. & T. Clark, 2005.

———. "God's Aseity." In *Realism and Religion: Philosophical and Theological Perspectives*, edited by A. Moore and M. Scott, 147–62. Aldershot: Ashgate, 2007.

———. "God's Perfect Life." In *God's Life in Trinity*, edited by M. Volf and M. Welker, 143–52. Minneapolis: Fortress, 2006.

———. *Holiness*. Grand Rapids: Eerdmans, 2003.

———. *Holy Scripture: A Dogmatic Sketch*. Cambridge: Cambridge University Press, 2003.

———. "Life in and of Himself: Reflections on God's Aseity." In *Engaging the Doctrine of God: Contemporary Protestant Perspectives*, edited by B. L. McCormack, 107–24. Grand Rapids: Baker Academic, 2008.

———. "Reading Eschatologically (1)." In *Reading Texts, Seeking Wisdom: Scripture and Theology*, edited by D. Ford and G. Stanton, 245–56. London: SCM, 2003.

———. "Resurrection and Scripture." In *Christology and Scripture*, edited by A. T. Lincoln and A. Paddison, 138–55. London: T. & T. Clark, 2007.

———. *Word and Church: Essays in Christian Dogmatics.* Edinburgh: T. & T. Clark, 2001.

Wengst, K. "Der Zeichenbegriff in Barths Kommentar zum Johannesevangelium." *Zeitschrift für dialektische Theologie* 16 (2000): 30–42.

Williams, R. D. "Barth on the Triune God." In *Karl Barth: Studies of his Theological Method*, edited by S. W. Sykes, 147–93. Oxford: Clarendon, 1979.

Wolterstorff, N. *Divine Discourse.* Cambridge: Cambridge University Press, 1995.

Wood, D. *Barth's Theology of Interpretation.* London: Ashgate, 2004.

———. "'Ich sah mit Staunen': Reflections on the Theological Substance of Barth's Early Hermeneutics." *Scottish Journal of Theology* 58/2 (2005): 184–98.

Wright, R.M. "Karl Barth's Academic Lectures on Ephesians Göttingen, 1921–1922: An Original Translation, Annotation, and Analysis." PhD diss., University of St Andrew's, 2006.

Yocum, J. *Ecclesial Mediation in Karl Barth.* Aldershot: Ashgate, 2003–4.

Index

Aberdeen, 2

Canon. *See* Scripture
Catholicism, 9n25, 19, 25, 31, 84, 142,
    154, 181

Eschatology, 48, 133n53
    Eschatological, 8, 11, 53n3, 55, 61,
        63, 66–68, 119, 126, 126n14,
        128n29, 132–33, 133n53,
        138–139, 142, 143n12, 143n17,
        144, 150, 157–58, 169, 169n20,
        171, 175, 183
    Parousia, 79, 81, 96–97, 132–33, 143,
        150, 162, 167

God
    aseity, 12, 103, 106–8, 123, 142, 145,
        183
    autopistia, 35, 96–97, 119, 183
    deity, 3, 3n7, 4n9, 5, 12, 13, 17–18,
        20, 23, 30, 39, 40, 45, 51–53,
        57–58, 62–63, 66, 71, 74,
        81–82, 86–87, 91–96, 98–105,
        107, 112–13, 123, 126n18,
        131n44, 133, 135n62, 137, 140,
        144n17, 145n25, 152, 155, 163,
        165, 168, 169
    vox Dei, 115–16, 161
    Son
        anhypostasis, 138
        christology, 10, 82n199,
            132n45, 161n111,
            168n17, 179

communicatio idiomatum,
    136n65
enhypostasis, 138
extra calvinisticum, 136n65
Fleischwerdung, 136n68, 137,
    139, 157
Spirit
    illumination, 2n4, 6, 12–13,
        26, 41, 48, 81n119,
        86–87, 89, 93, 93n180,
        95–96, 99n212, 100,
        104, 110, 114–15, 119,
        119n328, 120, 122,
        122n2, 123–27, 129,
        129n35, 130, 133–34,
        135n61, 139–40, 146,
        149, 163, 166n5–6,
        169n20
    inspiration, vii, 2n4, 6, 12, 21,
        26, 34, 38, 97, 115, 119,
        141n1, 156, 156n86,
        160, 162, 167, 169
    pneumatology, 4n11, 6, 10,
        12, 45, 69, 82n199,
        89n155, 92, 152, 175
    processio, 108
    spiratio, 108

Kant, 3n5, 8n20, 37, 106, 167n13, 179,
    182

Ontology
    epistemology, 3n6, 46n114
    ontotheology, 2n5, 3n5, 8, 8n20, 182

Index

Salvation
  harmatological, 19
  peccatores iusti, 3, 9, 11, 63, 74,
    161–162, 165, 170
  prayer, 44–45, 52, 74, 111, 129,
    129n35, 138, 138n82, 161, 163,
    170, 172
  regeneration, 2, 7, 13, 24, 53, 55, 60,
    74, 105, 115, 125, 127, 158, 159,
    161, 163
  soteriological, 2n4, 3n5, 9n24, 11,
    12, 13, 14, 16, 17, 22, 26, 32, 38,
    41, 44, 45, 46, 46n114, 48, 50,
    54, 55, 57, 63–66, 69, 71–72, 74,
    78, 80, 82, 84–85, 85n136, 87–
    89, 90n163, 91–93, 96, 98–101,
    103–4, 106–15, 117–20, 122,
    124, 129, 138n82, 138n86, 139,
    142–43, 146, 148n45, 149–50,
    150n57, 151, 151n58, 153n70,
    161–63, 165–166, 166n6, 167,
    169, 171–72

Scripture
  Canon, 2n4, 3n6, 6–7, 10, 12–13,
    16, 18, 19n8, 23n22, 34, 34n57,
    38–40, 53, 53n2, 55, 61,
    85n133, 86n136, 87n149,
    90n163, 93n180, 96n203, 97,
    99n215, 103, 105–6, 107n258,
    110–11, 112n293, 112n294,
    113–18, 120–21, 133, 140, 142,
    147, 147n41, 150, 150n57,
    158, 158n96, 159, 159n102,
    159n104, 160, 160n104,
    162, 163n121, 165, 165n1,
    166, 166n8, 167, 167n9, 168,
    168n15, 170–72, 175, 177, 183
  Scripture Principle, viii, 9, 9n25,
    11–13, 53n1, 55–56, 81,
    81n119, 83, 92–93, 96–99,
    102–3, 112, 115, 117–18, 123,
    135n59, 139, 141–42, 154,
    166n6, 169, 181
Verbal inspiration, 26

Printed in Great Britain
by Amazon.co.uk, Ltd.,
Marston Gate.